ANGELA DU MAURIER

It's Only the Sister

An autobiography

Truran

Published by Truran 2003
Truran is an imprint of Truran Books Ltd.
Croft Prince, Mount Hawke, Truro, Cornwall TR4 8EE
www.truranbooks.co.uk

ISBN 1 85022 178 2
First published 1951 by Peter Davies Ltd

Cover designed by Peter Bennett, St Ives

Printed and bound by Short Run Press,
Bittern Road, Sowton Industrial Estate, Exeter EX2 7LW

"One day a very gushing woman approached and effusively thanked me for all I had done for her nephew. She told me his name and I was able to say truthfully that I had never met him. Oh, I must be wrong, she continued, she had heard all about my kindness *and* that of my husband. The light dawned and—

'I expect you think I am my sister, Daphne Browning. I am *Angela* du Maurier.'

With the eyes and the voice of a Medea she turned to her husband, who was standing in the offing ready to be introduced, and cried—'It's ONLY the SISTER!' and with that she left me." (Pages 95–96)

Contents

Dedicated in love
To the Memory of
Gerald du Maurier, my father

To Angela

Upon the first of March you came
And made us glad.
Though we had never thought of you
As being ours
In all the hours
We'd loved, we'd never talked of you—
No! never had—
But, all the same,
I can't conceive the world would be
The happy place it is to me
Without you, dear.

I don't know why I love you so—
Ah! yes, I do:
It is because you're part of me
And part of one,
The only one,
The heart and very life of me.
Still! there is you
And well you know
How happily we both contrive
To love each other and to live
With you, my dear.

G. du M.

I

Childhood

"Wait till you come to forty year." . . . I wonder how often my father—Gerald du Maurier—said that to us when we were children. As, apparently, his father had quoted to him. ("As Papa used to say, wait till you come to forty year.")

And now that 'forty year' is quite a long way behind me it seems as good a time as any to look back upon years that have been full, and are now nostalgic.

What pleasure one gets at looking through old photograph albums, browsing through old diaries, exploring the hidden treasure of a forgotten bureau and coming upon a letter, a fan, a handkerchief or a piece of lace, that in one swift moment conjures up—not to the imagination but to a far more personal and precious sense—*memory*, of an occasion long forgotten, times of happiness, or sadness or despair. "*Do you remember?*" . . . I think my father and my grandfather were right. "Wait till you come to forty year." For it is not until one is approaching middle-age that one looks back with that nostalgic yearning, glad of the companion who will share one's 'do you remembers', oblivious of the yawns to be seen—and heard—of that new young generation to whom we and our elders are now becoming bores. For let us not delude ourselves. We are bores to the young. And so for that matter are the young to us! By which I don't mean children. Children are like puppies, one either likes them or one does not. They are not bores; unless made so by their parents; and then it is the parent who is the bore, as he—but generally she—yarns on, extolling the virtues or views of some child who has probably never said or done whatever it's supposed to have said or done in the first place.

I imagine the point of waiting till one was 'forty year' was that one would have matured in wisdom and simmered down, as it were; no longer the 'Miss Know All' that I was constantly accused of being. And yet, what do any of us ever know? What do we learn beyond that inescapable truth that the older we get the less we know? As to simmering down, that is something that I for one shall never do, if I live to be ninety, if it means losing one's youthful enthusiasm or equally lessening one's indiscretions. I suppose my father imagined one changed a great deal, that by the time that 'forty year' was reached opinions one had held at twenty would be scattered to the four winds. I wonder.

Recently I came across many old diaries which I had written in daily, and with great conscientiousness, in the days when I went to my finishing school in Paris and for some years after I 'came out'. They kept me engrossed, and bewildered. Was the author of these illuminating Ouida-like scripts, falling in love with a different person every week, *me*? Which only goes to show that both George and Gerald du Maurier were right; up to a point; but why only wait till 40? Why not 60, 70, one's death-bed? I think the answer is just that of the old French proverb: 'Plus ça change, plus c'est la même chose.'

Times may alter, people in themselves do not. We may think we do. The fact that our Débutante diaries may make scandalous reading when we're old maids of forty odd, doesn't mean that the old maid herself is reformed. It probably means she has learnt just that amount of wisdom not to keep diaries any longer!

Quite a number of people have said to me, surprisingly enough, "you ought to write your memoirs" as if I was a V.I.P.

And it is because I am very humble at heart and have knelt at the feet of many V.I.P.'s that I shall try to pay homage to at least some of them in these pages.

I once heard a little girl who shall be nameless grumble because she was always being asked if she was 'the daughter of' her father and her mother, both equally famous people. Instead of this filling her with filial pride it seemed to ignite a curious jealousy.

From the earliest of days I have been happy and proud to be the grand-daughter, the daughter and the sister of three very celebrated people. Until my father died I was never introduced to anyone who didn't ask "Are you a relation of Gerald du Maurier?" It was a glorious feeling to be able to say one was his daughter. There were times when I considered pretending to be a mere niece, and sometimes no relation at all, but pride and snobbery (I fear) got the better of me and I never denied it.

How long is the public generous enough to pay tribute to a memory? How long does loyalty last? I wonder, because recently I met a strange lady of my father's vintage who twittered on meeting me and asked if I were *George's* daughter. (He was born in 1834.) Explaining with pride that he had been my grandfather, and that I was *Gerald's* daughter, she wavered and havered and said, "Gerald. Ah yes, Gerald. And tell me what did he do?" Now that was either affectation or *putting me in my place*, because this lady was as I happened to know a most erudite lady, and certainly knew what my papa was. But will the actors of to-day—and the writers, and the singers and the poets for that matter—live on in conversation and memory and *history* as those in the past did? I should like to think that in fifty years' time my father's name will still be spoken of in connection with his work, as Irving is still spoken of, and Tree. I do not class Gerald du Maurier with Irving or even Tree, don't worry. He would be the first person to say 'careful' and tell me to stop before making a fool of either myself or himself on that score. But there is no getting away from the fact that no one has taken Gerald du Maurier's place. To-day there may be greater actors than he was; he was not *great*, he never pretended to be, he never played *great* parts. You cannot be a great actor unless you produce and play classics. Whether he could have reached the heights in these fields we shall never know, for he had a public who was loyal to the stuff he gave and refused to see him in anything but comedy, 'thrillers', or modern drama. I think myself he could have been a great actor for he was the finest mimic I have ever known, and possessed a voice that was perfectly capable of declaiming Shakespeare, or any other poet for that matter, had he been allowed to. Where he *was* great was in his own métier, that of producer. He was a highly accomplished comedian; and there was no one to touch his manner in the parts he created of Barrie's.

I said I was proud of my father. That pride I suppose dawned when I was about seven, perhaps sooner, when I began to realise the Theatre. I was equally proud of Mummie too. I was always so relieved that she was pretty. I did not go to many schools, but to those I did I was always aware that *my* mother was the best-looking, and the most chic, of female parents. Oh! the dreary dowdiness of most of the poor girls' mothers! I suppose it was easy for her; once you've been on the stage you get a dress sense that lasts your day, and if you have natural beauty too, well, you can't go far wrong. And Mummie was so pretty. When I was very small, four-ish, I used to love to powder her back for her when she was dressing to go out for a party. It was a great treat for me to see her in full evening dress. I loved to see her with her hair hanging down too, looking like a princess as I thought. I was very different to Daphne who could not bear to see my mother with her hair down. I can remember that she would let it down to tease Daphne, and Daph would go crimson in the face and pick grass, or if indoors keep her eyes steadfastly on the rug, as if she were being made a witness to something obscene.

How far can most people's memories go back? I have hazardous snippets from the age of two. Which is good, you'll allow. Not things I've been told about but things I remember. I remember my first canary dying. I was perhaps three. It was taken off in its cage, with a cloth hiding its poor little form; and in a day or two back came Dicky, full of song as ever, and I was none the wiser. That occurred several times. I remember wetting my knickers in Regent's Park, when dressed in my Sunday clothes. In fact that is my first memory. I wore a pink coat (pelisse) and a pink and beaver-edged poke bonnet, and white suède boots. I was very smart, and in either the Outer or Inner Circle of Regent's Park this shame befell me. One is always asked one's first recollection: that is mine. Another very early one is *dancing* to the hymn of 'Do no Sinful Action' and my mother turning from the piano and saying to me in tones of absolute horror, "Angela! what would Mr Shaw say?" Mr Shaw, the Reverend Bernard Shaw who christened Daphne, and was to become a very fashionable preacher in the West End, but who was at that time the vicar of Christ Church, Albany Street. Yes, that's a potent memory. I didn't know what Hell was, but I knew I had done something *very awful*. For a long time I had not the slightest idea *why* one could not dance to 'Do no Sinful Action', the words conveyed literally nothing. Any more than 'Suffer my simple city' did; ('suffer my simplicity'). Nowadays, if Daphne, Jeanne (my younger sister) or I are at sea about the meaning of a word, we always ask if it's a question of Simple City.

It has always been a source of great disappointment and sadness, that George du Maurier—grandpapa—died before my parents met and that therefore I never knew him. From early days I was brought up on his lovely drawings, and was never happier on visits to my grandmother than when allowed to sit with a massive volume of *Punch* in my lap and pore over *his* pages. I think I must have been very young by the time I could have spotted a du Maurier; certainly by the age of ten or eleven I would not have dreamed of mistaking his drawings for a Leech or Keene; and although this should be easy enough for an adult brought up to read *Punch* every week throughout the years, it must be remembered that until I was eleven my education where my grandfather was concerned was indeed only formed by the frequent perusals of the old *Punches* at my grandmother's house. I was twelve when I first read *Trilby*, I remember distinctly, it was during the first World War. How I adored it. It would have been wonderful to have known the creator of that and *Peter Ibbetson*, and all those glorious *Punch* drawings, and moreover to have called him Grandpapa, and perhaps have been drawn by him; so at least twelve-year-old Angela used to think, forgetting that little girls in 1915 bore little or no resemblance to the romantically and charmingly clad misses of the 'seventies and 'eighties. We were the only grand-daughters in the family. My father's beautiful eldest sister Trixie had married Charlie Millar and had produced four boys. The ravishing Aunt Sylvia (Llewelyn Davies) was the mother of five sons, Aunt May (Coles)—my godmother—had no children, neither had my very dear Uncle Guy, my god-father. So that we three were considered a great blessing and excitement in the family.

Gerald was the youngest of the children of George and Emma du Maurier. He was adored and I think rather spoilt, as we in turn were. We are in fact given to spoiling. He and my mother spoilt each other, and they in their turn spoilt us. But what does one mean by the term spoiling? One dictionary says 'to mar, to vitiate, to impair the goodness of, to decay' . . . the dictionary also says 'to impair the character by over-indul-gence'. I think the latter phrase is as good as any; at the same time if one loves anyone very much, it is the easiest and nicest thing in the world to over-indulge the other person. And sometimes whole families indulge in such-like orgies, and of such families are and were the du Mauriers.

Grandpapa and Granny lived once in Hampstead, in a charming-looking house near the Whitestone Pond called New Grove House. It still bears the plaque (ivy-covered) 'George du Maurier lived here'. My famous—or shall I say infamous—great-great-grandmother Mary Anne Clarke also had lived in Hampstead, in New End Square. Her house, an early Georgian one, was demolished by bombs in the last war. Daddy was born in that loveliest of all roads, Church Row, and he with the rest of his family now lies under the Yew-tree in the old churchyard at the far end of that street. Hampstead is in our veins, I feel that very strongly. Rather irritatingly too, because I so very much prefer living in the country. I do not like London, I do not like cities at all. But I'm a Londoner born and bred—and I have only to get out of the tube on the corner of Heath Street to sniff the air, unerringly like a horse nearing home, to realise I am home. To my mind there is no part of London with so much charm as old Hampstead. And when I say Hampstead I don't mean your Finchley Roads, Belsize Parks and Hampstead Garden Suburbs. I mean the Hampstead of Keats Grove and Downshire Hill; the Hampstead of Upper and Lower Terrace and Holly Hill and Holly Place; the Hampstead of Fenton House, Heath House, Cannon Hall, Squires Mount; of Jack Straw's Castle and the Spaniards. And above all the Hampstead of Church Row, and the old parish church at the end of it.

That Hampstead still remains miraculously intact, and untouched by land-mines and blitzkrieg. The Whitestone Pond may have lost its charm, and become a mere rendezvous for dogs, but lilies still grow on the Viaduct Pond, bulrushes and willows by the Hampstead Ponds beyond Kenwood, and the Vale of Health and the Leg o' Mutton will always have a charm

of their own. You can't get away from the fact that Dick
Turpin rode the Spaniards Road in the days gone by and held
up coaches in isolation there; that history teems about its very
air, that spirits of *ghosts* hang over Hampstead like a pall of fog,
even in this bomb-ridden and atomic age. Under the pine-
trees (or firs, to be exact) at the end of the Spaniards Road are
buried the remains of victims of the Great Plague of 1665. To
me there's excitement and romance there. I love too to think of
the old Queen Anne houses still intact and to imagine their
inmates of a couple of centuries or more back, bewigged
gentlemen, and ladies in sedan chairs. Where now a vast block
of flats is in process of being built (thanks to Hitler) was once
the Pump-room in Well Walk. And Cannon Hall, for long my
home, boasted of the 'lock-up' (or original prison) of Hampstead; a horrible dungeon with heavy iron bars across its glass-
less open windows. The Court room of the Hampstead J.P.
was my father's study; and last but not least, in our garden we
had the *first* Hampstead fire-engine, a mechanical device of
much ingenuity and strange design.

''Appy 'ampstead.' Yes, it *is* a happy place, a happy village
one might almost say. And no one was happier than my father
when, in 1915, he found Cannon Hall which was to become
our home until he died, and he was able to return to the
scenes of his childhood.

As a little boy Daddy was sent to Heath Mount to school
(which no longer exists) and then to Harrow. He was extremely
proud of his connection with Harrow, and as children sporting
cornflowers we dutifully accompanied him year by year to
Lord's where he became a far more excited and enthusiastic
spectator than many of the boys around us. Any 'old Harrovian' could be sure of a helping hand from him if in later
days he happened to fall on bad times, and I've often wondered why my father was accused of being a snob and an up-
holder of the old-school-tie idea because from time to time he

cast parts to type, and gave a job to an actor who had been to a public school when it was quite obvious that the part in question needed such a player.

Daddy was a Coming Young Man by the time he met Mummie. She was Muriel Beaumont, and they met and fell in love with each other whilst acting together in *The Admirable Crichton*. Mummie's people came from Cambridge and from Ely, and had not looked upon their daughter's career on the stage with great enthusiasm. She was very pretty when Daddy met her, and was usually snapped up by Managers to play ingénue parts, and was considered to be a 'mascot' as several plays in which she acted had runs of over a year.

My du Maurier relations were very happy at my father's engagement. He had had ideas of marrying before, people of whom (in spite of their fame) my dear Granny had had her doubts. No less a person than Ethel Barrymore might have been my mother once upon a time, and also Mrs Patrick Campbell. Stella I knew fairly well, for she always remained a dear friend of Daddy's. I thought her rather frightening and rather wonderful and although in my 'teens' I would listen spellbound to her stories (and often her rudeness) across the table of a Cannon Hall Sunday luncheon, my heart had probably sunk the day before on being told, "Stella wants to come to lunch to-morrow." How beautiful she was, how grand in stature. Her voice . . . how could one describe the voice of Stella Campbell to those poor unfortunates who never heard it? We who knew it can recapture it in our memories. It had a strangely pouting quality, it fell in staccato drips, as it were, like water falling in jerks, not limpidly. In deep staccato, contralto notes her words fell, words that could lift one to heaven or by their brutal truth plunge the wretched recipient into un-utterable gloom. She was always very nice to me. But she was surprisingly cruel or maybe just thoughtlessly tactless to my sister Jeanne who as a small girl was told to play the piano to her. At that time Jeanne was thinking seriously of taking up music as a career. She had a sensitive nature and I've often wondered what her inmost thoughts were when Stella said, when Jeanne finished playing, "Why don't you paint?"

As to Ethel Barrymore and her engagement, I really don't know how or why it was broken off, but I seem to think it ended on a tour in Ireland. They too remained friends, but as she lived in America I never knew her, and it was not until shortly before Daddy died and we gave, as far as I remember, our last big party at Cannon Hall that I met Ethel; for she was in London and she came, and remained on alone to supper, and Oh! how one fell. . . . There is a magnetism about Barrymores that only they have. A time there was when Jack was always up at Cannon Hall, and he and Ethel certainly cast spells. I only met Ethel this once, but I shall never forget her; neither her voice, nor her quite superlative eyes.

But Daddy met Mummie, and married her at St Peter's, Cranley Gardens, on April 11th 1903, and on March 1st 1904 at No. 5 Chester Place, Regent's Park, I arrived, with poor Daddy upstairs in bed with bad diphtheria, for which a cat was blamed.

I was a very fat baby, and as months went by I apparently became a vastly intelligent one, and from all accounts Gerald and Muriel du Maurier must have bored their friends by the hour telling them the perfectly amazing things Angela did and said. I was witty moreover (something I've never succeeded in being since I grew up, more's the pity). People were kept in fits of laughter by the miraculous imitations of animals at which I was, it seems, adept. I'm told my parents held strange conversations with each other in humdrum tones of voice, mentioning the words cow, and cat and dog and so on, and this Paragon of Childhood Genius outed with a moo or a bark or a miaow. Personally I've yet to meet the child who does not. But there was one story that I believe to be true, which was that at a big luncheon party to which I went (aged two) to collect my parents, on admittance to the dining-room Daddy lifted a glass and said, "The King," to which, totally un-coached and untutored, I replied swiftly, "God B'ess him." I wonder, I really do indeed.

How many people owe the happiness of their childhood to the nurse who brought them up? I do not know, I will only go as far as saying *all* my very happy early childhood can be laid at the door of my very dear 'Nanny'. She came to us when I was eight months old, and left when I was eight years old, and I know that neither of us has ever omitted a birthday letter to each other in the many long years since, nor forgotten Christmas greetings. She was one in a thousand, and I feel certain that friends of mine who have her now to bring their children up find her an unsurpassed treasure (even if they must get bored by the stories she loves to tell about me and mine). I had a horrible sense of loneliness when she left, it was like a child's first meeting with Death. Indeed the dying of my lovely Aunt Sylvia had left me much less bewildered. I can see Nanny now, going down the top flight of stairs and carefully shutting the gate behind her, tears pouring down her face, and only then myself being told she was going for ever. It was life's first misery for me. And all because with three children my parents had thought an under-nurse unnecessary! In those days under-nurses were symbols of *very* well-to-do people, and we in 24 Cumberland Terrace, Regent's Park, were hardly that in 1912, though in 1910 Daddy had become manager with Frank Curzon of Wyndham's Theatre, and things were certainly on the upgrade. But under-nurses were generally found in the houses which kept butlers, and the du Mauriers did not aspire that high. Nanny was no spoiler, she was firm but kindness itself, and a wonderful inventor of games and reader of books. Perhaps if I had had children of my own instead of nieces and a nephew and ten godchildren I should know more of children's books to-day than I do, but how my heart bleeds for the young of to-day who have no enthusiasm for Mrs Molesworth, her *Hoodie* and *Stumps* and *Us* and *The Cuckoo Clock*, to name but a few. How we used to listen with avid interest, almost knowing the stories by heart, our eyes fixed on to those blue and gold covers.

Perhaps children's books are happier to-day? Certainly there were miseries enough in the children's classics of my childhood; I remember howling over the slum horrors of *Froggie's Little Brother* and *Little Meg's Children*. We much preferred stories of people, children who sounded real, to fairy stories. And we worshipped our teddy bears and would not have said 'Thank you' for a doll. Dolls seemed most foolish and embarrassing bits of nonsense, except Hamley's wax ones which we were given for 'best' and only looked at on very great occasions. But our bears were children; I still have the two I was given when a year old. They lie on my bed, very dirty and furless, and are now joined by a queer little animal that Daddy was devoted to. I took them to school, pretending they were mascots. I had not quite the courage at fourteen to pretend I had to have my teddy bear.

I find people of my generation on the whole do cling to the toys of their childhood, far more than our parents of the Victorian era did. My brother-in-law's little bear goes everywhere with him, accompanied by one of Daphne's; they are known as the Boys and woe betide the day if they are left behind on a holiday. And little silly things like that seem to be lacking in the life of so many children to-day. Take Father Christmas (whom I will never call Santa Claus): there are so many children nowadays who hang up a stocking knowing full well that Dad and Mum are going to fill it. What an admission of failure on a parent's part! Fancy having a child and not letting it know Father Christmas. I knew he visited us, right down our nursery chimney. A wonderful old man. I was about seven at the time, and went white and speechless with excitement on his call to my humble nursery. I remember distinctly sweeping him a curtsey, and not until I was in my teens did I discover that a pal of my father's, Marsh Allan the actor, had been Father Christmas. I was nearly twelve when I discovered the Awful Truth—that there *was no* such person. That was Disillusion Number One in my life. It was during World War I and we were living at Chorley Wood, and I asked my mother if it was true, as someone had told me, that no Father Christmas lived. I asked her knowing that I should be told all was well and that of course he lived; the truth, when poor Mummie apologised and said, "I'm sorry darling, I'm afraid there *isn't,*" knocked the bottom out of childhood. With that piece of news went a bit of one's trust. Were fairies another lie too? (And no child brought up on Peter Pan as we had all been could possibly disbelieve in fairies.) That perhaps is the argument modern parents use: don't pretend to your children, don't bring them up in the belief of people who don't exist. I still think that never to have believed in Father Christmas and never to have believed in fairies is to have forgone some of the most exciting and happiest moments of childhood.

We moved from Chester Place to Cumberland Terrace for Daphne's advent. I cannot remember her as a baby, oddly enough, but I do know my mother has always said she was the loveliest tiny baby she has ever seen. For Daphne, and I think myself, we had a beautiful white pram, which matched our white front door. Mummie still acted in those days, and our lives were very much Nanny's. She never had a day 'off' and in all her eight years I can only remember her taking two holidays, but I suppose I must be wrong. We were beautifully dressed always, but I remember as I grew older how bored I was that all three of us used to be dressed alike. None of your white frilly petticoats or 'Hyde Park' nonsense, thank you.

We were dressed picturesquely; in lovely velveteens in the winter (exquisitely embroidered by Mummie) and charming linens in different colours, *with knickers to match*, in the summer. (Heavens! how we despised girls who wore *drawers*.) I was a plain little girl, and I got plainer. Luckily when small I was, apparently, amusing, but no one could deny I was plain. Time was when I had lovely curly hair, but unfortunately at the age of eight 'things' were discovered in my head, and instead of giving me a good petrol rinse, Daddy had me rushed off to a specialist in Harley Street who produced a killer of such strength that all colour and all curl left me for literally years to come. Daphne was always pretty, and became quite lovely by the time she was ten, and Jeanne the youngest of us won a beauty prize and was, I think, the loveliest child from the age of two till she was about six, I've ever seen. Luckily I never realised I was so plain, because I was deeply emotional and from early times I dramatised life in a fantastic way. There was an occasion, I still remember it, when I was having my hair washed in the big bath, by Nanny. Some soap got into my ears, and my screams and yells brought the minions from the two flights below, *and* my parents too. Ordinary childish cries and screams and tears? Not on your life! I called "Help! help! mercy! murder! I shall be deaf for ever." I suppose one was already acting.

People have been said to have been born in the prompt corner. I cannot pretend to that, but the stage influenced me and was part of my life from very early days. I have been a member of the theatre-going public since I was two. And proper theatres, not just pantomimes and a circus or two at Christmas. As a matter of fact as children we never went to pantomimes; I went to one, and was so disgusted and horrified by the Harlequinade at the end (something about a sausage shocked me at four) that I never went again until I was nearly grown-up. *Peter Pan* was practically our birthright. Indeed we were related to the Boy, and its author was one's Uncle Jim. As a tiny child he (J. M. Barrie) would take me and make me yell out all sorts of monstrous things to Hook and Peter and Tiger Lily from the box in which we'd be seeing the play. Daddy was the original Captain Hook, of course, and although he played it for several years I do not remember him in the part until he played it again with Jean Forbes-Robertson shortly before he died. No one could touch him in the part. I wonder if first things are always best, always favourite, and whether one's criticism therefore is just? To my mind there has never been a Wendy to touch Hilda Trevelyan—in fact I remember no others except Mary Glynne who was sweet in the part—and I have seen the play so many times that I can't remember. Equally Pauline Chase is *my* Peter. Oh! those heavenly happy days of childhood when our annual Peter Pan Day came round, and it was time to go to dress (accompanied by our teddy bears *also* dressed and sat to watch on the edge of the box), and go off to the Duke of York's Theatre and there collect our ticket from the 'Wendy House' which the Box Office was always transformed into in the old days when the play belonged to 'Dot' Boucicault. Lights went out. . . . Crook's music began. . . . I should think by the time I was seven I could certainly have prompted *all* the cast. Barrie used to visit us in our nursery and we used to act it for him by the hour. Daphne always bagged Peter, and I was Wendy and Mrs Darling and several of the pirates, Jeanne was Michael and I rather think Eliza. It was quite easy to act *all* the parts in turn, and we flew from chair to chair and swam as mermaids on the floor, completely without any fear or shyness that Barrie might be sitting on the fender watching us. Daddy, at such times, was probably Hook. On the occasion of our annual visit to the real Peter Pan' we nearly always went up into the tree-tops with Peter and Wendy in their little house during the last scene when they blew kisses and waved hankies to the audience. (I've always thought that music some of the loveliest I know.) And we used—during the interval—to be rushed round to eat tea with Peter, Wendy and Tiger Lily. I suppose we *did* know they were called Pauline Chase and Hilda Trevelyan and 'Budgie' Frazer but they were very real Peters, Wendys and Tiger Lilys, to Daphne and me.

Another play I remember seeing very early on was *Pinkie and the Fairies*. I don't remember much about it, but I was very frightened and tried to hide behind a stall. Frogs, giant frogs I think, were the cause of my terror. I also remember a revival of *The Admirable Crichton* to which I went very young. If one is the child of an actor, and especially if one's mother is an actress too, one is almost bound to be brought up in the theatre. And believe me it doesn't lessen one's enthusiasm or one's interest in plays and theatre-going. If one is romantically minded, and I was, one's appetite is whetted all the more. How I disliked the children, and still do, who must be know-alls and damp imagination by trotting out remarks like "Look at Peter's *wires*! He's not flying", or who look at one crying at some sad bit and say "It's only acting", in patronising tones. If you've theatre in your blood and in your veins you *murder* such people in your heart.

Of course we automatically saw all Daddy's plays, from the earliest ages; whether they were suitable or not. Curiously enough I don't remember going to many before he was in management, but as I was only six then perhaps that's not altogether surprising. This first venture was *Nobody's Daughter* and all I remember of that, other than the heroine being Rosalie Toller, is going to a matinée with Daphne (aged three) and hearing Marsh Allan saying "You know Angela and Daphne corner", for our benefit. *Mr Jarvis* came next, a Charles I or II affair which was a failure. Jeanne was born during this and Daphne and I and the monthly nurse went to a matinée and I sobbed because a bunch of flowers given by Daddy to the beautiful lady (Amy Brandon-Thomas) was either trampled under-foot or hurled on to the ground. It was too much for my tender heart. It ruined the play for me.

It was about this time that my manners were found fault with by Daddy. His stage manager was a certain Tommy Lovell (he was at Wyndham's for years with Daddy and I cannot imagine Wyndham's without him or him without Wyndham's). And at the age of seven I shook his hand with my left instead of my right. The heavens fell. I doubt if any child has ever had such a dressing-down for so small an offence. My goodness! when I think of the children nowadays who say how-do-you-do to one with a finger in the mouth and one leg lagging behind the other, and who put out the left if they consider one's worth a hand at all. Not so me and Tommy Lovell. But of course Daddy could not keep up the attitude of anger for long, and by the evening I was thoroughly enjoying myself shaking hands with legs of cupboards, handles of doors, curtains, fire-arms and the parlourmaid who was waiting (the 'lesson' took place whilst my father was having his early dinner before returning to the theatre). Daddy's admonitions were generally pretty good fun by the end; there was that time when he came upon Daphne and me bent on killing each other because one of us had said "Jeanne loves *me* the best". Jeanne, a year old, certainly knew nothing of the matter and certainly could not have cared less. Daddy immediately put us both in Court, became Judge, 'tried' us and doubtless punished us in a way to give satisfaction all round. Punishment, qua punishment, and corporal punishment of any sort was never meted out to us by anyone. As a matter of fact we were not naughty children. Perhaps little girls are not? We only had to be 'spoken to'. And as for Jeanne, she only had to be looked at. They had a way, my parents, of making one feel thoroughly small if one had done something displeasing. One thing we were never allowed to be and that was noisy. People say it is natural for children to shout, as it is nature for puppies to bark. Daddy could not abide noise, either screaming or jumping children, barking dogs, noisy traffic, or a singing blackbird at six a.m. As children in the Regent's Park days, our nurseries were on the top floor, over the rooms where Mummie and Daddy slept. They kept late hours, when acting, probably went out frequently to supper, and rarely were in bed before two a.m. How right therefore to disallow yelling little hooligans upstairs. Yes, we were brought up to walk and talk quietly, and to remember siesta hours. He always slept, his 'shut-eye' it was called, before he went to the theatre in the evening, and we crept about the house like mice.

"H'sh, Daddy's resting." . . .

And the du Mauriers were not alone there. Well do I remember Betty Seymour Hicks 'H'shing' me when her father or her mother would be asleep in the day-time.

I was six I think when I had my first portrait painted; by Wolfram Onslow Ford. His wife was Helen Henschel, the well-known singer and Daphne's godmother. I had my first and last meeting with Royalty in the Acacia Road studio. I took it very seriously, completely unaware of the amusement I was causing. To me Kings and Queens, Princes and Princesses were second only to fairies. (They still are, and are now alas even rarer. . . .) The prince on this occasion was Prince Alexander of Battenberg, none other in fact than Lord Carisbrooke. He came into the studio one day when Wolfram was painting me and Helen was reading. One supposes they must have said who he was, because I 'arose' from the dais, and swept him the deepest curtsey he'd ever had swept him, I'm sure. No one told me to, it came naturally—one behaved like that to princes in those days and curtseyed without being told to. My only other introduction to royal personages was when I, in company with Elizabeth Irving, Betty Hicks and Prue Bourchier had to present programmes and bouquets to Princess

Mary (as she then was) in a box at some big charity matinée.
We were all children, and she was barely grown-up herself.

My young days were the days of picture post-card beauties;
pretty actresses and their progeny, 'society beauties', and
Queen Ena of Spain. My own family was very averse to publicity and we were not nearly as much photographed (in
public) as other theatrical children.

The day that used to stand out in my young life, along with
Christmas Day and my Birthday, was that of the Theatrical
Garden Party. In those days it was a wonderful affair, really
élite, and had an Edwardian glamour about it—like the Gaiety
Theatre—which has gone further than any wind. In those days
it was held at the Royal Botanical Gardens (themselves no
longer the private and exclusive concern they used to be), and
men wore top hats and women Ascot frocks. And *I* wore my
Garden Party Hat; which was a creation of no less a firm than
Zyrot of Hanover Square who gave it to me when I was six,
and I wore it every year—a large white lace hat with blue
streamers and a bunch of tiny pink roses. No bride has ever
been more proud of a Molyneux trousseau than I, at six, of my
Zyrot Garden Party Hat. 'Dot' Boucicault always gave the
most superb luncheon party on The Day, with his belovèd
wife Irene Vanbrugh (Jeanne's godmother); and Daphne, I,
the Fripp children, Elizabeth Irving (I think) and Prue
Bourchier (Irene's niece) all sat at a small table to ourselves in
the dining-room, whilst at the big table sat the Stars of the day.
It was here, at 4 Wyndham Place, that as a little girl I first
clapped eyes on Phyllis Neilson-Terry, then in her late teens
and lovelier than anyone I've seen before or since: here that at
a later date I fell madly in love (in my *early* teens) with Robert
—'Bobby'—Loraine (the only Cyrano for me); Fay Compton
I seem to remember, Gwendoline Brogden, 'Bunch' Keys,
various Forbes-Robertsons, Ellis Jeffreys and her daughter
Evelyn (bridesmaid to my parents) and many others. Dot took

us children under his wing for the afternoon, and there wasn't a side-show that we were not treated to, nor a strawberry nor ice refused us. Dear little man in his silk top hat and sponge-bag trousers, shepherding a bunch of little girls . . . what happy times he gave us, how seriously he treated us, and listened to our prattling, and *how* I wished he was living to direct *Peter Pan* when the time came when I was playing Wendy.

Actors and actresses were the people we—my sisters and I—knew. I suppose there were other people too but I don't remember many. We came into little contact with writers, oddly enough, unless they were playwrights. Barrie, as I have said, was almost looked upon as a relative, being the guardian of our Llewelyn Davies cousins. There was dear old Alfred Sutro, living in Regent's Park; we used to meet him daily on our walks, with his beautiful Old English sheep-dog Peter; he wrote plays for Daddy so we knew him pretty well. There was Ernest Temple Thurston, and his wife Joan. (I remember unpacking for Ernest when I was about nine and he came to stay, and being simply horrified to find he had no trees for his patent-leather shoes. Daddy had a shoe-stand on which were arrayed at least two dozen pairs of shoes all exquisitely polished and treed. I was disgusted by what I considered Ernest's unsoigné mode of behaviour.) It was not until we were older, teen-agers (hideous expression) that Freddie Lonsdale, Roland Pertwee, Edgar Wallace, Rudolph Besier and others swept into our ken.

Musicians were nothing in our young lives either, more's the pity. Nor, and this is indeed strange for George du Maurier's grandchildren, did painters brighten our doorstep. I cannot imagine why. I cannot think how it came that our grand-father's son should have taken so little interest in the painters of the day. It is true that we were painted, but no painters sat round the table in our dining-room as had sat Whistler, Burne-Jones, Alma Tadema, when the same table graced New Grove

House. John painted Daddy (but the only time I met him was at a lunch Daddy gave at the Garrick); Collier painted him, but he never came to Cannon Hall; Harrington Mann painted him and Daphne too, but I don't remember meeting him. The de Glehns were friends and so were the Harrisons, but it was my Aunt May and her husband Coley who 'kept in' so to speak with painters, and I often think it was because I met so few, and we talked of painting so little, that I am so abysmally ignorant of modern art to-day. Daddy loathed practically everything that was modern. He hated modern music, modern painting, modern architecture and the modern way of living (with the exception of the motor car! and for business I suppose he admitted the telephone had its uses). Regarding painting and pictures, he was adamant in insisting that we knew all there was to know about the Old Masters. As we grew older History of Art was drummed into us, and superbly illustrated books were given us, and by sixteen I certainly knew a good deal about Italian, Flemish, Spanish, British and French painting from the time of the primitives until mid-nineteenth century. After that my education in this field stopped. The pre-Raphaelites had been friends of grandpapa's, and I know *their* worth, but I fancy Daddy had little use for French Impressionism, because we were never bought little books about Degas and Van Gogh and Manet and Monet. And Gauguin horrified him I do remember. I'm not at all sure it is a good thing to be as impressed by one's parents' ideas and opinions as I was by Daddy's. It takes one a long time to readjust oneself when one realises that he may have been wrong, and that quite possibly one thinks differently on certain matters. He had a favourite saying of his own, à propos of disagreeing with someone's ideas:

"Because X says so-and-so it doesn't necessarily mean it *is* so."

I've often found it a most helpful way to end an awkward argument. But I don't remember ever applying it to him!

I have said we were more or less brought up in the theatre and that therefore actors and actresses were the people we knew best. True we had friends amongst children who were what we'd have called 'ordinary'. One met them in the Terrace gardens, one's nurses palled up with *their* nurses (after dear Nanny's departure a veritable string came and went, *and* an under-nurse was promptly ordered in). We had cousins too, and we were a family of relations on both sides. Mummie's sisters were not quite so alarming as Daddy's. In the first place they were younger and unmarried and one called them Billy and Timmie (though Timmie eventually married). But Daddy's were very definitely Aunt. They began by being Auntie so-and-so, and became Aunt as we moved into double figures; odd. Uncle Guy was my hero, and my godfather. He was Daddy's elder brother and had written *An Englishman's Home*, and was a soldier. He brought me back superb clothes from India and other foreign places. I remember a glorious little Evizone's uniform when I was very young, and a quite beautiful coat from Kashmir. He was generally with his regiment, the Royal Fusiliers, in India or South Africa, and was killed, alas, when I was eleven, at Hill 60. My father had his war letters printed privately and they make very good reading, and my great grief as a girl and always was that I, his godchild, had not written to him when he was at the front and Daphne, so much younger, had. It was he who took me, aged six, to the Zoo for the first time. After which I developed a squint. Immediately I was carted off to a famous oculist who announced to my despairing father—"The little maid is flat-eyed." Whatever that means I don't know. All I do know is that I have worn spectacles ever since.

It was when I was six that King Edward VII died. Somehow in my mind he was connected with Peter Pan. I think this must have been due to the unmistakable picture by Rackham in *Peter Pan in Kensington Gardens*. Anyway, I remember being sad when he was dead but I was terrified by the constant tolling of the near-by church bell. We were living in Denham Village at the time, and I remember being made to sit all alone in the lavatory in terror both of the bell tolling and a large daddy-long-legs on the wall. I was a very frightened and nervous child always. As a really small child I would scream the house down if Nanny left the nursery floor for so much as a minute after dark and I was in bed. I was terrified of a drum-and-fife band, and even uneasy over the bugles which played Reveille and the Last Post from Albany Street barracks over which our nursery looked. I was frightened of gypsies, probably due to Mrs Molesworth's *Us*, and I was petrified of ogres and the possibility of witches, and was literally sick—'basin sick' as Daddy would call it—on being made to run round the garden alone in the morning when we were living in Denham.

Jeanne was born in 1911, when I had just turned seven. For years I'd been praying for a baby brother, but when (I was eating cold beef and beetroot in the nursery) Daddy and a doctor came in one lunch-time and told me I had a new baby sister I immediately got down from the table, went over to the armchair and said a prayer of thanksgiving.

We spent that summer, one of the hottest in living memory, at Croxley Green, and I connect it with: Jeanne's christening, with Irene Vanbrugh (then playing in *Passers By* with Daddy) who was one of the godmothers, and 'baby' and myself sticking in a Rolls-Royce on Scott's Hill and running backwards the whole way; with a Coronation garden party at Windsor Castle to which Daddy and Mummie went; some big strike—coal? railway?—; Mummie driving a pony-trap down all the way from London and everyone's surprise when the pony, Polly, foaled the following day; and last and certainly by no means least the dawn of Gladys Cooper into our lives.

It was a very hot Sunday, and Daddy and I drove off in

the Ford to Rickmansworth to meet the train off which a lady was coming to spend the day. We got to the station, and—

"Now Jill, off you get and meet her."

I did not know who I'd come to meet.

"Just pick out the prettiest face you see," said my father.

Under the tunnel and up to the far platform went I, *aged but seven*, and out of the train poured a very large crowd of people. Well, I was guided. Obviously. I went straight up to a very lovely person in a blue hat which matched her eyes, held out my hand, and Gladys and I went back to the car. I still think it remarkable perspicacity and a strange lack of shyness for a child of seven. But then I was never shy; nervous—horribly, yes— but never shy. We were brought up to look on shyness as a form of bad manners, and were probably sophisticated instead. Gladys came into our lives in 1911 and has never left. It is difficult to pay tribute to living people without causing embarrassment, but this is my book and from time to time I shall say what I like about people. Gladys has been a wonderful and darling friend to every member of my family. Daddy, as many people will remember, produced her in countless plays and I think she would be the first to say that she was never better than when produced by him. I think he taught her a great deal, and he believed in her capabilities as an actress more than in any other woman I can remember. She had her glorious good looks, and this was a handicap in itself, for many people were unkind enough to say (at one time) that she owed her success to these looks. This is palpably untrue. She had always immense intelligence, was a first-rate actress and worked like a steam-roller. Never sick or sorry, I have known Gladys play when other women would have been carted off to nursing-homes in ambulances. Daddy thought the world of her, especially in highly dramatic parts such as Paula Tanqueray, Magda and Iris. In 1922, when I was at school in Paris, Daphne (then aged fifteen, and a great adorer of Gladys) wrote, "It's Glad's first night to-night in *The Second Mrs Tanqueray*. Daddy says she is too wonderful. Beats Mrs Campbell, Mrs Kendal, etc, *hollow*. At the dress-rehearsal everyone became hideous with crying, and he says she looked more beautiful than he'd ever seen her before."

I do not think my father would have over-praised Gladys Cooper in a part created by Stella Campbell had he not been truly sincere. I know he did think she touched the tops in this part, and equally I know many disagreed with him. It's an unenviable business following in someone else's footsteps; there are always those to whom the First is the Only—rightly or wrongly.

In 1911 however Gladys Cooper was comparatively un-known. But in March 1913 she and Owen Nares together burst into fame overnight in my father's production of *Diplomacy*. Marie Löhr should have played Dora, but was having a baby (Jane) and so Gladys achieved her fame. *Diplomacy* has always been one of my favourite plays. I was eight when I saw it the first time, and seriously fancied my imitation of the wretched Dora's hysterical door-banging at the end of the second act. "Julian, Julian, Julian." I took it, as a part, in turn with Wendy to play in the nursery. Ellis Jeffreys played Zicka. Lady Tree, Dawson Milward, Norman Forbes, Arthur Wontner, Donald Calthrop . . . all were in that production; what names, what a cast, what a production, and what a success! We were living at Slyfield Manor, Stoke d'Abernon that year —I've always said eight years old was the happiest time of my life. Nanny was still with us, we were in the loveliest house I have ever lived in, we were having happy lessons with a sweet young governess called Miss Bishop who wrote fairy letters to us and dropped them about the garden, and I was madly in love with a farm labourer called Arthur.

Every year we used to take a house in the country from early May until the end of the summer, from which Daddy—and

Mummie if she was playing too—went up to London every evening. It was a perfect life for children, and this state of affairs lasted more or less until one day in 1915 my father fell in love with Cannon Hall, on Hampstead Heath, and did not rest until it was his. Lady Tree was with him at the time, and they both fell in love with the staircase. Lady Tree . . . Maud . . . I think she must have come into our childhood lives from *Diplomacy* days. Most people, adult people, remember her by her amazing wit, her vague eccentricities and—yes, surely—her gentleness. My memories of her are really a child's memory. I remember back to the quite fantastic and fabulous presents she would give us children at Christmas. I don't think a more generous person ever existed, nor do I think the ordinary grown-up would begin to take the thoughtful trouble Lady Tree must have taken in *thinking out* the presents she gave those silly little du Maurier children. One kept hers, on Christmas morning, until the end, they were always the Best. Never toys. Oh dear me no. Jewels, jewelled boxes, Indian scarves, pretty fans, trinkets, shells, holy figures, clothes in which to dress up. And if one went to spend a day in the country with her, or stay—as once we all did at Robertsbridge—we would be asked our choice of food, and given exquisite china off which to eat it, and put to sleep in rooms fit for princesses. Oh, she was amazing, even to little girls in their teens. Of the great and wonderful Tree himself I only have a hazy recollection, more's the pity. When we were staying at Robertsbridge in September 1914 just after the declaration of war (I was ten) he came for the week-end. I think he may have been bored with children, at any rate we were certainly not brought into his ken. I just remember his wandering about the garden like God . . . speaking and gesticulating, and oneself very much in awe and keeping as hidden as possible. Sir Herbert Tree, yes, there was a name. I was brought up on two great names to which to bow the knee, Irving and Tree. Daddy certainly knelt at the shrine of Irving and had a profound admiration and affection for Tree. There are no giants of their ilk now, say what you will. Perhaps one day. . . .

Sir George Alexander was a dear friend to me as a child. I knew him best when I was eleven and living at Chorley Wood where he and Lady Alexander had a house. Though he had none of his own he was devoted to children and particularly kind to me. He gave me a sweet little book and I have a long and affectionate letter from him, written in his own handwriting. I am sure children remember generosity. Or perhaps not when they are children, but in later years, looking back as now I do, the memory strikes deep and one tries—a little late in the day—to say 'thank you'. For many years Frank Curzon was Daddy's partner and although his was a name with which to conjure in theatreland, the same can be said of it in the nursery! Maybe a few cynics will say "Pooh! what's a tricycle to your partner's child?" but in the days when toys at Christmas-time were boxes of soldiers, dolls, *small* doll's prams and large boxes of plasticine, Frank's tricycles and see-saws and life-size dolls were things one remembered and treasured through the years. He was a very generous giver to us, I don't care if he was our father's partner. There were plenty of others I can think of who owed more than Frank did to Daddy who never gave one so much as sixpence or a box of crackers. No reason why they should, and all the more reason to remember after all these years a few names of men and women who contributed to make one's childhood a happy one.

You see, don't you, how the theatre and people of the theatre dominate these memories? It was, as I have said, our milieu. Doctors—didn't we know any? Except for professional reasons I can remember none but the Fripps' young family who were *our* friends, and there again that was probably because Sir Alfred was so kind to the 'Profession' and was in and out of dressing-rooms and operation theatres without any bills to follow. I always remember it was Lady Fripp who, unknown to herself, showed me how to introduce people to each other. My first post-1918 war dance was at the Fripps' house, 19 Portland Place. I was fourteen, and very excited because it was the first 8-12 party I'd ever been to. There were boys in Etons and young men in evening dress, and girls were not supposed to dance with each other. Lady Fripp bore down on me and introduced me to a young man with such exquisite decorum that I never forgot the procedure. How different to the slipshod days of the '30's and '40's, "Bill meet Flo", "Hi-ya, Bill", or the stupid way hostesses say to girls "You know Ted", or Gerry, or what have you, when it's perfectly obvious neither creature has set eyes on the other before. No, I'm old-fashioned. Give me Lady Fripp's "Angela, may I introduce Mr Snooks? Mr Snooks, Miss du Maurier." Even if one *is* fourteen. Manners are appallingly slack nowadays, deteriorated and slack. One mislays them oneself. I do, in spite of good bringing-up. Not so long ago I was asked somebody's name (surname). "I don't know her well enough," I replied without really thinking of the import of my words, "I only know her as Phyll." I ask you. Adults behaving in a kindergarten manner. It's with one's own people, the British people, I dislike this new insidious lack of manners and calling by Christian name. To me it's a step *forward*, a rather exciting moment, the first time the Christian name is used. The new post-war generation, I realise, begins at once now with the friendly 'Tom' and 'May', but I—born in 1904—take umbrage at being 'Angela' on the handshake to a man born, say, in the 'nineties! We should know better. I like all young things to call me Angela—and all Americans. But I still am old-fashioned enough to prefer being Miss du Maurier to men in their fifties and occasionally in their forties! And who knows? perhaps it's all because of Lady Fripp.

The Church was a World Apart to us. I'm very much afraid that all my father's family were allergic to church and the clergy. I know of only one parson for whom my father had much use, and that is Canon Elliott. I don't believe he knew him, but he heard him take Lady Bancroft's funeral when he was as then comparatively little known—I think at Sandgate, near Folkestone—and from then on Daddy had a great admiration for him. Mummie's family, on the other hand, were distinctly 'churchy'. They hailed from Ely and knew the Cathedral (and presumably its services) backwards, and Mummie and 'Billy' had been educated at St Michael's, Bognor, which entailed so much chapel-going that some girls were known to have had their fill there. Billy was very devoted to churchgoing and 'high' church at that, and my greatest treat (next to *Peter Pan* and the Theatrical Garden Party) was to go to High Mass with her at some very high Anglican church, and sway to the incense and bow to little bells, and emotionalise myself thoroughly. It started as a treat, and has gone on as such. *Peter Pan* is a thing of the past, and so is the Theatrical Garden Party (and it would be anything but a treat now), but Church 'and all that' means probably more to me than anything else.

Looking back to my childhood I am grateful that it holds so much happiness and joy in it. How often one hears the cry, "Thank God I'm not a child any more", and even, "I hated my childhood". Mine until I began to grow up was the happiest time of my life. And childhood should be, for everyone. It is the only time when it is possible for a person to be free from care, free from worry. Granted health, childhood should be blessed, and only by the fault of thoughtless, neglectful and cruel adults can childhood be unhappy. There is a tendency these days I think to over-spoil children and indulge them in excess, a new code is coming into being in which the word 'don't' has been left out altogether. This will not lead to happiness. No child and no grown person either is going ultimately to be happy in a life where no discipline has been taught, shown, learnt or achieved. That way madness certainly lies and not

2*

only madness but world chaos. Discipline—kind and tolerant discipline—makes for happy childhood. Happy children become contented and reliable adults. Adults lacking bitterness, jealousy and class-hatred make the best citizens, and when the citizens of a country are happy, and free from bitterness, then the world will possibly come into its own. Spare the rod certainly, but for everybody's sake do not let us delude ourselves by pampering our young to the extent whereby no punishment is to be fitted to any crime, when misbehaving is not only tolerated but looked upon as an interesting development of self-expression, and where in the schoolroom rudeness, wrong-doing and rank disobedience is the order of the day.

II

Growing Up, Adolescence, Love, Etc

"DON'T put your daughter on the stage, Mrs Worthington."
Do you remember Noel Coward's clever little song, with its
catchy tune? If you remember the tune, sing these words to it
instead of Noel's: "Don't tell your children packs of lies, Mrs
Worthington." My own adolescence, and I think my whole life,
came near to ruin by the well-meant evasion of all kind relations, grown-ups and above all my parents in telling me the
truth.

We were brought up on the angel-and-baby lines; pretty,
sentimental, poetic. Helped too by a large picture of a baby in
an angel's arms, descending to a house. That was the proof,
what else was needed? I don't think we ever asked for an
original explanation. One was aware, as one grew older, that
other children's newly arrived brothers and sisters came differently from under bushes, in bags. By sundry means and
ways. Subconsciously a seed of interest? curiosity? wonder?
was sown in one's mind. As I have said previously, at the age
of eleven and a half I was told there was no Father Christmas.
That had been Disillusion Number One. Disillusion, plus
slight bewilderment and the teeniest spark of distrust.

At twelve I went to a day-school. We had moved to Cannon
Hall by now, and Daphne and I, with satchels on our backs and
socks upon our legs, would march off sedately every morning
at 8.45 a.m. after feeding countless canaries and fan-tail pigeons.
I hated school, I admit that, from the start. I was terrified of the
mistresses, terrified of certain lessons (arithmetic in particular)

and bewildered by the noise of nearly two hundred girls answering roll-call, slamming down desk-lids, pushing and pulling at 'break'; in fact I loathed it. There were five or six nice quiet little girls in my form, and I liked them. We played quietly in the garden at break, formed 'crushes' on the head girl, went to tea with each other in each other's homes, and by fair means or foul discovered our Parents had LIED to us about *How* we had been *Born*. One little girl knew far more than any of the others and fairly made our hair stand up on end.

"My father would never do such a thing," I remember saying very indignantly. Miss Know All replied with the 'sez you' of her day, and that was that. The Underground Movement was on. It was 1916, we all knew about German spies in those days, and no secret agent could have worked with greater care or diligence than the five little girls in Form IVB (I think) of a certain reputable school in Hampstead, as to exactly how Babies WERE BORN. And in my heart at least was the *awful* truth that I had been betrayed. That I had been told lies from the beginning. And why? Why, I asked myself, should my father and mother lie? I knew the answer, or thought I did. It was because the truth was so HORRIBLE that they couldn't bear to tell it to me.

Into our fold was admitted one day a newcomer. She was different, rather prim, pretty and much better class! She turned out a Quisling. She TOLD HER PARENTS.

There followed a really dreadful and ridiculous row. I was blamed as torch-bearer and ring-leader, and the show-down as far as Cannon Hall was concerned put the Battle of the Marne (or whatever battle raged at that moment) into very second place. I was called for at school one day by our nursery-governess (who looked after Jeanne) who said in sepulchral tones:

"You've been found out."

I swear no pilot bombing Berlin for the first time knew the

fear that was in my heart. 'Now we see through a glass, darkly.' . . . Yes, and now I had stumbled on the truth 'face to face'. So what? Mummie had been summoned by the Head Mistress and I was threatened with expulsion. So she told me, as sitting by my bedside later in the day, an expression of utter misery and degradation on her face, she informed me of the heinousness of my crime. "It's all so beautiful if you only knew," I was told, and a fat lot of comfort I gleaned from *that* piece of information. Especially when it was added to by— "I shall feel I can never trust you again."

But dear God in Heaven! who was the one to lose their trust?

"Must Aunt May be told?" I whimpered.

(I cannot imagine why the idea of Daddy's sister May, one of my godmothers, should have filled me with such terror. I did not beseech Mummie to keep my Awful Secret from Eva Moore, my other godmother.)

Now, I can see that when my mother's eyes fall on these pages, she will say, "What a *fuss*! You *do* exaggerate."

Not one word have I exaggerated. Like an elephant's, my memory is horribly and at times painfully accurate. No, I had the truth at last. And I cannot be blamed for imagining that 'all that' was horrible, unnatural, repulsive, disgusting and ugly. How could I think otherwise? I was twelve, and absolutely innocent. The fact that I'd been told fables in the first place *stopped* me from enquiring from my parents. The fact that other children's parents had fobbed them off with lies too, only went to prove the shame all the grown-ups felt.

I became very self-conscious, imagining that people's voices would hush as I came into the room; I was the leper, so I thought. Mummie's old *'prenez garde'* was useless now that I knew at least that amount of French, and I would run a mile rather than meet any bride who might conceivably look different than when beheld last. Then a really unfortunate thing happened. I think all would have very gradually been 'got over' and 'got used to'—for after all one was young, and busy with lessons and homework (I wasn't expelled)—but for the occurrence of the Wounded Soldier.

On our way to school Daphne and I had to walk along a very quiet and secluded lane. It might have been miles in the country. Some months after the Facts of Life episode, on our way to school one day, a wounded soldier (in pretty blue uniform) was exposing himself in a manner which would have got him locked up. I have said I was a nervous little girl, by now I was a mentally bewildered little girl, and I was also an extremely ignorant little girl. The soldier was the last straw. Daphne did not notice anything, and I was much too aware of my elder-sister-responsibility ('you're to promise never to tell Daphne') to say anything to her. But there it was, and there was no one I could tell. Our 'Underground Movement' had been closed down, disbanded, there wasn't a soul to whom I could confide my terror or my surprise. Not for many years did I tell anyone, and for what it's worth not for more years than anyone would believe possible could I bear to think about a man, much less look at one.

I have given this rather pathetic and rather drab little story in detail because I think it is very very important indeed that other little girls should be neither bewildered, frightened, nor influenced as I most certainly was, by the misguided wish for permanent so-called innocence which my parents wanted for their daughters, which led to even greater fear when I saw for the first time the unpleasant spectacle I have related above.

★   ★   ★

Chester Place, Cumberland Terrace, Cannon Hall . . . those had been our homes up till now, with a fair sprinkling of entrancing country temporary summer homes, of which Sly-field was the gem. There were always visits, annual ones, to the seaside too, with spades and buckets, brown sand-shoes, dark blue bathing-dresses with white anchors (hideous they were too), and paddling-drawers. Visits to Daddy's mother 'Big' Granny (to differentiate her from 'Little' Granny, Mummie's mother) at her Regency house in Royal Crescent, Ramsgate, to the Guildford Hotel, Sandwich (to which my parents, both enthusiastic golfers, would go as often as holidays would allow), to Dieppe, Dinard, Birchington . . . to Mullion, the Isle of Wight, Bournemouth, Whitby. . . . We were in Wales, at Llanbedr, when war was declared in 1914. I was ten. We were at Bushey, where Daddy was training as a cadet for the Brigade of Guards, when it finished.

I suppose I began to grow up around this time. In some ways I had always been treated by my family as a person with whom to be reckoned. They never talked down to any of us where the theatre was concerned, our friends often enough were Daddy's own, we read fairly grown-up books and discussed them at length, generally over the dinner-table or at Sunday suppers. If we were not bright at our lessons it was not counted against us, although subjects like music, French, art and literature were encouraged more than maths. I shall always remember Daddy ringing up his business manager, Tom Vaughan, to do one of my decimal sums for me. Neither Daddy nor Mummie were any good at maths. (I floored our form-mistress by brightly informing her that Mummie had achieved four out of a hundred in an arithmetic exam, and that the four was for neatness. She could no longer flay me with sarcasm nor be rude about my mother; I had her.) Sums were pain and grief to me, and in tears I went to Daddy, who was probably about the mark I was—'long division' and no further. I can see him now, at the telephone, in earnest conversation with Tom, who ran Wyndham's and the Playhouse with such dexterity and brilliance but could not do my decimals.

Daddy always had an early dinner before going to act in the evening, and we ate with him. I started 'dining' with Mummie in the Bushey days—which I daresay was sardines for supper— but it seemed a grown-up thing to do, and once the war was over and Daddy back in the theatre I remained dining à trois until he died. Theatrical domestic life is different from the routine life of the business man, the countryman or that one-time gentleman of leisure. It's a question of late at night and late in the morning, and it's no use for well-brought-up conventional folk to sniff and become high-hat with their "my dear, they're never down till eleven" sort of talk. Try going to bed every night at two a.m. *not* having been up dancing but memorising a long Shakespearean part, or Shaw, or Tchekov. Or what must be much more tiring (and about which I know very little) singing and dancing—and trying to be funny—in a muscial comedy or revue. Evenings like these with two or three matinées added, probably rehearsals for other shows, and then, as my father would have said, "How d'you like your eggs boiled?" In other words, lay off criticising the Hours Actors Keep. In our home the hours were not so very peculiar; my parents breakfasted in bed, naturally, and were down by the middle of the morning. If rehearsals were on foot, Daddy left the house punctually at ten-thirty, to be at the theatre by eleven. He very rarely lunched at home, except on Sundays when he always did. But his rule of life was to be back by about six-thirty, have the early dinner, then half an hour's 'shut-eye' in a long chair in his study or the morning-room, and off to the theatre again. As theatrical children, once school was over and done with, we led the same life. Breakfast in our rooms, and *why not*? Continentals of all ages do.

My bouts at schools were short-lived and not particularly successful. The day-school at Hampstead lasted for four terms, during which we had German measles, ordinary measles and chicken-pox, and when the school announced the intention of putting us all into uniform we were whipped away. No nice little neat blue gym tunics for us, with our pretty chintzes. But the relief came in the nature of zeppelin raids and bombs. People of Hitler's war have forgotten how very unpleasant indeed were the air-raids of the first war. I frankly became a terrified and shivering child, always anticipating the nights with large full moons; somehow the daylight raids were not so alarming, though I shall always remember the first full-scale raid by a large number of Gothas one Saturday morning as I was picking raspberries at the bottom of the garden : the far-away hum in the skies that sounded like bees, the shouts to us from the house, the pointing of frenzied servants and behold! the swarm—as it appeared—not of bees but German airplanes. It was the night raids that frightened us, me at any rate; being woken from a sound sleep and made to sit in a cellar, and listening to the terrific report of the big anti-aircraft gun which was close by at the Whitestone Pond. And then Mummie took it into her head to go to the theatre to be with Daddy, which was worse. Finally a house was taken for us at Cookham in late 1917 and I was restored to a less gibbering funk.

Daddy's war-time productions were many and varied. In September 1915 came *The Ware Case*, George Bancroft's great drama which gave Daddy one of the finest parts of his whole career, as the murderer of his weak brother-in-law; it was a long time since a murder trial had been portrayed on the London stage and the first time to the best of my belief that the scene actually depicted the Old Bailey. Marie Löhr played Lady Ware, and Arthur Hatherton the pathetic little tramp whose evidence gets the murderer off. Everyone who saw my father in *The Ware Case* must, I'm sure, remember the expression on his face at the close of the play when Sir Hubert Ware, returned—free—to his home after the verdict had cleared his name, hears the cries "We want Hubby Ware" in the streets below, and the man's sudden realisation of the whole farce of the lie, the look of hopeless hatred and bitterness which came on Daddy's face as he turned to the window, his cry of "You bloody fools, I did it" before committing suicide with poison, and crashing to his death on the stage. It was a tour de force throughout, and the end magnificent, and even in these hard-bitten critical days could not be labelled Ham.

This was followed next March by Barrie's *A Kiss for Cinderella* with Hilda Trevelyan. Next, in December, came *London Pride*, which was a big success. It dealt with the war-time record of a London cockney costermonger and as the heroine Mabel Russell staged a brilliant come-back. In September 1917 there was a revival of *A Pair of Spectacles* with Sir John Hare; the first first-night of my life, this; the occasion on which I elected to fall in love (thirteen) with 'Bao' Campbell, Stella's son, and a great favourite of Daddy's. I added his name to a growing list to be prayed for nightly, but alas—he was killed.

When we were at Cookham Daddy saw fit to introduce us to Dumas and Harrison Ainsworth. How we both, Daphne and I, revelled in *Old St Paul's, Windsor Castle, The Lancashire Witches, The Tower of London*. These great romantic novels appear to be neglected from the modern child's education, and surely there could not be a better way of interesting a child in history? I personally always found Scott very heavy going, but there wasn't an Ainsworth unread by either of us after a few weeks, and certainly my subsequent interest for French history came into being after I had been introduced to the Court of Louis XIII by *The Three Musketeers*, and the many sequels that followed.

We returned to London early in 1918, the raids had abated and Daddy was now playing his greatest of all successes, *Dear Brutus. Raffles*, one of his earliest and best loved successes and a war-time revival, he always swore brought him ill-luck, but when I look back on that original cast of *Dear Brutus*, a biggish cast at that, hardly one player is alive to-day. Brilliant and attractive Hilda Moore—dead, long before she was even middle-aged; she died whilst nursing her boy for a strepto-coccal throat which she caught and from which she sub-sequently died. Faith Celli, Barrie's dream for all parts surely, and never more perfect and enchanting than as Margaret. Why do people decry Barrie's bursts of sentiment nowadays? I only know there was never a dry eye in the house when Faith's poignant and heart-rending cry, "I don't want to be a might have been", rang out. . . . I can cry now at the very memory of it. Norman Forbes, Arthur Hatherton (the creator of Lob), Sam Sothern, Jessie Bateman, Maud Millet, Will West, 'all all are gone. . . .' Only Lydia Bilbrooke I think is alive of that cast to-day and Doris Lytton.

I went to boarding-school at this juncture, taking with me as keepsake and mascot Hilda Moore's pink tam o' shanter which, as Mrs Dearth, she carried in her hand as—happy with her husband at last—she passed by the open window in search for the Dearths' second chance. I adored Hilda, one of my earliest and most profound adorations, and her pink 'tammy' helped to keep back the tears of homesickness that lay heavy on me. The day I left for that far-off destination, that Tibet-like quarter of isolation, that Siberia (i.e. Wimbledon Common), my cousin Gerald Millar came to lunch. It was a Sunday, and he was about to rejoin his regiment in the thick of the worst fighting in the worst year of that war. No one gave him a thought, we were all weeping our eyes out for me and the front to which I was off. I went at half-term, and I returned for good at the end. I could not take it, let's face it. I was a timid and nervous homesick silly of fourteen, and although I made friends with quite a number of the girls I just could not bear to be from home. So back I came, to do lessons with Daphne (with Jeanne at another table), with the excellent 'Tod' who taught me all I know really and who for the last years has been trying to din knowledge into Daphne's own children. I enjoyed my lessons at home, one could learn the things that seemed important and useful, and not bother about Latin or Algebra, both of which my parents thought unnecessary. Tod came along too when we moved to Bushey to be near Daddy when he 'joined up'.

Poor Daddy! how he loathed army life. There he was, well over the age in the mid-forties, in company with boys straight from school. Every cadet in the place was eighteen; he had one crony only of his own age, Burghard (who now lives within half a mile of our home in Cornwall). He and Daddy were allowed to share a room; one supposes in recognition of their Great Age. Even the officers were mostly younger than my father, and in any case he did not take kindly to orders. How he *loathed* his sergeant, *and* a certain officer whose name perhaps it is even now more discreet to forget. Ebenezer Pike was the C.O. His wife Olive Snell did a crayon drawing of Daddy in khaki, but though she has given a pathetic look to her sitter it misses the abject *hungry* misery which his face showed so often. He was taken of course as a 'joke', a 'lark', by most of the cadets, and really one cannot blame them. He used to bring some of them back, in twos and threes, to our dreary little villa for tea. I was now fourteen and falling in love right and left. It was wonderful, all these brilliant young men in khaki, about to be killed in action (I could not know Armistice Day was nearing) straight from Eton, Winchester, Shrewsbury . . . there were several with whom we kept in touch for years, but only one who drove me suicidally inclined for Love. To me he was Apollo, Mars, God, Romance, IT. He was very good-looking, and kind to me in a patronising fashion. He had slight side-whiskers and should obviously have worn his clothes in the mode of 1820; the uniform of a private in the army of 1918 was definitely not a style he would have chosen for himself. He caught the Spanish 'flu, and I contemplated suicide quite seriously one afternoon in the Watford canal. He 'lasted' for quite a long time in my throbbing heart; he went as far as sending me a box of chocolates from Paris, from a shop called (I think) the Marquise de Sevigné (I know I kept the box for jewellery for many years after the sweets had been eaten!). The arrival of this box of chocolates so shook me that I quite literally did shake nearly all day, and the red-haired 'children's maid' who was my confidante suggested I should end my letter of thanks to him with the words 'toujours à toi'. Which I did. It was this young man (I really think he must have been rather nice, with a sense of humour that certainly I had not) who later took Daphne and me to the Military Tournament; by this time I was either fifteen or sixteen and still as éprise as ever with him. I had chosen for the occasion to put on a pretty low-necked pink frock, in which I looked my best. On coming down to lunch Mummie took one look and sent me upstairs to change, and put on the matching frock to what Daphne was wearing; there was nothing to do, we were children who obeyed these sorts of orders and knew better than to argue. Tears welled in my eyes, my bust also swelled high in my tight mauve linen frock (which was the sort of frock one got hot in too). Daphne looked a dream as always, and by the time my swain had called to take us to Olympia I was red-nosed with heat, discomfort, mortification and a fit of the sulks.

I have fallen in and out of love one way and another all my life. It started, I think, at Mrs Wordsworth's dancing class with a little boy in a sailor suit. That was easy, and in fact encouraged. The difficulty came when one fell in love with a mere face, or someone out of one's class (I should not have known what class meant in those days, I doubt sometimes if I do now), but I knew just enough to realise my adoration for a curly-headed baker's boy in Albany Street would get me no further, nor a village boy in Llanbedr village, nor the farm labourer Arthur (for whom I pinched Daddy's cigars and as a reward was allowed to cling to his back as he rode me through the farm on a cart horse); nor several of the wounded Tommies who were patients in the Fitzwilliams' wonderful Milton where we used to go and stay during the war. I certainly saw myself 'married' to all these people in turn, and it was a difficult business trying to organise it in my mind, as I grew from ten to eleven, to twelve, thirteen, fourteen. There was the Prince of Wales too, whose photograph hung over my bed—honour shared with Bobby Loraine—the smudges on the glass frames showing all too clearly the devoted kisses I emplanted upon them. There was always the hope that one day I could conceivably marry Bobby Loraine; but even I saw no future as a Queen of England, and the nearest romance ever got with my wild dreams over the Prince of Wales was that somehow I would rescue him from a burning aeroplane. Through all these great romances however there was one Love to which (? to whom?) I remained faithful; my cousin Gerald. I well remember that whilst fighting was at its heaviest in 1915 (I was eleven then) I would lock myself into the drawing-room of our house in Chorley Wood, take out the only photograph I had of him (at the age of nine in a smock), and gaze at it with rapt adoration as I listened to my favourite record: the drinking song of *Cavalleria Rusticana*. . . . This to me, in 1915, was the high spot of Love and Romance. And when, at thirteen, I fell equally in love with the head girl of my school I arranged it all very nicely in my mind that she and my cousin Gerald should meet, marry and live happily ever after. *That's* the kind of nice innocent little thing I was. No complexes, no inhibitions; Love to me meant romantic young soldiers in khaki, Keeping the Home Fires Burning, the Prince of Wales, Handsome Actors, Beautiful Actresses, and all falling in love, and no sex in any of it.

That is the most curious part of all. Even after the Hideous Revelations about which I have written had so upset my equilibrium, I still did not connect falling in love with any physical change in myself. When I made up romances between all these exciting people and myself sex just never came into it. I probably imagined myself being kissed like the princess in The Sleeping Beauty, even the imaginary children I was always giving myself were most miraculously conceived! I pushed the nightmare of that horrible memory away from me, refusing to remember it, loving people with a Juliet-like innocence that few people have given me credit for. A worshipper at shrines, that was me. And ragged and teased mercilessly by my family when they saw signs of a new love. "Puffin with her swollen look" was Daddy's gibe. (That was a nickname I came by at seventeen which has remained ever since.) Swollen looks after a time can be camouflaged! And let me add one word of warning : DON'T always tease your children when they start to fall in love, it can be dangerous. Confidence which might alter the course of a person's life may be withheld for want of tact and understanding. Actually I did not mind being teased, I knew it was kindly meant always, besides which by the time I had reached the age of sixteen I realised if one couldn't be the beauty one might as well be the butt. Nearly everyone, with the exception of my mother, has teased me all my life, but nicely, with affection and love. But I still think one should 'go carefully' when dealing with adolescents. They'll take a lot from their contemporaries, but from an adult, c'est autre chose.

In my young days we were called flappers, now the expression used is teen-ager, or even bobby-soxer, though what the latter means I cannot for the life of me fathom. All silly expressions, but I prefer flapper and the flappy plaits which doubtless gave the name. I was beginning to be a flapper I suppose when Frederick Whiting painted the colossal portrait of the three of us ; taken supposedly on the Heath, but painted in reality in his Kensington studio whither we trekked from Hampstead in the tube. I was extremely bored with the whole business, the more so as I realised I should be handed down to posterity with a flaming shining nose, and Daphne looking rather like a flaming shining Jeanne d'Arc. My position was a tiring one moreover, sitting with my whole weight resting on one hand. I shall never forget my tears when told that the whole of one precious Sunday was to be given up to posing. Perhaps that was the day the nose shone so palpably that Mr Whiting was determined to put in the red light. It was a fine piece, however, acclaimed throughout the length and breadth of England at the various exhibitions at which it was lent. It now hangs in my sister's house at Menabilly.

Round and about this chrysalis stage the Lonsdales came into our lives, Fred and his family I mean. Happy Birchington days those were, so many holidays spent at the (then) little Bungalow Hotel, and the Lonsdales living up the road in a small house. Fred was the famed author of *The Maid of the Mountains*, and had not yet begun writing those sparkling comedies which made him perhaps the first worthy successor to Oscar Wilde. His three daughters Mavis, 'Frankie' and Mab, were about our own ages, and though younger than me Mavis was parcelled off for my friend, Frankie for Daphne and Jeanne for Mab. My first recollection of them now even goes back a great deal further, to a party given by Frank and Isabel Curzon for Cecilia Cavendish (Isabel's daughter) when I, a plain little eight-year-old in a home-made Dutch 'creation', had my eyes riveted to three little exquisite cherubs in almost diaphanous scantiness; they looked like three wax dolls from Hamley's, and were three little Lonsdales. They were always charming, and aged twelve, eleven and nine, wearing butcher-blue linen frocks were, I should think, as attractive a trio as could be seen. Later I was bridesmaid to Mavis. Freddie was rather an alarming parent; not to his children but to his children's friends. He would forget one's age and ask point-blank some serious question which needed an adult answer. And he was no sufferer of fools. My memory of him will always be a youngish girl's one, and of Birchington days; Freddie in white socks, no hat, and invariably stroking his nose; his sentences always prefixed by the words "Ha! my dear feller" . . . somewhat furiously as he pins you down. And he would be, it seemed, as keen for the opinion of one of us children or his own, about some problem, or line in a play, as he would have been for the opinion of a real brain.

Birchington in those days had a galaxy of brains too. There was Lord Carson (Sir Edward still I think), one of the kindest and most charming men I ever remember. Gill the K.C., Sir Butler Aspinall; and there was dear Fred Norton, the composer of that evergreen *Chu Chin Chow* which has given pleasure to so many millions; and one Christmas I remember an influx of Bancrofts. Dear old Sir Squire—but of course we knew him well anyhow, a fairly regular Cannon Haller—Lady Bancroft (Marie Wilton), who actually advanced the theory that I had talent, when dressed up in sheets and playing the part of a nun (we children acted some hair-raising play called *The Sacrifice*, written for the occasion by Daphne). Gladys Cooper, her children and her sister Doris were frequent visitors to Birchington in those days, and in fact were on many holidays with us, at Dieppe, at Frinton. . . . Emily Brooke entered the fold sometime about now to be Daddy's leading lady in Besier's *The Prude's Fall*. She was an enchanting person, a very real person—and there are plenty of theatrical folk who glitter and seem un-real—but Emily brought a breath of the country, a little of her native Irish peat, into the air and atmosphere, and proved also what a good actress she was, sending an extraordinary sense of sincerity across the footlights. The stage suffered a loss when she left it to marry Atty Persse, but one felt she was leaving to return to a life that she much preferred, and perhaps wisely she did not try to combine marriage and acting.

In 1919 Alfred Sutro wrote his play *The Choice* for Daddy. I must have been about sixteen I think, fifteen or sixteen. And it brings me to that inimitable and indomitable Viola. Viola Tree, the most brilliant, most witty, most amusing—and at times most maddening—woman it has been my pleasure to have known. How one misses Viola! there are so many occasions on which one longs to hear her generous laugh, ask her advice, tell her a story. She swept across the lawn of Cannon Hall in mauve and black, her gestures large and expansive like her father's and her voice a woman's echo of his voice. She had a way, a habit, of reiterating her words as she spoke (as I believe Tree used to).

"Sir, sir" (she always called Daddy 'sir'; "Sir dear," . . .!) "I see, I see," "I know, I know, I know," "yes, yes, yes," spoken in short staccato jerky movements, yet with a deep-throated lilt. One just was contented to sit listening to Viola talking. Or tears would run down the face with laughter if she started on her imitations, or you could cry naturally and unaffectedly if you were lucky enough to get her to sing to you. I would as soon have listened to Viola singing German Lieder or an old Scottish ballad at the piano of one's own drawing-room, than pay the earth to hear some of the greatest singers of the day. She sang generously, spontaneously; her heart in the song she would be singing, her Milan training preventing the vulgar 'catch in the throat' which so many singers try to achieve and which merely ruins a great number of songs; an evening of Viola singing to the accompaniment of her attractive and talented husband Alan Parsons was a 'treat', and her repertoire was as varied as it was generous. She could be plaintive; she could be 'highbrow'; she could be so vulgar as to pass belief. The field of Viola's talent was explored by one as the years went by, but she came into our lives through *The Choice*, in which she astonished London by appearing on the stage in a replica of the Bluecoat uniform, yellow stockings and all. Very handsome she looked too. The most endearing quality of Viola was, I think, her complete lack of 'side', the absence of any conceit, and the whole-hearted way in which she thoroughly enjoyed fooling. Viola could look a million dollars if she had to, but nine out of ten times her natural carelessness and lack of vanity precluded her from making the best of herself, and she was *never* above painting her nose red and adding a touch of boot-black to get a laugh when one was needed. Not many women can get away with making frights of themselves, causing real mirth and not merely an embarrassed attempt at it, by cloaking good looks and clowning, but Viola could, and one never felt hot under the collar. She adored amusing people, especially my father, who ragged her at times unmercifully. I always think the funniest occasion in my memories of Viola was the time she paid her first real visit to us, at Fowey, arriving one morning by motor-boat, and falling *straight* into the harbour, fully clothed and with a rather smart hat on her head. Utterly undaunted, and in full view of a number of people, including—naturally—Daddy, Viola turned tail and went for a swim, her smart hat becoming more and more rakish as the waves rippled it. That swim nearly cost her her life, for she caught a severe chill and within a week was desperately ill with acute peritonitis.

I suppose *Bulldog Drummond* will be claimed by many people to rank in the forefront of Wyndham's and du Maurier successes. Even if it was one of the 'thick ear' variety of plays (as my father labelled them) it certainly in no way diminished his popularity as actor-manager or producer, however much the highbrows wailed. 'Sapper' and Daddy between them got a lot of amusement and fun out of *Bulldog*, and the first night was a riot of enthusiasm. Who can forget the polished suave manner of 'Bertie' Hare's Dr Lakington, or Alfred Drayton's truly brutal Petersen? Or the fooling of my father, Basil Foster and Ronnie Squire putting on the carpet to the strains of

'Avalon' as the curtain descended on the first act? Daddy and Bertie Hare had one of the greatest stage-fights ever produced at the end of the second act; now that films have taken such a rooted hold on the imagination, people are apt to forget—and even now forgo—the thrills that legitimate acting on the stage, with flesh and blood instead of celluloid, can produce. Certainly the Drummond-Lakington fight in the doctor's consulting-room, with bodies falling, men screaming and finally the massive medicine-armoire crashing, was one of the most exciting spectacles the London stage had seen, in 1921, for many a day. *Bulldog* was running in the New Year, 1922, when Daddy was knighted, and the ovation that night at the theatre was something that his family and his friends felt very proud over.

In January I went to school again, this time to a finishing-school in Paris. As in the old Wimbledon days I was agog to go; and just as before was even more agog to return, but this time I was not listened to with quite such sympathy. Betty Seymour Hicks and I were to go together, although when the time came I had 'flu and went later, escorted by Gilbert Miller's charming wife Margaret, always a veritable fairy godmother to me, and Nelson Keys, of all people. I had never been to Paris and was wildly excited, especially by the Crillon Hotel where I stayed with Margaret for the night before she dropped me the following afternoon near the Tour Eiffel. My school was a very famous one, full of very 'smart' girls; the sort of girls neither Bet nor I were ever really likely to come into contact with in later years, whatever we felt then. However, we both made two or three friends who still count as *real* friends in our lives, so what matter if we felt a little disturbed when passing the open door of one of the Mesdemoiselles X to hear ourselves described as 'filles d'artistes', moreover to hear ourselves spoken about patronisingly as really very 'bien élevées'; had they imagined, one wonders, that we were going to dance the can-can, or pollute the aristocracy with a little jargon from Billingsgate and eat off our knives? I cannot say I learnt very much, and this is no discredit on the excellent X's. I do not see how a horde of English misses will ever learn anything en masse. My French, which had not been bad with 'Tod', deteriorated, there were two or three girls who spoke exquisite French 'more French than the French', but the accents on the whole were pretty deplorable and our sentences and conversations were the usual mixture of the two, "avez-vous vu le blotting-paper". . . . Again, and no discredit meant, I must be the only girl who has ever achieved two terms at a Parisian finishing-school without one visit to the Comédie Française. I was mad about music, especially opera, and as names were put down for attendances for *either* opera or Comédie Française, automatically I'd put mine down for the former, and was never found out. I had ambitions in those days to be an opera singer myself (!). To-day when I think of the money that has been spent on that hoped-for voice of mine. . . . I still think it was not money wasted, however, any more than was the money spent on piano lessons for years, for I learnt a lot; enough to criticise, enough to appreciate, enough to want to spend my last penny at Covent Garden rather than at Chanel or Molyneux. We all have our extravagances, music is mine.

My singing lessons in Paris were given me by Madame Ritter-Ciampi, then one of the greatest names of the Opéra. She saw a 'future' for me, and after my first lesson I returned to the Champs de Mars on wings. She was a tall, extremely handsome woman, the conventional idea of the prima donna. Only two or three of us had singing lessons, and the thing to do obviously, I soon saw, was to develop a grande passion for Madame Ciampi, which passed her by completely, and she was perfectly apt to toss one's meagre bunch of Parma violets across the room if she felt that way. Now I may as well admit that I have to be encouraged; whether over a short story, a song, a love affair or the receipt of a bunch of flowers. I was not used to spending pocket-money on flowers for Hilda Moore, Emily Brooke, Madge Titheradge, to have them chucked aside; they did at least give me a kiss and one saw one's flowers vased at once and popped on to a dressing-table; not so the Diva, who, if one came a cropper over one's F sharp or wobbled on Middle C, behaved as though the Huns were at the gates of Paris, and oneself just the most imbecile of an entirely imbecile race. I was terrified. And when I become terrified I can do nothing. All poise, all sense leaves me. I am not of the stuff that can be screamed at. I wilt and tears run down my cheeks. It was useless for the great Ciampi to be a Dove on Friday if she'd behaved like a Jay the preceding Tuesday. I was 'through', I'd had it. The great diaphragm, the stupendous voice which was to shake the foundations of Covent Garden, quivered and was still. I learnt no more singing in Paris.

I wonder how many teachers realise how dreary it is for students to learn nothing at all but scales and exercises? Whether it is for the voice, or for piano-playing—or even for dancing. A great many people learn to sing, to play, to dance for their own amusement and edification. They are *not* budding Melbas, Pavlovas, Menuhins or Myra Hesses, they do not even wish to be. But occasionally a teacher will think fit to re-start a new pupil—aged, for sake of argument, eighteen, nineteen— putting him or her back to the five-finger-exercise school. If the pupil has been badly taught in the first place and has serious ambitions to become a public performer this is one matter; but it is literally soul-destroying for the boy or girl of sixteen, seventeen, eighteen, who perhaps has not very great confidence in him or herself, but enormous love of music and a longing to express themselves. For years I had played the piano, fairly creditably, enough to keep myself thoroughly happy; though always a nervous performer with a great distaste for 'playing my piece' to Sunday visitors. Paris killed my piano-playing stone dead: a man informed me my knuckles were out of joint, that my hand 'slipped' in a disgraceful fashion and that for a term at least I must do hand and finger exercises on the lid of the closed piano . . . *that* for a girl who loved nothing better than playing through operatic scores in duet-form by the hour, who really enjoyed trying to master symphonies in piano form, who revelled in Debussy (and to hell with wrong notes). There must be, I am sure, hundreds of cases where young, eager and impressionable would-be students of music (I won't call them musicians) have all natural inclination and enthusiasm damped to zero by over-zealous and entirely unimaginative teachers. I would liken it to a stoppage of all private enterprise of the soul.

As at my Wimbledon school I found the few rules—and admittedly there were but few—irksome. Bet, who had battled at Roedean for a number of years, found them in Paris to be almost negligible. The X's themselves were highly cultured, extremely attractive sisters, with a flair for clothes which made most of us look dowdy to the extreme. 'Crushes' raged fast and furiously, and the petty jealousies reached when an X said good-night to Y, and not to Z, only go to prove how entirely correct are such stories as *Mädchen in Uniform*, *Olivia*, and one or two others I have read. It's such an entirely natural thing, this 'falling' for older girls and mistresses, that I cannot think why there is always such a song and dance made when novels deal with the subject. Victorian adults put their heads together and mutter "Unhealthy"; what is there unhealthy in putting someone on a pedestal and giving them violets? Or hoping—in bursts of homesickness—to be kissed good-night? The only unhealthy matter is when an older woman battens on a young girl's adoration and cruelly persecutes her mind by maliciously seeing how far her power will reach. There is precious little sex and so-called Lesbian affection in girls' schools, whatever some people imagine; there is a rather pathetic and innocent longing for love and understanding, and much sentimental pedestal-worship.

I was frankly homesick that first term in Paris, kind as the X's and all the girls were. But in March a wonderful stroke of luck came my way. My family wrote that they were going to Algiers for a holiday. It did not take much persuading on my part to be allowed to go too, a trip which the X's were most understanding about, for it did mean missing some weeks in Paris.

Off we set, Daddy, Mummie, the three of us and Billy (Mummie's sister—incidentally my father's secretary), Ronald Squire and H. V. Esmond. Daddy always had to have a pal or so on a holiday to play with, or I think such a 'parcel of women', as he termed us, would have got him down, and who shall blame him. He liked to play golf, and bezique in the evening, and have cronies with whom to swap stories over the port and cointreau. We travelled very much 'en prince' whenever we went anywhere with Daddy I may as well say, with a plethora of cabins and couriers and all laid on, and if suites booked did not meet with approval Daddy would shoot an agonised glance at my aunt and say, "Billy darling, this is damn awful, go and see so-and-so and have it all changed, will you", and soon some wretched manager bowed to the knees with grief would emerge and some Rajah would be turned from comfort and ourselves installed, and—"Send the chap a case of cigars, Billy darling," Daddy would remark, gazing from the window over aquamarine bays and palm trees blowing in the breeze, as he secretly wondered why on earth he'd left Cannon Hall, which he adored, and the Garrick Club where all his friends were.

Daphne has written so much about him in *Gerald* that I find it difficult to paint him again. Purposely I have not re-read her life of him, in case subconsciously I might seem to 'crib', and in fact I have not read it since it was first published in 1935.

In the matter of holidays he was difficult to please. For he adored his beloved London, and was never really happy when away from it. For a town-dweller he had odd pursuits, however, for he was never happier than on days spent in the country, eye-glass in pocket, a delicious picnic lunch put up for him by our wonderful Mrs Leigh, and bird-watching by the hour. He was almost as good an imitator of bird-song as he was of his fellow-men, and in that there was none better. In the summer, in spite of our lovely garden at Hampstead with its lawns and tennis court and flowers, he would invariably order the car for the middle of the day, and—matinée, rehearsal and other engagements permitting—drive off, with a favoured crony, to watch birds on Berkhamsted Common or Bookham or somewhere. Queer, for he did not like living in the country, nor did other aspects of country life hold any attraction for him. He had a rooted objection to taking life, loathed the very thought of hunting and shooting. I knew him to fish, but he was no fisherman really. He certainly had not the patience to dry-fly, and as for deep-sea fishing I think he only owned a boat for the enjoyment of his friends as he himself would lie outstretched sun-bathing on deck. He loved to surround himself with friends, adored the companionship of his fellow men and women, and was equally loved by both. On the occasions of holidays taken abroad he wouldn't have been happy without the lot of us, and a friend or two in tow. If the trip was beyond some pal's means it didn't matter at all, the whole world could be Daddy's guest as far as he cared.

"See Tom about it, will you," he would say, and if the play had been a roaring success with the expectations of another to follow, Tom Vaughan was always willing to ante-up with the necessary. Tom Vaughan's name was synonymous in our family with not having to bother: "Ask Tommy", "could you ask Tom", "Tommy says it'll be all right".

It was even in use in the schoolroom. I cannot remember what lesson I was having, but I was once stumped over the answer to some vital point, and thought I could get out of it by saying, "I should ask Tom Vaughan". "You won't always have Tom Vaughan around", I was told tartly, and that was the first time the awful realisation of such a catastrophe ever dawned on me. That the du Mauriers could get on without Tom Vaughan seemed an impossibility. Alas, when he died it became all too evident that life without him was a sadly complicated affair.

I don't suppose a more astute business-man ever lived, nor a man who had his friends' and clients' affairs more at heart. He wasn't always easy, but even as a very young girl I would sit entranced over Sunday suppers listening to the intricacies of London theatre management—and of secrets therein—as he and Daddy would talk and argue by the hour. It was Tom who arranged my 'allowance' when I first came out. Tom was a true and great friend, and when he died it was found that in spite of his business brain and the fact that he had two small sons he himself had left no will. Extraordinary.

I was just eighteen when the Algiers holiday took place. Eighteen, rather plump, hair just up (and in consequence always falling down), desperately serious and very much under the influence of *The Garden of Allah*. Not only did it seem to me the greatest book ever written but also the greatest play I had ever seen. (Films, I would remind readers, were still in comparative infancy, and Drury Lane sand-storms *were* sand-storms.) I was ready to find a Boris Andrevsky under any palm tree, and was certainly Domini Enfilden (or whatever her name was) myself. I think I should mention now that so heavily in love had I fallen with Godfrey Tearle that I named a dark green canary Boris after him. (Could love and admiration go further?)

Algiers ... the desert ... sheiks ... monasteries ... camels. ...

Into the lounge of St George's, Mustapha, walked Roland Pertwee; and Godfrey Tearle and Boris Andrevsky went with the wind (or should I say sand-storm?). Roland has been amusing about me in his *Master of None*, so now I shall, I hope, pay him back in his own coin. He was thirty-six at that moment, and not very happy as he was recovering from a mistake, his first marriage. Just ripe he was, in fact, for a very sentimental eighteen-year-old who before a fortnight was through had fallen hook, line and sinker. I must say on looking back (and on reading through my 1922 diary) Roland behaved in a way deserving knighthood for gallantry. If ever anyone threw themselves—unconsciously—at someone's head, I did. And all he did was to have his photograph taken for me *riding a camel*. It was too much. When he and Daddy and Harry and Ronnie trekked off to have fun in the desert I was left behind brooding but happy, for I had been given Roland's stick to take care of. Sunsets and sunrises, all were grist to the mill of my emotion. The fact that by the time we women had joined the men at Bou Saada my nose was cherry-red and peeling in the centre of a rather pale face in no way deterred the welling emotions of my heart. By the time the Sahara was reached I was all the heroines Hichens, Hull and Dell had dreamed of, though not I fear Mr Pertwee. However, walks in the moonlight, tête-à-têtes at dawn, hand-holding in the back of cars ... I do not believe I hoped for more. I should imagine my family were not a little perplexed by the turn of events, and wished they had left me at school, for (diary) "Smoked a cigarette, liked it. Hair washed and waved, looked topping, row over it however, but Roland liked it." Moreover it seems he kissed my hand.

How very innocent, naïve and altogether charming was my

first Grande Passion, and I wonder how many other men would have behaved as well as Roland did, for I cannot help thinking there must be a fascination in initiating a pupil in the art of love who was as ready to learn as I was. True the eagle eye of my papa was always on me! Also that of Ronnie Squire, determined to be in on anything that was going. I'm afraid that was the holiday that earned him a rude—but affectionate— name, the cot-quean ('He who busies himself in the affairs of women', vide dictionary). We left Algiers, almost en bloc; Roland taking the place of Harry Esmond who left us mysteriously one day. We were not to know then that we should not see him again; he died in Paris a week later, a horrible shock to all his friends, and to us at that time in par- ticular, for he was an extraordinarily lovable man, a poet, a dreamer. My father had always been devoted to him.

To Cannes we sallied and (diary) "Trained from Marseilles, arriving nearly midnight. Some difficulty wangling R's hand in train as —— and —— were both there. He said Bless you." (Which must have been very nice, and pleasant hearing.) But alas, I had to become a schoolgirl again, and Roland and Ronnie took me back to Paris, leaving me on the X's threshold rather as one leaves a dog at the vet, with some slight misgiving all round. A lump in my throat doubtless and who knows, a tear? and I should think relief on Roland's side, for it must have been quite a part to play, though I am convinced men take to pedestals with greater ease than we do.

Who can remain impervious to the charms of Paris in early summer? May and June with the lilacs and limes . . . the flower markets . . . the Bois in all its glory, exciting visits to the Pré Catelan and Château de Madrid. Certainly I enjoyed my second term far more than the first, and even shed a tear at my departure. But I was now eighteen and a half, ready to 'come out', ready to . . . I wonder what most girls do think they are ready for, when all is said and done. In one word: marriage.

I feel certain that nine girls out of ten have marriage as their goal at nineteen, whatever they may feel later. I certainly did, and Bet (Hicks) and I would swap ideas by the hour as to whom we'd have for bridesmaids, where we would go for our honeymoons, what we would call our children, what sort of husbands we'd *like*. And as each young man drifted into one's life—and out of it again—one wondered.

III

' Out '

'COMING out' used to mean big dances, balls every night, an allowance, chaperones, smart clothes, feathers and being presented, and then, in a triumphal climax, St Margaret's, Westminster.

Balls and parties gave me a certain 'kick', but I was not really the usual débutante. Always the theatre, and my father's theatre most of all, were of paramount interest. But there were other excitements, and if I were asked now what I enjoyed most in these early years of 'grown-up-ness' I would say the annual lawn tennis championships at Wimbledon. My father was a member, and every year my mother and I set off for our centre-court seats, and would not have missed a day for anything. Like the people who say no one will ever touch Pavlova, so I echo "No one will ever touch Lenglen". But we all had our favourites, Daphne and Jeanne were eager enthusiasts too, and we had to take it in turn as they grew older as to who should go with Mummie, till Daddy in his usual generous extravagance bought everyone seats. Part of our education, he maintained (and how right he was), as in the past he had bought boxes for all the Saturday matinées of the Gilbert and Sullivan operas, which he insisted we should know by heart. My Wimbledon days are, alas, long since over, and I confess to wondering whether to-day's players—glamorous as the Marbles and 'gorgeous Gussies' are reported to be—are as fine to watch as Lenglen, Helen Wills, Elizabeth Ryan, Helen Jacobs, Mrs Lambert Chambers, d'Alvarez. . . . Tilden,

Borotra, Perry, Austin, Cochet . . . they were giants in their day and how happy and exciting the hours I spent watching them, and later enjoying the friendship of some of them.

Racing was not one of my pleasures, and I cannot imagine why not. Daddy was a gambler, up to a certain point, and up to a certain point I have inherited that streak from him. But when I think that for many years Frank Curzon was his partner, and indeed how many actors and managers *are* imbued with the 'sport of Kings', I do wonder why he took so little interest in it. He would win vast sums on bets placed because he liked the name of the horse—there was Felstead that won him the magnificent sum of five hundred pounds (which you'll admit is a magnificent sum to win when the only reason for backing the animal is that Fel reminds you of your sister's house FELden and STEAD of your own HampSTEAD). Elton was another win in the same category, because it was one of the characters in *The Last of Mrs Cheyney*, which play he was doing at the time. Frank's Call Boy I feel sure he must have had a packet on. When he had a win of that magnitude we were all given lovely presents; I was invariably hard-up and over-drawn from my allowance, and a handsome cheque would be given one with a kiss. Racing in those days only meant to me the Derby and the Grand National, and I shall never forget the day I was tipped Master Robert for the National by my hairdresser (it came in subsequently at 40–1). I meekly put on my shilling and would have withdrawn it if I could on the pompous 'never heard of it' which I got from a very knowing man whose opinion I asked.

It was 'Sommie' Tattersall who took me to my first Derby, and surely no better person could have initiated me. It was the year Papyrus won, and I backed it. What a kind man he was, always so really charming to the young. It was he too who really introduced me to the greatest love and interest in my life: grand opera.

I returned from Paris in 1922 to find a revival of *Dear Brutus* at Wyndham's. Only Faith Celli, Norman Forbes, possibly Arthur Hatherton and my father, remained in their original parts as far as I can remember. Madeline Seymour who was to become a very great friend played Mrs Dearth, and a newcomer who had uttered a cry 'off' in *Bulldog Drummond*, and who, after this revival was to play the lead Phyllis Benton—in the subsequent Christmas revival of *Bulldog*, played Lady Caroline: Audry Carten.

In 1923 Audry came to fame overnight, and if she had remained on the stage I am sure she would be among the foremost in our front-ranking actresses to-day. In 1923 Viola (Tree) and Daddy wrote together their play *The Dancers*, and in it two unknown-to-London young actresses flashed like comets through the night of February 15th; and from that moment London could talk of nothing but the genius of English-born Audry Carten and the American Tallulah Bankhead. Yes, that was Tallulah's advent to this country. I suppose the play was what would now be described as 'Ham', but it was d—— good ham! Melodramatic, sentimental, certainly. What of it? London ate it, begged for more. I shall never forget the first night, and when at the end my father came in front to make his usual speech, with Audry on one hand and Tallulah the other, and led them to the front, the audience applauded these two with acclamation that I've seldom if ever heard given except to acknowledged stars and favourites. They were both of them young, in their early twenties, and the success each of them made was richly deserved. By the time the production of *The Dancers* was in hand, I knew Audry well, because as I have said she had been schooled, through the past year, in the *Dear Brutus* and *Bulldog Drummond* revivals. Not only was Audry an exceptionally clever actress, but she had a brilliant perception of character and understanding of human nature which later led her to write well. She was at all times the most perfect companion; funny, witty, the most appalling tease, and she had the most attractive laugh of anyone I've ever known. Her pre-Raphaelite appearance was only one of her many attractions. Alas, sheer nerves drove her from the stage I believe, which is something I can well understand. Whether that is the truth of why she gave up acting I don't really know, but I was told it was the reason. It is a pity, because she had an Albanesi quality which hadn't been seen on the stage since brilliant Meggie died.

Audry had a penchant for playing practical jokes; there was no 'dare' that she would not have taken in these early 'Twenties. I remember one evening she and I went to a Prom at the Queen's Hall, and passing some people on the stairs (total strangers) who made some remark or other, Audry—sotto voce —answered. They turned and said, "Did you say something?"

Most people would have hurried away in shame or denied having said anything. Not so Audry.

"You don't remember me?" said she. "How shattering."

The other woman, somewhat perplexed, admitted she did not.

"Don't you remember Shanklin?"

"Yes," said the stranger. (Most unfortunately!)

"I can't bear it, it is Peggy isn't it?" said Audry.

"Yes," said the woman. Audry, up to her knees in it by now, started an utterly ridiculous conversation embroiling herself further and further. Finally giving the woman a smacking kiss and saying, "I must fly," she took my arm and we rushed as fast as our legs would carry us to the exit.

It is so long since I've seen Audry, but her name amongst many of my friends is synonymous with deeds of daring.

"What would Audry do, or say," is constantly said to me by people who never met her but who are fascinated by tales of her behaviour in the past. How often do I find myself saying or thinking: "If I were Audry, now, I'd do such-and-such a thing . . ." as some impossible occasion arises. She had a wonderful, if sometimes odd, sense of humour. Certain sentences would make her rock with laughter, sentences from plays, or new words, and she would have them written on the handle of her umbrella. She gave me the umbrella, so I know. One sentence read: "Do you get much tennis at the convent?" My extremely youthful ignorance and innocence amused her no end and I can still hear the echo of her infectious, somewhat ironical laugh which greeted my rather prim: "I've read *Three Weeks*. . . ."

It was re-quoted in and out of season to me if ever I put on airs. "I've read THREE WEEKS" Audry would whoop in glee.

Some of her jokes were not always so funny or perhaps our senses of humour had declined a little. There was the time when she and some of her friends had a bone to pick with us. We found the fountain in the courtyard of Cannon Hall filled with empty champagne bottles one morning, giving our rather respectable home every semblance of having enjoyed a Bacchanalian orgy.

After she had said good-bye to the stage as an actress, she began to write, and later, in 1929, Daddy produced *Fame*, which she wrote with her sister Waveney, at the St James's. Nora Swinburne, Cathleen Nesbitt, Naomi Jacob and Frank Vosper were all in it, and my father played a violinist who married into the 'county'. It was highly dramatic, and deserved a longer run than it had.

Yes, my chrysalis stage was to me exciting. I seemed to be part of so many worlds, to be on the fringe of many sets. One's Paris school friends, with whom one kept up for the first year at any rate; Daddy's exciting stage and literary friends who now that I was grown up asked me to all the parties to which he and Mummie went; my Etonian cousin—that year in the XI—and his glamorous contemporaries (or so I found them). There was a wonderful week spent at Stanway, the Wemyss's beautiful Gloucestershire house which Barrie took yearly for the 'boys' (in other words my cousin Nico Llewelyn Davies and his cricketing friends) and filled with a bevy of beautiful women and entrancing youth. My diary records it, at the end of my visit, as 'the happiest week in my life'. Lady Cynthia Asquith was our hostess, there was a full Eton XI staying in the house, matches were played in surrounding districts daily (through a scorching September end-of-summer), dancing and charades took place at night, and my heart—forgetful, after a few months, of Roland and desert days—fluttered in full measure for the young gods who were my temporary companions. It was rather difficult not to lose one's head and one's heart at eighteen! One young man far outshone the rest in my estimation; he had a gay panache about him that broke many young hearts in the years that followed. In my incredible innocence and ridiculous ignorance (still!) I wrote and asked my aunt if she thought I was going to have a baby because he had kissed me good-night in my bedroom and I felt sick the next morning.

Diaries report I went to dances night after night, and that I enjoyed them, which I now find difficult to believe, for although I remember loving the sophisticated parties I went to fairly often with Daddy's friends at the Embassy, Ciro's, Savoy, etc, I remember being distinctly bored at private affairs. The 'sitting out' on stairs with boring young men . . . dancing one's favourite tunes with the *wrong* young man . . . and then if one was enjoying it the Cinderella act that I and later Daphne had to put up with: 'Allan' had come for us. Allan was our chauffeur, and we were never allowed to keep him waiting. He'd had 'a hard day, and had to be up early'. Half an hour was the most liberty we were given. On the other hand we were *not* allowed to be brought back alone by young men in taxis. Nor to come home in taxis by ourselves. Hampstead was a long way and who knew . . . At boring dances, as 'Destiny' fiddled its way slowly at eleven p.m. and 'Tippy

Canoe' followed it, and one's taffeta frock was being crushed
and crumpled by a damp hand, and claret cup was the best
offered, one longed for Allan with an almost filial longing. On
the other hand, if at one-thirty a.m. after caviare and champagne, and one was well away with a 'god' to the strains of
'Limehouse Blues', one had blue murder in one's soul.

"*Got to go home*???"

"Yes," I murmured feebly, "the car's waiting."

"My good girl, send it away. I'll drive you back."

Oh! for the courage to have taken the bull by the horns, sent
the Packard on its business and given oneself up to Romance.

"No, I must go now. You see . . ."

And I would make up some ridiculous excuse, not daring to
admit Mummie lay awake till one tip-toe'd past her room. And
that there had been times when Daddy's face was to be seen
peering through the landing curtains on the rare occasions one
had been 'seen home'. And my goodness! the catechisms.

"Who brought you home? Who is he?"

". . . . ."

"H'umph. Did he kiss you??"

Hardly to be wondered at if we eventually took to lying.
Daddy was an amazing mixture of Mr Barrett of Wimpole
Street and a schoolboy brother. He hated us growing up;
loathed the idea of one 'losing one's bloom'. And yet he was
inordinately pleased at any success we had. There was one
great rule, one order, one maxim, however: Thou shalt not
make thyself CHEAP. How we had that dinned into our heads.
Having His Daughters Kissed was the last straw to poor
Daddy; I do wonder what he'd have made of sons.

I think the most precious memories I have of him are our
wonderful Sunday-night supper talks. They would linger on
and on, and finally my mother would knock on the drawing-
room floor above to make us leave the dining-room ("they
must clear the table"), for Daddy would be yarning on to me

as if I was a son, and later to Daphne too, to both of us. Argument would wax long and loud; sometimes we would have terrific disagreements, sometimes the conversation would be strangely bawdy ("Really Gerald! the things you and the girls talk about!"). And he was friend, brother and—yes— father too. And these are evenings I love most to recall, and what I am most grateful for. Those were the times when his "Wait till you come to forty year" would ring out, and other oft-said expressions that became household ones: "Man's a hunter" (if he thought one's behaviour was getting on the 'cheap' side, inclined to do a bit of hunting oneself maybe . . .) and "I can always go and live at Jack Straw's Castle" if we were all 'at him'. (For those who do not know Hampstead, Jack Straw's is an old coaching inn at the top of the Heath.) Very happy—and sometimes unhappy—discussions on life, and love, and the past . . . his family, so many by now had gone; our future; and then our young and immature opinions asked about men and women who came up to Cannon Hall. Why did we find so-and-so attractive? . . . and either he would look at one with a swift piercing glance and say, "You're very like me", or else he'd be miles away and I would be told to pour out another cointreau—in which case I joined him.

There were certain things about which my father was adamant. Good manners, efficiency, punctuality, being soigné, behaving with savoir faire and being what he called a good citizen—in other words not shirking responsibility. Some of them are difficult to live up to.

I suppose the young of to-day certainly 'pull their weight', as my father would have put it, better than I did. When I look around and realise the real hard work which the débutante daughters of my own ex-girl-friends have to do to-day, in the so-called years of peace, the housework and the cooking and 'earning their own living', quite apart from any social good- works they may take up in their spare time, I am speechless with admiration; and I also sigh in unwanted and unasked-for sympathy, for I would not be a girl to-day, by choice.

"My dear! they feel sorry for *us*! you needn't worry or have any sympathy for them!", a friend of mine said who was telling me how her daughter bicycled daily to her job in the city, and then danced at night. They are, these post-war products, pretty wonderful I think. When I re-read my débutante diaries and learn of days spent entirely in going to parties and plays and films, in playing golf and tennis, in shopping extravagantly and endlessly . . . and remembering the 'divine' and 'too marvellous' conversations of myself and my contemporaries, I begin to think that wars and hard times produce young women who, though they themselves may be harder and less sentimental than I was, are better equipped to fight the struggles and grim reality of to-day.

They say that every generation looks back with nostalgic yearning. That every cry from the heart of the elderly man and woman is "Ah—when I was young. . . ." Those dear dead BAD OLD TIMES, as the Labour Government and their supporters insist on calling them. Well, maybe they were bad old days for some people, but for those with a child-like enthusiasm for enjoyment, who grasped gratefully the pleasures that leisure gave, they were Good Old Days, and I for one would rather have had them and lost them than never have had them at all. I never cease to count my blessings one by one, from the highest to the lowest, from the most sublime to the most ridiculous. From treats like sitting with Ivor Novello listening to Kirsten Flagstad's Isolde, or at fifteen being allowed to make a fourteenth at dinner when Arthur Rubinstein played the piano in our drawing-room, and Maggie Teyte sang, and Désiré Defauw played the violin; to the fact that *once* upon a time three trim alpaca-clad maids brought tea to one in the garden . . . that underclothes were mended for one . . . that your car was washed every day and you took unlimited petrol for granted; and that nobody would have been admitted to the stalls of a theatre unless wearing evening dress. To sit in the stalls of Covent Garden wearing tweeds, with possibly the Queen of England in the royal box, is to me The End. That was the greatest post-war shock I have had. As Sir Squire Bancroft used to say to my father, "I no longer understand".

First nights played a big part in our life, not only Daddy's but those of our many friends. Next to Daddy's, those of Gladys (Cooper) were to us the most exciting and the most important, but we went to all of them. It was always a source of amusement to me, who had been brought up in the theatre, to be asked in tones of awe by the uninitiated what 'the back' was like. Had they had ideas of Aladdin's caves, and open drops and fears of never emerging into life again? I have never really enjoyed the dressing-room visit personally, and after a 'first night' least of all. A surging mass of people crowding into a tiny room . . . fulsome and exaggerated praise which is the usual outcome and expectation after a success, and worse—the studied bright making of banal conversation if the play's a flop. The gushing "darling, marvellous, utterly divine", dropping from male and female voices (one's own amongst them) irrespective of whether the addressee is also male or female. Parties on the stage or at a restaurant after the play is over are a different matter. The affair takes on a different setting, even conversation *can* change to other matters. We used to have wonderful parties on the stage at Wyndham's, done by Gunters; and Edgar Wallace first nights were generally followed by an enormous supper party either at the Carlton or the Wallaces' flat in Portland Place. Most parties given after first nights, however, used to be small and private, generally at the home of the author or producer. I cannot remember other on-the-stage affairs quite like ours, where anything up to a couple of hundred people collected; to be fed on champagne and foie gras and either to praise or 'pan' the evening's entertainment.

I loved first nights, but they also made me horribly nervous. I have sat through some literally shaking in the fear that someone might 'dry up', or that the gallery or pit would show disapproval at the end by unkind cat-calls, boos and hisses. Once I had to leave our box on one of Daddy's first nights and walk about outside, I could not bear the strain. Like waiting for the result of news from an operating theatre. And oh! the hideous seconds, which seemed like hours, at an obvious dry-up and the over-loud voice of the prompter from his corner. One of my jobs was to hear Daddy his parts; this was a job I adored, and at which I was, so he said, very good. But it made for nerves on a first night, for as far as *he* went I knew to a T. just the little bits he might be uncertain of, and for five minutes before such-and-such a sentence was due, I felt the sweat on my forehead and the palms of my hands go cold and clammy. Actually I never remember my father drying up. It is not a failing which comes and goes with experience, it's just something one's born with; either you have a memory or you haven't. Nerves too. Or do I mean nervousness? There are plenty of actors and actresses whose nerves would be very hard to detect but who go through agonies consistently through the run of a play; on the same basis perhaps that some sailors are always sea-sick!

From very early days I read all the plays Daddy had sent him. This was occasionally rather mal vu by authors who did not know either him or me, or the set-up of our family where everything was openly discussed. I fancy more than one disgruntled playwright uttered: "And the man takes one's play back to a child to read. Pah!"

I wasn't too bad a judge of a play; I certainly knew the type of thing that would lose my father's interest after a few pages. Very often I would insist on his reading something which I had liked; only to be told "You must be mad". The only play which was subsequently someone else's success about which we disagreed was Priestley's *Dangerous Corner*. I raved about it, but he could not see it was a vehicle for himself, anyway.

One of the worst things that ever happened to me occurred over the first reading by Fred Lonsdale of his play *The Last of Mrs Cheyney*. Fred came up to supper on purpose to read it. Now frankly I say this: to *hear* a play read immediately puts a strain on one; few people read aloud well anyway, and I am sure the merit of any book or play is enhanced to its full degree only by reading it alone, in private. However, be that as it may —and I know that many writers prefer to read aloud their works—Fred came to supper, Daddy was tired, and presently to our horror and acute discomfort he fell asleep. There was no denying the fact that Fred was not only hurt but dreadfully insulted. He chucked the Second Act over to me and told me to read it. I would willingly have sunk through the floor. At twenty-one as I was then I was rather alarmed by Fred, who was famous by that time, and I was fully aware that not only had I a lisp but that I read very monotonously too. The evening was, as can be imagined, a fiasco; a bad time was had by all. I think Fred found it a difficult thing to get over and forgive for a long time, but I remember he was very sweet to Mummie and me as he bade us good-night. Fate however obviously meant *Cheyney* and Daddy to come together, for he finally produced it with Gilbert Miller at the St James's with Gladys in 1925, and it was one of the biggest successes he ever made.

At Cannon Hall, Sunday was our great day. To begin with it was Daddy's only day of rest. (*How* against Sunday shows and Sunday acting he was. Not, I fear, on religious grounds, but because he knew that the human frame must have a day on which to relax.) Sunday morning he spent first reading practically all the Sunday papers, and then either a walk on the Heath or a visit to the Zoo, accompanied nearly always by Daphne and Jeanne. This would be followed by a lunch party. These varied as to the season. If it was summer people came who afterwards would stay on to play tennis, remaining to tea and often to supper. If it was winter the lunch would be more serious perhaps, followed by a nap, more newspaper reading and sometimes people to supper followed by bridge or bezique. Maybe it would be Viola, in which case amusing talk and some music; or Tom Vaughan, which meant an absorbing business talk; or Garrick Club friends (cards; and Mummie and I would retire to read undisturbed); or relations—which brought conversation to the Past and probably arguments would start; or just an evening alone.

The summer was by far the greatest fun, when the garden looked perfect, 'roses, roses everywhere', and the Shakespeare border a riot of colour: and there would be tennis perhaps, with John Drinkwater and the 'Bunny' Austins. . . . Irene Ravensdale, Mary Newcomb, Madeline Seymour, Audry . . . (I realise I'm picking years and dates at random) and the Bobby Loraines would come up or the Guitrys (if they were in London). 'Bart' Marshall and Edna Best, Ronnie Squire, Melville Gideon, the Nigel Bruces; Basil and Kate Loder, darling Leslie Faber and Gladys; Mary Tempest and Willie, Victor and Bridget Paget, Heather Thatcher, Betty Pollock. . . . Tennis would be played for hours, with new Slazengers for every set (one of Daddy's many extravagances), and the silent grey-alpaca-clad maids brought terrific spreads of cakes and cucumber sandwiches and iced coffee and tea, to the terrace.

They were wonderful Sundays: I loved them, Daphne couldn't bear them. As a child she detested parties, and Cannon Hall Sundays were frankly anathema to her. Jeanne, good at tennis from the age of fourteen on, always played; neither of us was shy, we were interested in people and although unlike me she was not always falling to the right and to the left, she found these Sundays good value. And Daddy of course was the centre, the life and the soul of them, and Mummie was a wonderful hostess. Just occasionally we would have a quiet Sunday, when a play had to be read, or someone didn't feel well, and our evenings would be either a session of four-pack bezique (which Daddy always called pinochle), or the long and varied conversations which were, as I've already said, unlike those generally and conventionally enjoyed by fathers and daughters.

Christmas parties were like Sundays on a vast scale. A quiet day—so that the kitchen could have their fun (and we were taken to lunch at the Savoy, or the Mitre at Hampton Court)—and our big party in the evening, with anything from twelve to eighteen people to dinner, presents on the guests' plates, a conjuror to follow dinner and a gambling game—roulette, petits chevaux, or the like—with which to end the evening's festivities. Course upon course followed each other and Mummie would quickly, neatly and deftly carve the twenty-six pound turkey *off one side only* for everybody in the room (which used to remind me of the feeding of the five thousand) and nobody ever seemed to be kept waiting. Most of our Christmas friends were culled from the homeless, family-less and the lonely, and it used to be great fun. I think perhaps the reason Daddy never really cared for living in the country was that it meant a cutting-off from the people he liked to see; he didn't want new friends and new occupations, and however much he enjoyed lying in the sun or watching birds for an hour or two, it didn't give him what his daily visits to his beloved Garrick Club did, nor his yarns on the telephone to some particular crony: and I truly believe he would have chosen the view across London, as seen from his bedroom window on a summer evening, to any the world could have offered. And certainly if you enjoy a panoramic view over a city, I doubt if a finer could be found—all London lay below us, St Paul's, Tower Bridge, the Tower, Westminster Abbey, the Houses of of Parliament; in the distance the Crystal Palace, and even Epsom's grandstand with the Surrey hills beyond could be seen on a clear summer's evening.

I am amazed, as I read old diaries, at the abandoned state of my feelings in these early days of 'grown-up-ness'. I appear to have loved so many people, so often, so quickly and so hectically! The pages are strewn with such phrases as "Oh! I love him." "Oh Fred, Oh Fred" (not Lonsdale). "He is the *only* man" (not Fred). "M. came up, I *adore* him." "Took J. to the dance, he's divine, I mustn't love him too much." "Walked round (golf) with R., he is heaven." "Saw B. at last, thank God. I love him, I love him, I love him."

And a fat lot of good it did me. For here I am, the maiden aunt, happily sitting on Parish Councils and reading over my past hopes and sorrows with a smile and not, thank goodness, bitterness. I would not have you imagine however that I was fast, naughty, or—as Daddy would have it—'heavily kissed'. Most of my young men (some of them not so young either) had far too healthy a respect for Daddy's eagle eye and his spies to try any nonsense with his precious daughters. No, I was madly and irrevocably romantically minded, and given to exaggeration; and extravagant both with my cheque book and my heart. I was generally overdrawn with both, and of the two worries only the financial gave me lines on the forehead and sleepless nights.

Daddy and Mummie were the most generous of parents, and yet I could never bring myself to go to either and say, "I'm terribly sorry, I'm overdrawn. Could I have a bit of my next allowance, please?" I never borrowed, I sold and I even pawned!! There seemed some sort of shame attached, in my mind, to over-spending and I never dared admit to my bouts of poverty except sometimes if it became absolutely hopeless to Billy, who would speak to Daddy; nothing was said and my advance would be paid in! Shame covers me as I remember not the debts and the overdrafts and the extravagances, but the methods I adopted to straighten myself; the sale (unknown to the family for many years) of a diamond brooch given me by

Barrie . . . and another sale of a book of historical autographs
and letters. . . . I was young and very silly, and afraid; and of
all young girls in the financial 'soup' I, less than any, had cause
to be afraid of what my parents would do. Certainly there
would not have been the type of row which had come into being
over the famous Facts of Life case, or which later materialised
when I loved someone who was not their idea of a son-in-law.

At twenty I was the most extraordinary mixture of naïveté,
primness, common-sense, knowledge and childishness. A
museum-piece I should be considered to-day. We had been
carefully and most strictly brought up in some matters (giving
the lie to those many people who used to fancy that anything
connected with the stage spelt immorality with a large I). I
sulked, I lost my temper, I frequently burst into floods of tears,
but even at twenty I still obeyed. In those days I had not as yet
learnt the glorious art of deception or I should most certainly
have written other words than these:

"Mel (*Melville Gideon*) rang me up and asked me to lunch.
They won't let me."

Throughout most of 1923 I had, aged nineteen, been
happily enjoying a most harmless crush for this Co-optimist.
The Sundays he came up to Hampstead were above counting,
and on evening festivities he had been well to the fore. He
couldn't have been sweeter to three children than he was to the
three of us, and I'm sure he only looked on me as an overgrown
schoolgirl, though diaries absolve *me* of any such feeling!
Indeed the "I adore Mels" simply cover the pages of that year.
But there it was, I was not allowed to lunch alone with Mel
at a restaurant (and certainly nowhere else!) in my twentieth
year. When I think of the girls of to-day! (No wonder my
contemporary's daughter felt sorry for us.)

Dear Mel, his voice came back on a gramophone record in
Housewives' Choice recently; I knew it at once, and I was
twenty again. He had more than his share of charm.

The famous Dean of St Paul's, Dr Inge, has written his autobiography entirely in diary form. I don't propose to follow his suit but I am going to give a few examples of the type of naïve, sometimes solemn, sometimes wildly enthusiastic little silly I was at twenty. (Italics in brackets are my comments now.)

March 8th. "First night of 'Diplomacy' (*one of its many revivals*) which was fearfully enthusiastically received, and rightly. (*!*) Sir Squire Bancroft and Jack (Barrymore, divine) came in our box. Gladys was *marvellous* and both Irene Browne and Boris Ranevsky scored huge successes. Went round after, great fun. Ivor (*Novello*) there."

The presence of Ivor anywhere always made the day for Daphne and myself. We had first met him when Gladys was playing in Maeterlinck's exquisite *Betrothal*. We were seventeen and fourteen, and dressed alike in new tweed suits, our faces tear-stained beyond recognition, by the play: we met Ivor in Gladys's dressing-room. Daphne and I adored him from then on, and she decided she'd marry him when she was old enough. I should have liked to, too, but she fixed it that she was to have Ivor, and I Bobby Andrews who had also been present. Well, there it is. . . .

May 10th. "Went to the opera 'Salome' with Viola and Alan (*Viola Tree and her husband Alan Parsons*), which was lovely though very, very modern. (*!*) Never knew Strauss was like that. (*!!!*) Ljungberg was wonderful. Packed and all very pre-war. (*1914–18 war.*) Went on to ——'s coming out dance. Got off with a silly old man and a rather frightening divine Russian artist who wants to paint me."

July 5th. (*Wimbledon*) "We took Bridget (Paget) down, she is a darling and I sat with her in the open stand; very nice. Helen Wills and Mrs Wightman beat McKane and Covell. My darling Borotra beat Lacoste in terribly exciting match, and dear Hunter and Vincent Richards beat W—— (*?*) and Washburn. Helen Wills actually knew me (*!!*) and smiled,

and Borotra signed my P.C. so it was a successful day. Jeanne and I played in the evening." (*What a climax!*)
July —. "Went down to Taplow to the Desboroughs. Great fun. About twenty of us, all girls. Margaret Bingham (*now F.M. Lord Alexander's wife*) so nice. A very beautiful Pole-Carew, and a sweet American, Maurice Baring's niece. Played tennis and bathed. Trained. Went to Daddy's play evening. Queen of Spain there. Afterwards to Jimmy Dunn's party at Savoy. Fun. Diana (*Lady Diana Duff Cooper*) looked ravishing, Oggie (*Olga Lynn*), Tallu (*Tallulah Bankhead*), Barbara Back, Viola and masses more."
Sept. —. "A most lovely day, not feeling *awfully* well. Ronnie (*Squire*) came to supper. Afterwards I had a ghastly time à propos of ——. They are adamant about her. Oh God help something to happen to get them to change their minds."

Nothing did! I was fighting a losing battle. My 'crush' on a notorious figure with supposedly ancient Greek ideas was doomed from the start. She must obviously remain nameless, but in all the weeks and months I knew her I never met anyone kinder, more generous, more amusing and so utterly uncontaminating in influencing the impressionable girl I was. She had every opportunity under the sun and never said a word on any subject that could not have been shouted from the housetops. Or more to the point, at Cannon Hall, Row à propos continued, it seems, for—
Oct. 29th. "Dreadful scene with Daddy over X and Z (*another friend*). He stormed like a madman. Went to dentist, awful time as he injected me with cocaine and jabbed a colossal needle into my jaw. Extraordinary feeling. Lilian and Joyce to lunch. (*Lilian Braithwaite and Joyce Carey*). Spent rest of day making frock. Polling Day—exciting results on wireless."

Typical of me in these days to be far more taken up with

scenes about personal friendships than the result of the General Election.

It had been an emotional year for me, but then on looking back, what years were not! What with Roland still hovering in the background, and Mel, and a certain Fred in the South of France, and the frustrated friendship with the 'Greek' and a great many other sentimental attachments. My great and loyal stand-by was away moreover, Betty Hicks. In Australia with Seymour and Ella. It was on this tour that she met Beverley Nichols, and he and I became so well acquainted by post, that when he arrived back at the end of the year, in reality a perfect stranger to me and at that time unknown, I wrote: "*Bev* has arrived. Too exciting. Rang up this morning."

The next night we met—"Went to supper at the Carlton. Daddy and Mummie and Ian (*Hunter*) and *Bev*. He's charming, I like him very much."

My parents thought I should have something other than people and mere gadding-about with which to occupy my mind, or perhaps they felt they had been a little unreasonable about certain friends of mine, but at any rate one evening in November 1924 Daddy suddenly said in the middle of dinner:

"Do you know who is to play Wendy this year?"

I said, "No, who?"

"You."

I could have jumped over the moon with glee. It had been my ambition ever since I could remember, to act that part. Nearly everyone has wanted to be Peter Pan himself I know; I never did. And I felt I knew Wendy and the whole play backwards. Gladys was going to play Peter for the second year in succession, Ian Hunter would double the parts of Hook and Mr Darling (he was playing Julian to Gladys's Dora in a revival of *Diplomacy* in the evenings), and Stella Patrick Campbell ('young' Stella as she was generally known to differentiate her from her mother) would play Mrs Darling.

IV

The Stage and I

Yes, I suppose I was spoilt. I had, in so many ways, been allowed to do as I pleased, been given rein and not had to conform and knuckle under to rules and regulations.

With real enthusiasm and keen ambition I threw myself whole-heartedly into rehearsals, thinking that as I already knew the part (and the play) backwards—for I had not missed a year since the age of two—I would have little to learn. But how true are the words 'Pride comes before a fall'! Dot Boucicault was dead, and the production was in the hands of a very worthy old gentleman, no actor himself, but a man with an exaggerated love of tradition. Because Hilda Trevelyan had found it natural for *her* to make some little movement I must needs follow entirely in her footsteps, making exactly the same turns of the head, or the exact little giggle or exactly the same tone of voice. I had been brought up to watch Daddy directing his rehearsals (and a finer producer of modern plays did not live) and he allowed the actors and actresses under him to think for themselves.

"I don't feel *natural*, Gerald, when I say so-and-so"—or, "I feel all wrong doing it like this."

And he would say, "Right. Do it your way, and let's see what it's like."

And if the effect was better he would always tell them—"Far better. Do it like that."

But the production of *Peter Pan* in the hands and in the eyes of X was sacrosanct, and my spirits sank to zero and I chafed under what I considered unnecessary tradition. I wasn't 'putting on side', though I daresay there are—and were—plenty of people to say, "Chit! Just because she's Gerald's daughter she thinks she can do so and so."

I was terribly anxious to be good in the part, terribly anxious not to seem the stupid nincompoop Wendy *can* be unless naturally handled.

Another thing that horrified me was the exceedingly dirty (or so I thought!) *old* clothes I had to wear! No new Wardrobe for a hardy annual like *Peter Pan*! My diary quotes that my senses revolted at "clothes dreadfully shabby, ghastly old shoes". But I loved rehearsing and the rehearsals, in spite of being annoyed with the way they were taken. I always have enjoyed watching rehearsals, they have a drug-like fascination for me. I was never happier than sitting in dust-sheeted stalls watching Daddy conducting rehearsals on a bare and empty stage, the actors with their parts in their hands (sometimes), and going over and over the same scene until perfection was reached. To watch a play shaping . . . it's like watching a child growing up. If a good play or an attractive child, quite absorbing.

My days were full, rehearsing all day and generally out at night, and one snatched a hurried lunch in the hour spared one somewhere 'round the corner'.

Nov. 28th. "Rehearsal morning. Did ship scene. Ian, Gladys and me. X. (*the producer*) turned up, rather silly old man. Lunched —— (lunch party). Back to another rehearsal. Diana (*my cousin Diana Beaumont who understudied Peter and played a Lost Boy*) was Peter, very good. I do love it. Rushed home to dinner, and went to 'The Vortex' at the Everyman with Vaughans (*Tom and his wife*) marvellous play of a sordid nature (!!) Lilian *wonderful* and so was Noel Coward. Molly (*Kerr*) awfully good too. In fact all."

Nov. 29th. "Rehearsal morning. My God! X. will drive me

to suicide or murder. Not one thing can one do on one's own initiative, nor Ian either nor 'John' nor anyone. Old fool. Gladys only there a second, she's divine though. Had lunch in a squalid place in the Strand. Quite nice though."

——. "*Terrible* day, pitch black fog. Rehearsed all day, ship scene mostly and bits of nursery. Daddy came and did a bit of it. Jill (*Esmond: played Nibs*) came along and lunched."

——. "Rehearsal all day 3rd act morning. Daddy came down and I was very bad. Lisped worse than ever, spoke quickly and forgot my words. Lunched Jill. Last act afternoon. Ian so sweet, I had to prompt him and he said 'Bless you'. I am a fool. (*How true, how true!*) Went to 'Patricia' evening. Dorothy Dickson too sweet and Cicely Debenham too perfect."

——. "Daddy drove me down and stayed most of the day. Ship scene morning and nurseries afternoon."

——. "Rehearsed at Wyndham's. A *filthy* stage (*!*) Gladys only there in the morning. Uncle Jim (*Barrie*) there, rather terrifying. But he was very sweet. Lunched with Aunt Eva (*Eva Moore*). Walked to Savory and Moore for some toothpaste. Car fetched me and I fetched Jeanne." (*This was rather a treat, for I mostly tubed it.*)

Of the first time I 'flew' I recorded it as '*too* terrifying', and Oh! the memory of that awful harness contraption of thick leather which girt one over the shoulder and between the legs, for all the world trussing one up like an unfortunate bird, with the addition of a heavy steel plate on one's back to which the wires were fixed. Such an affair could only give the appearance of a hump, and it was exceedingly uncomfortable to wear. Needless to say one only put the flying harness on in the acts where it was needed.

——. "Drove to theatre morning. Daddy took rehearsal most of the day. It was a very jolly day somehow, specially the afternoon when we rather fooled. At Wyndham's.

Flying rehearsal at Adelphi (*where the play was produced*).
Lunched with Gladys at the Ivy. She's a darling to one. All
the lights went out in the house. Washed my head."

Dec. 16th. "Dress rehearsal. Very exciting. At theatre all day.
Lunched in Gladys's room. Mummie made me up. I think I
was quite good, and it went all right but for bits. 2nd Act
muddled and 2nd nursery a bit. Felt a little nervous at first.
Uncle Jim very charming to me."

Dec. 18th. "My *First Night*—or rather afternoon. Went up
with Daddy; not feeling too well. Did some shopping,
flowers, etc. Lunched Samovar and then. . . . I had *the* most
marvellous flowers sent me—masses, and shoals of wires.
Went awfully well and everyone very pleased with me.
Marvellous flowers from Z. (*the 'Greek'!*) and divine
thimble (*Peter Pan's kiss, you should know*) from Gladys. Ian
sent a wire."

Well, there it was. I was launched. It was all very exciting
and rather bewildering and sometimes nerve-racking and even
at times boring. There were days when one knew one was
better—or worse—than on others. Friends came, and it was
great fun having people like my darling Madge Titheradge
(a heavenly Peter once) come and see *me* in *my* dressing-room,
and knowing that perhaps Jack Barrymore was in front, or
Tallulah, or Roland with his two little boys, or my own sisters
(obviously the most critical of one's Wendy, remembering old
Cumberland Terrace nursery days). It was fun having tea in
the dressing-room, and in other people's dressing-rooms too,
getting an invitation to the Lost Boys' room for instance. . . .
And one had so many little jokes, jokes that could amuse no
one except the people immediately concerned. In fact it was
like living in a jolly school, I would say on looking back, certainly much jollier than my real schools were. I think all might
have gone smoothly but for the fact that Fate singled me out as
a target to destroy. The most incredible series of accidents

befell me, and by the end of the run my nerves were shattered.

There are people who believe in premonitions. I had never thought of the matter, but one afternoon, just as I was preparing for my 'flight' back to the nursery in the last act, I said to the man whose job it was to fly me (every 'flier' has his or her own wire-puller): "Have there ever been any accidents?" He pooh-poohed such an idea as being out of the question. Well, the fact of the matter is or was that in two minutes time *I* was lying *in the orchestra*. Wendy, John and Michael all fly through the window home to their nursery, alighting in the middle of the stage. It had never been a flight I cared for, one felt always rather as the first Atlantic solo pilot must have felt, as one met that dark gaping void facing one, which truly enough was only the audience and the auditorium, but it always felt vast. That afternoon I crash-landed; right on to the footlights, and then toppled over, taking the double-bass with me, along with double-bassist. . . . A more uncomfortable, nerve-shattering *and* painful experience I have never had. There was a hush throughout the whole house, quite obviously it was thought I was seriously injured, if not killed. The next few moments are hazy because I do not know just what did happen, but I recovered my 'wind' which had been knocked out of me, and when I came to I realised from the orchestra pit that my understudy had been hurriedly pushed on. In great pain I crept under the stage and up, and came in collision with old X. Our heads met and the impact of that was even worse than the hurt I received in the fall into the orchestra. As bad luck would have it, poor Daddy chose that moment to pop round to see the end of the performance and was met by an hysterical "Wendy's gorne!" . . .

When I felt certain I was going to be neither sick nor faint I gave the signal that I'd go on again. Poor Wendy II crept off the stage, and I crept back via the prompt corner, into my bed where luckily Wendy had to lie for a good five minutes in peace and silence. The ovation which greeted me was almost frightening. The audience stood and clapped and yelled, and with tears running down my face by then (from emotion not pain) I blew them all a kiss and then the play went on. It was a most terrifying experience, and I never made that particular flight again without a prayer. Of course I was black and blue in the body, and shaken both physically and mentally. It didn't help that I dined-out on the story for months to come, so much so that amongst my family and most intimate friends 'an orchestra' means a long tale of disaster and mishap. That was Mishap No. One.

One isn't encouraged to be sick or sorry if one acts; I think probably unconsciously this is one of the reasons why I was unable to take it up as a permanent career. I was used to slacking and spending the day in bed if I wanted to with a bad head or a tummy-ache, and that sort of thing just isn't done in the theatre. I do not think it is a question of jealousy and the fear of an understudy playing the part possibly better, that keeps an actor or an actress in harness, it's just 'one of those things', one of the unspoken traditions. Anyone who didn't turn up for a performance because he or she had a cold in the head would just be thought not to be taking his or her art seriously. And that would be considered a Very Grave Offence. I've no patience with people who say, "I hear so-and-so is always off", and worse, "I suppose Y. had gone to X.'s first night". Such abysmal ignorance of the theatrical profession is enough to make the blood boil of someone like myself who has known men and women go through performances with appendicitis, miscarriages and husbands lying dead. 'The Play must go on' is as deep-rooted a Last Word to every true artist as ever was 'Calais' on the lips of Bloody Mary. But not, I say it with shame, was it mine. However, even through these few weeks at the Adelphi I tried hard to ignore aches and pains, and the appalling bouts of pain which I suffered from for years before it was finally decided to remove my appendix. The day after my flying débâcle for instance there was no question of staying in bed resting, but—

——. "Daddy took me up. Everyone very kind and enquiring after me. And I tried the last flight over two or three times."

Another time there was—

——. "Didn't feel at all well all day. Beastly pain in chest, felt sick and awful retching attacks. Lunched with Molly (*Kerr*) in Soho then she came and watched from the O.P. all afternoon."

But I was thoroughly enjoying my life, and the fullness thereof. Jack Barrymore was rather to the fore at that time (not my fore!) and came up a lot. He criticised my performance very adversely, I remember, saying that the day he was in front I *giggled* and was obviously on to a joke. This of course is thoroughly naughty, and he was right to warn me and tick me off. It is desperately hard at times not to have a joke in the middle of an act, but it is a shocking business if members of the audience are aware of it.

Jan. 12th. "Awful fog. Jill and I lunched together. Jolly matinée. Daddy there with the Cholmondeleys. Bev and I went to Meraud Guinness's dance. A very good one and then I went on to the Carlton to Josephine Victor's party for Daddy. She is very strange but *divine.*" (*She had taken London by storm with her performance in 'The Pelican'.*)

It was during this run of *Peter Pan* that Daphne and I went to Cecil Beaton's coming-of-age party. He and his younger brother were great friends of ours and we very often went dancing. I recorded his party—"Great fun. Very nice men. Had supper with Kinsey Peile."

I think Daphne and I were two of Cecil's earliest 'sitters'. I distinctly remember we went to be photographed by him in the nursery, and I rather think his helper was his old nanny. There was a lot of shilly-shallying with small cameras on tripods, and we all thought it a heap of fun. The result was Daph's and my heads appearing magically under wine-glasses. Certainly neither of us have ever had lovelier (or I'm afraid, more flattering!) photographs done than these in the old days taken by Cecil in his advent. Mine hung in Naomi Jacob's house in Sirmione till the Germans came and I rather think that has 'had it'.

Which reminds me. During the run of *Peter Pan* a well known and rather peculiar photographer asked me to sit to him as Wendy. He had a name as a photographer—and for other things as well of which I in my innocence was unaware. I trotted along, and the first time all was well. "Come back again," he said, "I should like to do you as you are." So off I went again. This time I was draped, and presently undraped. And later, much to my astonishment I was asked to pose in the nude. About to demur I was told to: "Look on me as a doctor." . . .

So I looked on him as a doctor. I was regaled with stories of my grandfather's *Trilby* who had stood for the nude. Gullible I was, and still looking on him as a doctor I let him take quite a lot of photographs. I thought perhaps I just wouldn't tell them at home . . . one never knew . . . but I thought he was a nice kind old man interested in photography. . . . And besides, Trilby. . . . It was only when I went the third time, saw the proofs (most unprepossessing and disappointing!) and was asked to sit again that it dawned on me that all was not what it should be. I became very prim, and suddenly affianced myself. (I had a crush on Ian Hunter anyway, and it was all one and the same to me.) I told Mr Thing that I was engaged and that I didn't somehow think my young man would like it. He was very nice about it, and it wasn't for years that I heard quite by chance that it was a 'thing' of this man's. A doctor! . . .

My crush on Ian was known to no one but myself, with I suppose the exception of Daphne to whom I have always told everything. Yet—

Jan. 17th. "Rehearsal in the foyer for young Bushell as Mr Darling. He's *very* young, but nice. Ian's last day. *Too* desolating, he is such a perfect angel it will be quite bloody without him. Michael Arlen in front."

Poor Tony Bushell! However—

Jan. 19th. "Horrid afternoon—no more Ian (though Bushell very nice—sweet in fact). But Luff brought his sword down on my nose during fight. Awful cut—blood, etc, will leave a mark for ages I should think."

And that was Mishap No. Two, and then my nerve really did begin to fail me. With Ian Hunter's departure and with Tony Bushell such a boy, Hook was played for the rest of the run by William Luff (Ian's understudy), the 'Cecco' (a pirate) to date. Gladys, with more courage than good sense, had insisted on the fight with Hook being fought with real swords rather than wooden ones. Till that day all had been well. Everyone with the smallest intelligence must know that a stage fight should be, and generally is, rehearsed to the smallest detail. I think perhaps in this case it had not been! Anyway, as the wretched Wendy rushes to be of aid (much more of hindrance) to Peter on board the ship during his fight with the Pirate Captain, the wretched A. du M.'s nose was nearly severed. I could do nothing; blood spurted up like a geyser. The pain was excruciating, but one could not make a fuss. I had to remain fighting too till it was my cue to retire, and then I burst into tears. I couldn't help it. The end of the ship scene is played in near darkness, so little of the mishap was noticed, but for the remainder of the matinée I had to put my hand up and shield my 'spouting' when and how I could. Poor Mr Luff, it was beastly for him too for he obviously felt badly about it. As to the scar, I carried it for ten or fifteen years. Luckily it looked like the marks spectacles leave across the bridge of one's nose.

The day before the end of the run I nearly met my end by a near crash into the iron curtain (not Russia; merely what is known as a Safety Curtain). The flying went wrong again. This time at the end of the first act, when the children all fly away. For some unexplained reason my wires went wrong and instead of flying out of the window I was carried backwards and forwards and round and round—everywhere but where I should have gone—and then out towards the iron curtain which was at that moment descending. . . . With no care for what the audience thought but only for my own head (and safety) I put my hand out, caught it, and was by the movement propelled back across the stage, finally coming to rest *on* the stage, which didn't matter as by that time the curtain was down. . . .

I was sad when the run was finished, but I felt very nervy, and not awfully well, and for that reason I suppose turned down an offer to play in *Are you a Mason* (revival). The fact was, of course, that Wendy was far too important and big a part for a beginner. For I *was* only a beginner for all my knowledge of *Peter* from the front, and being Daddy's daughter and having spent most of my life in and out of the theatre. It had been a case of trying to run before I could walk, and my nerve was shaken in more ways than one. Yet—

Jan. 24th. "Last day of 'Peter'. Terribly sad in a way, made me awfully depressed at the end. And I felt so rotten at the beginning of the afternoon. All the good-byes so dreary. Ian came round. It's been a wonderful time my first acting in spite of accidents."

I was, I remember, thoroughly tired by that time, and with the mishaps which had occurred my nerves had gone. Like most young people too I always tried to burn the candle at both ends (and sometimes in the middle) and no one who

really takes up a stage career seriously can afford to work *and*
gad. So for a time I determined to forget words and fights and
swords and noses and flying, and give myself up to the process
of enjoyment once more. (I should think I was highly
unpopular amongst the young people who were yearning for
jobs. For naturally I was offered parts and—unnaturally—I
turned them down.) I was a butterfly, let's face it, or a moth?
A *flutterer*, loving to hover on the fringes without having to
take on the responsibility of a definite job.

In February that year (1925) I went to a party given for
Ellen Terry at Claridge's—"Great fun. *Masses* of people I
knew. Darling Josephine V., Marie (*Löhr*), Athene (*Seyler*),
Lady Colefax, Blossom (*Forbes-Robertson*) and her mother."

Alas, I never knew Ellen Terry. You cannot call meeting a
person and kissing a hand *knowing*. As a little girl I remember curtseying to Pavlova and being kissed by her, now I come
to think of it. How and where? I fancy it must have been at a
Theatrical Garden Party.

March the first was my twenty-first birthday. This should
have been a wildly exciting day but a bitter disappointment
occurred two days previously, when Daddy took to his bed
with 'flu, putting the party I was to have had out of the
question. Yet the day seemed to have been one of great enjoyment.

March 1st. "My twenty-first birthday. Some lovely presents,
lovely dressing case from Mummie, mirror from the Bruces
(*Nigel and his wife Bunny*). Jeanne and I went to Holy Com-
munion. Bridget (*Paget*) and Billy to lunch. Gladys and John
(*her son*) came to tea, she looked *too* lovely. Dined at the
Berkeley with Nigel, Bunny and Ian. Ian divine. I do love
the Bruces."

And with his usual generosity Daddy saw that I was not done
out of my real twenty-first at the Embassy, which was held a
fortnight later, to which came Gladys, Marie (Löhr), Victor

and Bridget Paget, Jack Barrymore, Ian, Charlie Cherry (playing then in *The Pelican*), Bev, Laurie Grossmith (a very old
friend of the family) and one or two girl friends. Supper at the
Embassy was my idea of a Perfect Evening. And indeed why
not? I can't think of a better birthday party.

Gladys was playing in *Iris* at this moment, which Daddy had
produced for her. Harry Ainley was magnificent in it, as was
Gladys herself. Whether Ivor Novello was in it from the start
or not, I don't remember, but—

April 16th. "Theatrical Ladies Guild committee meeting
morning. Quite jolly. Then lunched at the Ivy with Daddy
and the kids (*! must mean Daphne and Jeanne*). Everyone there
including Marie T. (*Tempest*). Saw first act of 'Iris'. Amazing
difference with Ivor. Went on to —— her birthday. Dress
show at Piccadilly Hotel, not bad. Dined with the Towles
(*Sir Francis and family*) at the Metropole, great fun, and on
to Stage Guild Ball at Covent Garden. *Such* fun. Had a box."

In April too the Hicks family returned in triumph from
Australia. With a crowd of their friends, including Bev, Ivy St
Helier, Kate Loder, Hilda (Hanbury) Fox and her family, Peter
Page and Russell Findlay, I paced Waterloo station for three
hours waiting for their arrival. It was like the return of one's
own family, for Bet was as dear as a sister, and I was devoted to
her parents. But we were soon to be parted again, for adventure
stared us in the face in the guise of our First Holiday to ITALY.

Once again I had to make a sudden choice, this time between
a holiday in Italy, or Edna Best's part in *Spring Cleaning*. I do
not regret having chosen Italy, I do not at forty-five regret that
after 1926 I definitely turned my back on acting, but I do realise
that a girl of twenty-one, whose father was Gerald du Maurier
and who had started a possible career with one part and that
part Wendy, should have had her behind smacked for daring to
say no to such a part as Edna's was. But I longed passionately
to see Italy (or anywhere else for that matter) and I kept telling

myself that foreign travel was an Education. I think I was right, not that Lake Como has anything educating about it beyond its incomparable beauty.

We drove there in the Packard. Daddy, Mummie, Allan the chauffeur, Jeanne and I. Daphne was in Paris, and flatly refused to leave her school. To me was given the task of planning the route. Unperturbed and with a rather antique Michelin guidebook I undertook this, and gave it great study and thought. Not for me the A.A. and all their bits of paper! We went to Italy *my* route, visiting the Loire Châteaux on the way which I'd already 'done' at school, and now I acted as cicerone to the family. Then on to Geneva, Brigue (where the car had to be put on the train because the Simplon was snowbound) and thence to Como.

Italy dawned to the du Mauriers in a downpour which lasted so long that my father, as he paced up and down the pile-carpeted lounge of the very English-seeming Hotel Victoria, Menaggio, swore that he would give it one more day to clear and if it did not, then back to England for the lot of us.

God must have heard my prayers for we awoke the following day to a morning of sun and blue skies that only Italy can give.

It was during this week at the Victoria, before we moved to the enchanting hillside villa which we took from the British Consul, Mr Melius, that we met—and loved from thenceforth —Agnes and Lil Mackay, the two dragoon-like sisters of the Vicar of All Saints, Margaret Street, Canon Mackay. They bore down on my father, rather to our astonishment, for they themselves also bore the stamp of the Church (Agnes very militant on earth), and it transpired that in days gone by another brother had been on the stage, and a dear friend of Daddy's moreover. A book in itself could be written about these two women, maybe one day one will be. They were a tall pair, Agnes a Scotch fir, Lil a pine, both six feet I'm sure, and they were, I guess, in their late fifties. Agnes, it seemed, led and

Lil followed; they were like stalwart saints in a medieval age. Both would have gone to the stake without a murmur for their faith and their beliefs. At home they shared a house in Maida Vale but spent their Sundays at the Vicarage in Margaret Street and were, I'm sure, a source of help, strength and vitality to their celebrated brother, one of London's leading churchmen. Lil was the most human and understanding, but Agnes unfurled a spiritual banner from which, if caught, it was impossible to escape. She was at that time a visitor of Holloway's Women's Gaol; I begged to be enrolled by her for welfare work of the same nature, but somehow that never came off. Maybe she thought that at twenty-one I was too young to be of much help to thieves and prostitutes. Agnes was very narrow in some ways, I used to think; at that age I could not understand her tolerance for tarts, and the venom she displayed against divorcées and Lesbians. As regards the latter she literally snorted. "I can smell them a mile off. Dear child, why do you *know* such people? And do wipe that hateful stuff off your pretty lips."

One of my 'treats' was to sit with Agnes and Lil at High Mass at All Saints, listening to the sermons preached by Canon Mackay and Geoffrey Heald and basking in the music of the church's incomparable choir. Agnes had a very uplifting influence on me in her lifetime. She looked like a dragoon, and a serjeant-major at that, but I adored her and derived a morbid pleasure in wallowing in as many sins as I could conjure for her benefit as I sat at her feet at tea, beside her and Lil and their red chow.

I remember I was desperately badly poisoned by lake fish whilst staying at the Victoria and was discovered in most disorderly array on the bathroom floor of the Hotel. We stayed a week and then moved up to the enchanting villa from which we played two rounds of golf a day and listened endlessly and at all times to nightingales. Viola Tree came out to us, amongst others, for Daddy always had to have one or two people other than his family on a holiday. It was a happy time, but tragedy was looming near us for it was while we were there that the news came that Daddy's remaining sister May Coles, 'Aunt May', had been struck down by the fatal illness from which she was to die later in that year. I have always been superstitious; about ordinary common-or-garden superstitions, and I invent my own as well. I perfectly remember that the news of Aunt May's illness and operation followed the bringing of may into the house. (I can never see one magpie without both spitting *and* crossing myself; I don't really care for lighting three cigarettes with one match, I dislike intensely sitting thirteen to a table, and always feel I should get up first, and I have plenty of private superstitions of my own. As to breaking a mirror...)

We stayed out there for two months and then drove through Milan, Turin and Grenoble back to Paris, where we stayed out at Versailles at the Trianon Palace and took Daphne out from school.

My first impressions of Milan were not as awe-inspired as they should have been, I cannot help thinking—"Terribly noisy city. After much looking about put up at the Cavour which is very nice. Went out in the evening and dined at Biffi's, *marvellous* place in an amazing sort of arcade place. (*I daresay as good a description of the Galleria as any!*) Pouring wet evening. A very thrilling place rather vicious looking." (*!!! The Galleria or Milan as a whole?*) And as to the Duomo (one of the seven modern wonders of the world), all that I could find to say about that was "Milan cathedral simply *marvellous* and enormous".

It was soon after our return from Italy that the evening débâcle took place when Freddie Lonsdale came up and read *The Last of Mrs Cheyney*.

At the end of July that year I paid my first (and so far only) visit to the Channel Islands. By the time Guernsey was reached

I was praying for the boat to sink and me with her. However after nine hours of torture St Helier was reached and I fell in love with Jersey—and one of its inmates. There must be something very special about an island that gives Lily Langtry, Seymour Hicks, Fred Lonsdale and Ivy St Helier to the world.

October the twenty-third was a red-letter day in the life of a mere twenty-one-year-old. Daddy gave a lunch party at the Garrick Club—I think for the Boucicaults prior to an Australian tour—I was of course allowed to go to it and the people were: "Wells (H. G. *too* sweet) (*!!!*), Melba, Augustus John, Boucicaults, Roland, Sir Squire (*Bancroft*), Harry Graham. *Such* fun."

I know I did sit next to H. G. who was perfectly enchanting. I was over-awed by John and sat far away from him, but I think I was most excited about Melba for whom I had (rightly) boundless admiration. One of the most exciting evenings of my young life was when later in Paris she took me and Mabel Mitchell to the Opera. *To go to the opera with Melba* . . . I was speechless and I'm sure tongue-tied. The woman who showed us to our box curtseyed, I remember.

I was staying at the time with the second Mrs Gilbert Miller —Margaret—my fairy godmother. It was one of my many lovely visits to her in Paris. What a wonderful time she gave a young impressionable and enthusiastic girl! Nothing was too much trouble to her. Her energy, like that of most Americans, far surpassed my own. It was Margaret who introduced me to the Paris of glamour and excitement, a Paris far different to that of one's school-days. I saw Melba more than once during my Paris autumn of '25, and one evening she took Beverley Nichols, Mabel and myself to the Revue des Nègres after dinner at the Café de Paris. It was a good trip to Paris and what with one thing and another I learnt quite a few things. . . . I discovered Mistinguett and the Moulin Rouge—"*marvellous*" —saw Gaby Morlaix in *Les Nouveaux Messieurs* and Sergine in

La Nuit à Nous. Lunched and spent glorious days at Fontainebleau and Versailles and Barbizon, danced till the dawn with
exciting foreigners and finally left for England with Bev as my
escort.

But London was depressing to return to. Daddy had an
operation two days after I got back and on November 20th
Queen Alexandra, that much loved figure, died. In those days
when kings and queens left us we wore mourning automatically in respect. I wonder whether we should now?
Mourning rather died its own death after the first World
War, and I for one dislike such trappings for personal loss. But
I am sure that it should be worn for funerals, and as respect for
one's sovereigns.

Throughout the whole of 1925 I had, at periods, woken in
the night in cold sweats thinking I was still playing Wendy.
My relief in realising I was but dreaming was boundless. And
yet by December I was rehearsing once again for it! This time
Dorothy Dickson was my Peter. In December too I had the
fun and honour of playing for the first—and alas only—time
with Seymour Hicks. I was the Boy Scrooge in a big matinée
for the Press Fund. Seymour of course played his celebrated
rôle and Bet and I were the two youngsters. They were
strenuous days for me, more or less an amateur, rehearsing at
the Shaftesbury all day for *Peter Pan*, rushing off to the Lyceum
to a brief scene for *Scrooge* and going to balls and parties the
evenings I was not playing two performances.

Dec. — "Shopped morning, matinée afternoon. Lots of
things went wrong. Gladys's birthday. Ivis (*Goulding: sister
of Eddie Goulding: she was playing Nibs*) and I went to 'The
Green Hat' in the evening. I enjoyed it and Tallu was divine.
Perfect party for Gladys at 'Uncles', got to bed at five.
Bruces, Henry (*Daniel*) Frankie (*Levesen or Lonsdale*)
Audrey (*Coates, I think*) Ronnie (*Squire*) Freddie (*Lonsdale*)
Doris (*Gladys's sister*)."

4*

But if I had been tired by the *Peter Pan* of 1924, the season of
'25–'26 was even more exhausting with two performances
daily once Christmas was past. Prue Bourchier (Prudence
Vanbrugh) played Mrs Darling, and we shared a dressing-
room and had the greatest fun. We had known each other all
our lives and also shared a birthday. Dorothy was an adorable
Peter. Fey, if perhaps rather fey à la Américaine. Elfin in
appearance, most certainly. She was charming to be with, and
I loved that catch in her voice; she made Peter a very pathetic
little boy, forlorn when he was lost but definitely naughty
when he felt on top.

Rather curiously the press and the critics who had been kind
and generous to me my first season slated me in my second. I
do not think myself that I had varied in the performance of the
part, but then one is seldom the best judge of one's own work
whatever it is. One very celebrated critic took it upon himself
to give me the bird in no uncertain way, thereby incurring
Daddy's wrath and enmity for ever! Bless him, he could not
bear what he considered to be *unfair* criticism and he thought
that this particular man's notice was all that and hell too. It's no
use of course to take umbrage at criticism, whether merited or
not; if one is in the public eye one has to lump it. I should like
very much to be a critic, both of books and of plays. I should
probably err on being too kind. Frankly I think a new form of
criticism is needed; why is it necessary to over-praise or
alternatively 'pan'? Why cannot papers employ a new type of
person who sets out merely as a man-on-the-spot to *enjoy*?

By the time *Peter Pan* of Christmas season '26–'27 had
finished I had made up my mind once and for all that I did not
want to act. I was too young and silly to realise that probably
in character parts (or even low comedy) I might have had a
future, but I had just enough sense to realise I would never be a
Juliet. I hadn't the face or the figure, or for that matter the
what-it-takes, for the conventional ingénue, and in any case

I knew that I was not ambitious enough to work hard enough; and always there was that sick feeling in the pit of my stomach —was I going to forget anything? As a child, and a grown girl, it had been torture for me to play the piano or sing a song for the benefit of my parents' friends in the drawing-room at Cannon Hall, and I realised that acting was only like that but much worse. I had no self-confidence at all. It was a pity, I think sometimes, because had I remained even a mediocre actress I might have graduated by now into a producer. I say this without cynicism, for it is a fact that there are plenty of excellent producers who do not shine when acting themselves. But I wanted to be a good actress, and with a name like du Maurier I could not afford to be a bad one. Possibly too much is expected of the children of the great; I would definitely say, in fact, that both as an actress—admittedly of only one part—and as a writer, I have found my name as big a handicap as ever it has been a help. As Wendy I was Gerald du Maurier's daughter—and it had been an amusing 'stunt' to try me out in a star part straight off. And when my first book *The Perplexed Heart* was published in 1938 (or '39, I forget) it was as Daphne du Maurier's sister that I aroused interest.

And what about this little story, whilst I am on the subject. I found myself on a holiday, in a fashionable hotel, a few years ago, 1946 to be exact. I had at the time four books to my credit, and one about to be published. Being unmarried *and* my father's eldest daughter I use, quite naturally, the name which is mine, and as Miss du Maurier had registered so in the hotel book. One day a very gushing woman approached and effusively thanked me for all I had done for her nephew. She told me his name and I was able to say truthfully that I had never met him. Oh, I must be wrong, she continued, she had heard all about my kindness *and* that of my husband. The light dawned and—

"I expect you think I am my sister, Daphne Browning. I am *Angela* du Maurier."

With the eyes and the voice of a Medaea she turned to her husband, who was standing in the offing ready to be introduced, and cried—

"It's ONLY the SISTER!"

and with that she left me.

I dined out on the story for quite a time, for as a piece of rank bad manners I think it takes a bit of beating, but it gave me a laugh at the time and still does, and when asked, "And are you the writer?" I find myself denying any such idea quickly, or else rather apologetically saying in a small voice, "Not THE one."

At the end of the run of *Peter* I went almost immediately to look after Daphne who was ill in Paris. We stayed together in a small hotel, but she was far from well and it was all very worrying. Some quack of a doctor, recommended by a dear well-meaning friend, was giving her every form of injection from sea-water to garlic. By the time I reached Paris she was the colour of a banana, smelt like a Calais porter and burst into tears over the smallest matter. I had arrived out there with a glorious invitation for both of us: we were to spend a month on the Riviera with the Towles at the beautiful Beaulieu Bristol. Daphne, who was very fond of Frank Towle, merely burst into tears. I took her back to London after a couple of weeks, and she became a different person the moment she was out of the quack's hands. The Towles, who had really given the invitation for Daphne's benefit in view of her bad health, said that I was to go anyway, and for one month I lived a life of sheer and perfect luxury with 'Uncle Frank', Lady Towle and their daughter Mollie. I had my twenty-second birthday with them and what has happened to southern weather now I do not know, but in those days winters in the Riviera were springs; one wore white, and basked under perpetual blue

skies in brilliant sunshine. Tennis tournaments waxed furiously
the length and breadth of the Riviera, and I spent my time (as
usual) falling in love with one star after the other until what
appeared the Real Thing arrived in the shape of a truly god-
like individual in the entourage of Prince Chichibu of Japan.

This was IT at last; and I regret to say it was *I* that gave *him*
a ring. And he took it. For two months life was at its most
blissful, and Casanova himself wrote no better letters I'll swear.
Like a meteor, however, this creature came, saw, conquered
and—left. For the first time I was up against what seemed to
me a bewildering state of affairs, a tragedy about which I could
neither do anything nor tell anyone. All my previous romances
with my undergrads, my actor 'crushes'—even Roland—had
been run on happy lines; exciting lines but happy ones. Here,
there was no getting away from the fact, I'd been jilted! My
family knew very little about it all, Daphne of course did and
Bet, but only in my own eyes and heart had I at last visualised
the long walk up the aisle, with delphiniums in preference to
lilies, voices breathing o'er Eden, and Bet and Daphne heading
a goodly retinue of all my Best Friends.

It just did not work out that way and with great philosophy
and a shrug of the shoulder I set about to Forget (as Stephen
Leacock would say).

I walked into Selfridge's and there found the person who
was my one true love for fourteen years. She cost me six
guineas only, and she was Chinese. I called her Wendy.
Wendy Pansy Posy Lollypop Stone-Martin. (Penelope-Anne
for short.) She was a *tiny Pekinese*. Just three months old.

V

" These Have I Loved "

"Oh lord, a dog crank——"

(Well, no one need read this chapter who doesn't want to. For I am now going to pay tributes to the dogs I have loved and known. Other people's dogs, for I never had but Wendy.)

"Of course the poor thing's an old maid. They do get so *silly* over animals."

"Fancy calling a dog a person. . . ."

"I like a dog to *be* a dog."

"Can't stand what-d'you-call'ems, *Pekes*—horrid snuffly bad-tempered little brutes."

Wendy, or Penny as she was mostly known for all her string of names, was a Person. She had a quite astounding vocabulary. Pekes *are* clever at words, there's no denying it. Any dog knows words like 'walk', 'dins', 'drink', 'master', but Pekes know the names of individual rooms. Wendy certainly knew the difference between beddy-room and Gran's beddy-room, and Auntie Daphne's (or Jeanne's) beddy-room. Or kitchen. And 'in the gardy'. She only had to be told to fetch me in such-and-such a place and she would do so. She could spell too. She knew jolly well what C.H.O.C. stood for, and she knew the names of all my greatest friends and at the mention of their names would leap off a chair (or possibly up from the floor), wag her tail furiously and tear off to greet the person. Luckily she always liked my greatest friends. She had a temper of pure gold and anyone could do anything with her. Her 'points' were non-existent as was my knowledge of what they should have been, and one of the only things she ever had up against me was that at a year old (or thereabouts) I showed her. It was a ghastly faux-pas. Off we set in the car to Alexandra Palace and when we entered the ring the two of us might have been ghosts. Just not looked at. . . . She was not only rather hurt but terrified by the noise and ungemütlich atmosphere of the place.

Like all Pekes she had a completely deaf ear to what she had no intention of hearing. There is no such word as Obedience in the Pekinese language; the Peke will no more obey if it feels it wishes to disobey than it will eat if it's given something it doesn't like.

"I'd rather *starve*," they'll tell you. And starve they will.

"'E'll eat if 'e's 'ungry."

How often I've heard that remark from the lips of someone ignorant of the fad of a Peke palate.

Wendy would no more have eaten a nice dish of biscuit, gravy and green vegetables than *I* would eat something out of a pig trough.

Wendy was a terrific sport. None of your little tippety high-heeled lap-dog behaviour about her. She was once (unbeknownst to me) made to walk up a mountain, seventeen miles in all, by Jeanne who took her for a holiday with a Labrador. She reeled at one moment, so I was told. . . . She and one Chen (a Cornish-bred parti-colour, owned jointly by Mummie and myself) chased sheep one day from Hampstead to Highgate. And the beatings they received when I finally caught up with them put my hand out of action and left them cold and undismayed. Wendy caught and killed her first rabbit at the age of twelve, on Mull. She was also a very fine mouser and rat-catcher. Musical too, and there we also shared similar tastes. She would roll over in ecstasy when she heard the Fire Music of the *Walküre*, and in fact quite obviously enjoyed the dreamy parts of *Tristan*, and quite a lot of Debussy. Chen, dear little soul, was all for the Savoy Orpheans (he was one of their vintage) and panted with enjoyment (and not a great deal of sense) at a military band. Wendy could go anywhere, meet anyone (human or dog) and one knew there'd be no awkward moment. I took her from Lostwithiel to the Isle of Mull in a train once, our only change was in Glasgow. She was as good as gold and was neither sick nor sorry. The only time she travelled badly was once when we were crammed into a third-class smoker and some man smoked a singularly foul brand of cigar. She bore it till Dawlish and then was sick. The man then went to the corridor window and followed suit, *blaming Wendy.*

"Your dawg."

"My dog—as you call her—would not have *been* sick if it hadn't been for your cigar, sir."

It wasn't a very enjoyable journey.

She gave me untold devotion, and although she loved me more than anyone else, she was extremely fond of the whole family and certain friends. She was sensible if I went away and I knew she would neither fret, run away nor get run over.

Now take Miss Muffet—Tuffy she is known as, and sometimes Tufnell Park and Lambird.

("The woman is getting beyond a joke—*lambird* for a dog....")

Lambird is my 'niece'. She belongs to Jeanne who spends far more time away than at home and I am left holding the baby. If it were a baby, a human one, Jeanne would have to think again. Tuffy is five? six? and quite quite beautiful. She is one of the most unpopular dogs I've ever known, is completely a one-person creature, and while she is my shadow during Jeanne's absences, I count for nothing when she returns, beyond tolerance and common politeness. Which *I* find endearing, for that is what I call loyalty. Jeanne is her life, and when she is at home Tuff will remain in a hot bedroom where

Jeanne will be glued to an easel, rather than come for a walk—which she adores—with me. She bites, which is why people do not care for her, also her snores can be heard from Land's End to John o' Groats. She is queer, with many lion-like traits. Her regal appearance bears a striking resemblance to Metro-Goldwyn's trademark, and the slow wag of her tail, like that of a lion, does not mean she is suddenly overcome with bon-camaraderie, but the contrary, that she's ready for the kill. It's an alarming and a lying sign, and very disquieting to puppies who mistake the gesture for friendship.

Muffet has also, like Wendy, a good vocabulary, and like Wendy too is a keen music-lover. Jeanne plays the piano a great deal and Muffet will lie at her feet for hours. Once I took her for a walk in the village and the sound of a piano being played came from a cottage. She stopped stock-still, looked at the cottage and wagged her tail. The following story is also completely true: Jeanne used to play part of the famous second piano concerto by Rachmaninoff; one day the wireless was tuned in to a concert, and the concerto was played. At the point where Jeanne's 'part' started, Muffet looked up, pricked up her ears and went over to the piano and lay down by the stool. What about that?

Jeanne is 'Mummie' in a certain tone of voice to her, and I would no more say that word, or "Here's your Mummie" to her, when Jeanne is away, than I would deliberately set out to be cruel to either a child or an animal. 'Missis' is a word she doesn't know; I am to her—and a great many children—Piffy, for some reason. She knows that name, for my mother has often said to her in a very normal voice (not the silly ones Jeanne and I use), "Here's Piffy back", and she'll fly out to greet me. She knows the sound of one's individual cars' hooters too, and sometimes when I've been to see Jeanne at St Ives—and have not seen them for some weeks—Jeanne has come out into the street and told me that she has been engrossed working and deaf to the outside world, but that Tuffy recognised the horn of the Morris. In 1949 she nearly died of multiple and desperate diseases, and it will be a long time before I shall forget rocking her, soothing her in my arms, after she had rolled from her basket screaming and in a fainting condition, waiting for Mr Jackson the vet to come, wondering whether he would 'make it' before the last ferry closed down for the night. He came, took her away because only injections could save her, injections given frequently, and for the first time in her life she departed from us, only half conscious. Daily I went to see her, just for a few minutes, to give her confidence so that *she* should know *I* knew she was there. She used to look at me, give a tiny tail-wag and go to sleep. When she was fit enough to return I fetched her and continued the nursing at home. The Jacksons are the *only people* I will leave her with, on the occasions I have to go away when I am in charge. Tuffy is not a person who can be left with servants, friends or relations. She is nervous, unhappy, knows no self-reliance, sits or stands still at the sound of approaching traffic and does—bite. But I can do anything with her now, except remove a tick from her face, and the greatest surprise I ever had in my life was when I saw her behaving normally and friendlily with the Jackson children—when she goes to Mr and Mrs Jackson she lives in 'as family' (*no kennel-life for her*)—for children as a rule are anathema to her.

My Wendy died the week war was declared. She knew something had gone wrong; she could not understand blackout, and not being able to have torches and lights on for her last walk at night. Her little mind went, I was told she had meningitis. Her last night was the worst I have ever spent—for I had to give her overdoses of luminal and hear her breath becoming more and more stertorous, and just wait-wait-wait for the daylight when someone would come.

I sometimes think that there are one or two (or three or

more) little dog saints. Or do I mean little saint dogs? Little creatures without any guile in their entire make-up, who suffer little hardships and little miseries with fortitude and gentle licks, who watch their owners with blind worship, who are completely unselfish and who, possibly without much courage and without great intelligence, give all they have. Blossom was such a one, my mother's parti-coloured Peke who looked every inch a princess of Ancient China. Blossom (also called Flossie) was so gentle that she never did a thing for which she could be scolded. She worshipped my mother, and merely existed, she certainly did not call it *living*, if Mummie went away, yet she would remain at home on these occasions as good as gold, giving no trouble, and loved by everyone. When she was a year old I found her with my needle-book in her mouth. A quick X-ray that evening showed the worst: a needle in her colon. She was operated on immediately, and with thirty stitches in her tum she was brought straight back and we took it in turns to lie throughout the night on the kitchen floor with her. At one point, in pouring rain, she intimated she wanted to go outside; she was the cleanest person in the world, nothing would have induced her to misbehave indoors, and so afraid were we that she might be worse if we didn't let her go into the garden that we carried her out, wrapped a sponge-bag over her and followed behind with an umbrella, as she tottered slowly to the performance. Blossom recovered, and during her con-valescence it would have been difficult to find a more patient and understanding little mite. She died in tragically unneces-sary circumstances at the early age of six, from an injection as a preventative for a disease from which she was not suffering. My mother found her a quarter of an hour later, as she thought asleep. She was dead.

The other little saint I know is Mouse Browning. He is a West Highlander. He is as sentimental as a spaniel, as devoted as only Saints for Causes can be, and his cause is Master,

Master's children and His Mummy. Mostly Master. If Muffet is beastly to him (and she can be) he smiles rather pathetically, looks at her and at me, and walks slowly away. He never dreams of going near her food, and is the least greedy dog I have ever come across. If he sees signs of Going Away he wilts like a flagging snowdrop and creeps—alone and despondently —to the nursery. He is jolly and full of gaiety but this air of sanctity and goodness pervades; I see a little silver halo on his white head as I used to see a gold one over Blossom's.

I do not think as yet I can dwell on the memory of tiny Carlotta; she left us and the world on the first day of Spring 1949 . . . meningitis was the cause. She was six months old, the gayest loveliest girl that ever came from China. As a village woman said to me when she heard of her death, "She was too beautiful to live."

Once I knew a Tiny Man who was never quite sure if he was a Black Pekinese or a Bumble Bee. He belonged to Olive Guthrie and lived his little life in the loveliest of all lands, the Isle of Mull. He had one black eye—bright as a piece of burnished coal—and one blue one. But for this his fame and fortune would have been immense. For myself I found it one of his greatest attractions. He had a tail the like of which any débutante would have given her eyes for as a fan: it was an ostrich feather. (Remember the line in E. V. Lucas's poem on a Peke "and plumes where tails should be"? Impy Guthrie's plume was magnificent.) He had the most enchanting mannerisms, would always kick up his tiny white back feet if he was excited, and his play with Spillers Shapes was a joy to behold. A car ride was what he enjoyed above everything else in the world, and he would lie by the hour at the top of the stairs in the front hall of Torosay hoping, hoping. . . . He was very intelligent but never could see the necessity of petrol rationing. His nature was angelic, he was an exemplary and welcoming host and the only jealousy I ever knew him suffer was for a particularly courageous robin who used to attend regularly the weeding of the rock garden, Olive Guthrie's own province. Imp thought Birdie an outsider on the job, and saw him off whenever he got the chance. He lies now, sweet little man, by other dearly loved Guthrie dogs, high on a hill, where the chasing of bunnies was their delight, with a view that must be as beautiful as any in the world. I wonder if little ghostly dogs sometimes cast their tombstones aside and chase each other madly through the bracken as the moon rises above Cruachan, and Loch Linnhe—a silver sheath—lies spread in beauty beneath her.

Belinda was another of ours, also known as Lindy Lou. She was my mother's, and really cared for no one else though she was I think fond of Jeanne. Aristocratic in her tastes, whether in the matter of people or food. She found children difficult to tolerate, and intensely disliked rough-spoken folk. No lover in fact of the hoi polloi. She had a penchant for dates, which were procured from Fortnum's especially, for—my mother told me in all seriousness—"Belinda did not like the ones in the Fowey shops". She died, poor love, of peritonitis, the result of a rabbit bone in her food.

Brutus was a sturdy fox terrier, given us as a Sealyham. He goes down to fame and posterity with us in Frederick Whiting's big portrait. He developed a passionate adoration for one of the Hampstead vets and we finally had to give him to him. One bank holiday he disappeared, it was obvious that he had been stolen. Weeks later, with pads swollen and cut, body thin and torn, Brutus returned and fell exhausted on the vet's doorstep, having walked from heaven knows where, probably Epping or maybe even further. He had a mania for football, and we only had to say "Brutus (or Foon) where's the FOOTBALL?" to make him lose all sense of proportion, and he would tear off pell-mell, collect the football and rush round and round the garden with it dangling from one of the laces in his mouth.

Betty Hicks had many dogs in her time but the two I remember mostly were Henry, an Aberdeen, and Rover, a—well, no one knew. He looked a mixture of Alsatian and Cairn! And most people feared him as his temperament was more Alsatian. He was given to taking nips (legs, not alcohol), but he and I were the greatest friends and there was one occasion on which I suddenly found Rover *in* my bed with me. Tucked down like a hot-water bottle. He was an independent man-about-town and would never have permitted the theft of himself like poor Henry, who luckily was returned from the East End dog mart by the good offices of Edgar Wallace who knew the ropes. Henry was very pretty but like so many Aberdeens (and Cairns) was given to barking too much. He also enjoyed a fight (like most Aberdeens) and his house manners were definitely not of the best. Viola Tree's Gyp was one of the most amazing man-about-town types of dog I've ever known. He was a very tall fox terrier, and walked all over London. And from anywhere in town Viola could turn to him and say, "Go home, Gyp", and he would. He also used to go home in taxis alone.

Dogs are very like children in that it is impossible not to have favourites. There was a Cairn in a hotel in Loch Rannoch that really wove itself into my heart, Bumble by name. Rather like a holiday romance he was, 'ship passing in the night' kind of thing . . . for I only knew him ten days or so, but I shall remember him. One of my greatest loves however is Naomi Jacob's Baldo. He speaks both Italian and English with equal facility, and is human. I spent a month once in his company, and neither of us could face the parting when it came. He has white gloves and shoes, and a very passionate face. Ginger in colouring (need I add he also hails from China). What walks we had, along with Mario the chicken-bandit. Mario so exquisite to look at, a tiny fox-terrier, smooth, brown and white, with the manners of the best type of Etonian and the morals of a gangster. What women were to Heath, chickens were to Mario, and walks in the hills of Italy with a murderer is not conducive to peace, even if olive trees and a vast blue lake are all that the eye can see. Hundreds, nay thousands, of lire must fill the pockets of the owners of Mario's victims, and sad, sad to relate one day Mario never returned to the Casa Micki. Some beastly squalling bird had been avenged.

Dachshunds are little foreigners with whom I've rarely come into contact, but I know a sweet pair of demure sisters on the Lago di Garda. They are rough-coated, their names are Hexci and Purschi. They are aloof and were told when young never to talk to strangers, I imagine. But they scamper the hillside daily to Bezzuglio and San Michele with their master, my friend Dario Giorgetti, and on these walks appear to shed their otherwise nun-like mien.

Mary Newcomb had a Cairn, Miss Sweetie, who was utterly adorable and spoke to one in long trembling tones with her mouth open, trying her hardest to copy the human voice. She was a dear friend of mine and always gave me a warm welcome to Stinsford.

Then there is JUMBO. With a name like that his breed should not be difficult to guess: he's a large floppy slobbery bulldog, and he belongs to my cousin Nico Llewelyn Davies and his wife, and he rules 22 Campden Hill Square and the lives of Nico, Mary, Laura and—Kate. He has colossal charm, and if you arrive on the doorstep and ring the bell you presently hear a noise like the slow approach of the Cornish Riviera express backing into Paddington. Nylons are not really very safe to wear and it is better to be on the wrong side of nine stone or one is likely to be knocked over by his exuberance—and weight. His charm, as I have already stated, is terrific like the rest of him. And when his family sailed to America for business purposes for a few brief weeks and were forced to leave him they *all* cried. (And who shall blame them.)

I once knew a rather beautiful Kerry Blue, and when the day came for her marriage she was sent off in a bridal gown designed by Idare, which was not altogether surprising as she belonged to Eileen Idare; and surely it must have been a pleasure and a change for the vet, or breeder or whoever the Officiator was, from the usual apparel of harness, lead and collar.

As a Christmas present once upon a time Daphne composed a magazine for me, with stories, poems, 'gossip', news, etc, as would have been written and spoken by the Dogs of our Acquaintance. It was brilliant—and would have been thought so by the usual insane sort of persons that I, and many of my friends, are who give 'special' (and beloved) dogs their own funny voices and their own comic likes, dislikes and ideas.

I know cats are beautiful and charming but to me they are people from another world. I like them to sit on my lap, and they are of course enchanting in looks and ways often enough, but I always feel at a disadvantage with them; rather as I do with some people, that 'all feet and hands' feeling, when one trips over mats and speaks ungrammatically; that's how I sometimes feel in cats' company. Their fantastic independence also puts me at a disadvantage; our own Timoshenko is kind to me and quietly tolerant, but like that character on the radio I always feel 'I AM a FOOL'.

Horses I don't know about. I've fallen off the back of every horse I've ever sat, sometimes giving almost circus-like demonstrations so doing—and anyway I'm frightened of them.

But dogs. . . . If you have a dog you need never feel alone. Their companionship is one of the most precious things in life. I have gone out for a walk with Wendy or Muffet when I have felt so miserable that I have been unable to cope with human companionship and they have given understanding, and even help. Their very silence can show their affection, and the expression in a dog's eyes will give its heart away. I have cried with them and blasphemed in their company, and they have quietly looked up, and perhaps licked one's hand, or even put their paws on one's lap. The dog that loves its owner and who is loved in turn always knows when something is amiss.

Muffet has helped me write my last three books (I realise that asks for a brickbat of some sort—but I find amazing solace in her company, even when she is snoring). Her very presence is a help, an inspiration. She cannot criticise, which is so blissful for one's self-esteem, and now and then she will look up with her eyes as large as florins, and in them is neither censure that one has forgotten her walk, nor greedy expectation for the meal already overdue; merely relief that one is there, and once again there comes to the ear the comforting sound of the plump little soft body's thud on the floor; the snores start again; her trust in one is complete. That, I think, is the key to man's affection for his dog. It is the realisation that their trust in one is so profound, so all-believing that if one were capable of wittingly betraying it, one is not the person who should enter the Kingdom of Heaven.

I know perfectly well that there are thousands of people who deplore the 'overdone affection' some dog-owners give their animals. To my mind there is something fundamentally lacking in the type of person who does not believe that animals have souls. Maybe they are not on the same plane as human souls, but I would suggest to this type of person that they begin to learn a little of the teachings of St Francis.

Animals *can* be just—animals. And certain animals, like certain human beings, can be devoid of intelligence. But there are few dogs, brought up and living their life through with a kind and loving master or mistress, who will not repay that kindness and love with devotion rarely found in ordinary friends.

VI

Those Twenties

THEY had rather a bad name, those early Twenties. They were
the beginning of those glorious Bad Old Days which I am
personally grateful enough to have lived in. For we shall never
see their like again, and doubtless that is a good thing too. But
'better to have loved and lost than never to have loved at all',
and I frankly say 'better to have *lived* and lost . . .'

I daresay I am ripe for the tumbril, I daresay a great many of
my early days were fraught with unworthy and selfish play,
but at least sections of the community in some of the days preceding 1939 were able to gain real if possibly unnecessary
enjoyment without descending to Black Markets to enable
them to do so. Such simple things were fun in the old days; you
did not have to be a millionaire to fill your car with a few
gallons of petrol and go for a drive over the Sussex Downs, or
into the New Forest. There was none of this ghastly so-called
Class Hatred which politicians ladle one out with nowadays
like spoonfuls of soup from an inexhaustible tureen. Manners
were far better in every section of the community even if
morals were not; as to the latter I daresay they have not altered
one way or the other. Only the really very rich chucked their
money about. Money qua money, as a subject was not discussed. Only bounders spoke of their incomes—and 'what it
cost'. Money, like food, was taken for granted. Nowadays both
subjects take up the greater part of most people's conversations,
moreover neither topic is considered sordid in the least degree.

One hears of the Naughty Nineties and I believe the Dirty

Thirties; I should myself definitely like to coin Forlorn Forties, but what about these 'twenties? Empty Twenties? For some, alas, they may well have been, but on the whole my own were better I think than the proverbial curate's egg.

In 1926 a man and his play came into our horizon which altered the whole course of our lives. The man was Edgar Wallace, the play *The Ringer*.

To be accurate I think that Edgar—or 'Krazy' as his family called him—had come into Daddy's ken the preceding year, but the fruits of this meeting were fulfilled, if I may mix my metaphors, when Daddy produced *The Ringer* for him at Wyndham's in May 1926. It was the first of the many of Edgar's thrillers and was an instantaneous success. As a writer of book 'thrillers' he was of course already famous, but until then I do not believe he had written anything really notable for the theatre. I cannot think of two men less alike than Daddy and Edgar, yet they were soon devoted friends, and it was during the first night of *The Green Pack*, his last play, that one heard of the serious illness which had seized him, and from which he died almost immediately; the last play too in which my father was to act at Wyndham's.

Much has been written about Edgar. A brilliant biography by Margaret Lane, apart from many biographical sketches. I remember him as an incredibly generous man, a frightening man; a superb host; a brilliant conversationalist at times, a story-teller without equal, a wonderful friend—and I should imagine an implacable enemy. To us, as a family, he was amazingly kind. I can see, at this juncture, the cynics murmuring, "And why not? didn't Gerald du Maurier make him as far as the stage was concerned?" *That is not the point.* My father helped a very large number of people, but even if they 'won through' they sometimes preferred to forget it; Edgar was generous to us because he liked us, and I should think for no other reason. And because he *was* a generous man when he had the world's goods. He adored parties, and giving presents —and spending more than he should have. People who have been poor either become miserly if they one day achieve riches or they chuck their money about right and left. Edgar was a chucker, and there must be many people alive at this moment who look back on his memory with affection and gratitude.

The production of Daddy's plays nearly always brought new friendships with them. One was bound to come into contact with the people concerned, one attended rehearsals, actors and actresses came back to Cannon Hall for multitudinous discussions, and before long I (at any rate) would be busily inscribing in the diary possibly exaggerated but real affection for a new friend.

The Ringer brought in its train, as well as the entire Wallace family, two people who were to mean very much to me personally. Naomi Jacob and Leslie Faber. 'Micky' Jacob at that time had, I think, only one book to her credit, and was in fact an actress. Maybe if her health had not given way, forcing her to live abroad, she would have remained on the stage. For she adored acting, and I know still loves anything to do with the theatre. She was brilliant in character parts and the stage is poorer for her absence. However, what the theatre has missed, readers-at-home-by-the-fire have gained, for surely no more prolific novelist is alive to-day, and Micky richly deserves the great success which as a writer she has achieved. Her 'Me' books have told the world about her, but she cannot tell the world what her friendship means to the people who are lucky enough to have been given it. For twenty-four years now Micky Jacob has given it to me, and has been my comforter and help and adviser and tear-wiper on more occasions than I care to remember. It was to Micky that I went after my father died, it has been to Micky that I have, for nearly a score of years now, turned and said, "What shall I do?" Her generosity is spontaneous, and childlike in its enthusiasm. We share a great deal in common, of course, our passion for Pekes, Italy and opera. I was twenty-one when I first met Micky, impressionable, still childishly sophisticated, thinking I knew everything and actually having no knowledge of anything but what I read about, or saw with my own eyes, or listened to across the dinner table at Cannon Hall—that table which in my grandfather's home had been graced by such talkers as Wilde, Ainger, Whistler, Burnand. . . . Micky was a wonderful friend then, as she is now. But it's easier to be the friend of the hard-boiled spinster of forty odd than it is to the girl of twenty-two. She was wise, and she was amusing. She was courageous and she was good. Her friendship throughout these years is one of my dearest possessions.

Leslie Faber, alas, was to give one but a few years of his friendship and affection. Barrie had a great deal to say on the subject of CHARM. I do not think I have ever known anyone have that strange elusive grace to a greater degree than had Leslie Faber. Charm is a quality hard to define (though I once wrote an article for Daddy on the subject with his signature (!) and made the splendid sum of twenty pounds!). Barrie, in describing it in women, called it 'a kind of a bloom'. It has nothing to do with looks, although Leslie Faber was one of the best-looking men I've ever seen in my life. It has I suppose something of a Pan-like spirituality which understands and recognises the ego in other people, at the same time remaining god-like and aloof. To have charm and to be charming are not necessarily synonymous to my way of thinking. I know plenty of charming people but I would hesitate before I paid them the fuller compliment in saying they actually radiated charm. Charm is a spontaneous and unseen smile, it is the soft beguiling mist of the mountain-tops.

And it was Leslie Faber.

How curious it is that often by what the world would consider relatively insignificant 'happenings' friendship—and love

—can be made—and broken. By such small things for instance as Leslie's quiet and perfect understanding (and the letter he wrote me afterwards) when one morning just as he and Daddy and two other men were about to start off for a day's golf, I arrived home from a walk broken-hearted and completely collapsed by the sudden horrible accident which had befallen Daphne's golden retriever. The dog was out alone with me, when he was run over; and he bled to death—in the ambulance which caused the trouble. It utterly unnerved me and I retired to the house with tears pouring down my face feeling like a murderess, the more so as he had been left in my charge whilst Daphne was in Berlin on a jaunt with Viola. Everyone was kind but Leslie was just that little more, and indeed how much it was.

What a brilliant actor he was too; no one has taken the place which he created for himself. Whether he played an old Scottish doctor with a preposterously unbecoming make-up as he did in *The Ringer*, or a suave enchanter as he was in *By Candle Light*, or a hardbitten backwoodsman as in *White Cargo*, he was never less than perfect. His parts bore in fact that perfection, that 'tout ce qu'il y a de plus fin', which one rarely, alas, finds on the English stage. The British stage is full of fine actors, brilliant actors, sometimes even great actors, but rarely is there to be found that Mozartian acme of perfection which Leslie inevitably brought to the parts he graced. What fun he was too! At parties or just talking to one or when—eyes lit with the fire of the zealot—he was on quest for that which lay very close to his heart, a BOAT. He was mad about boats and I shall always remember the day Daphne and I spent at Burnham-on-Crouch one dank autumnal October looking for a yawl or a ketch. In 1926 I doubt if a better-looking couple than Leslie and his beautiful Gladys could have been found anywhere, and for a few brief happy years we du Mauriers enjoyed their friendship and I think love.

Another newcomer to Wyndham's in that production was Leslie Banks, who played then an important but not big part, and who was to rise to the front ranks of the London stage. Franklyn Dyall played the villain of the piece, Bet (Hicks) the ingénue, 'Nod' Forbes-Robertson (Norman Forbes's charming son, who later gave up acting for art) was her brother, Val Gielgud of B.B.C. fame was a policeman and the heroine was none other than Dorothy Dickson. Micky and Bet shared a dressing-room, and that is how I came to know Micky, for I was often in and out to see Bet. 'St Chad's' was formed—St Chad's being the name given, I think by Micky herself, to the collection of youth which pervaded the play among the cast and the understudies (and of which I became an hon. member), and which collected in full strength in this particular dressing-room. Micky of course was a fairy godmother and 'mother'-confessor to the lot. What fun it was—I can hardly believe it was so long ago. I can even remember clearly some of the frocks I wore in those days. I have forgotten one important member of not only the cast of *The Ringer*, but also of St Chad's, Nigel Bruce! He played an inspector in a bowler hat if my memory does not lie; (in training maybe for the future when he would be Sherlock Holmes's famous partner).

The first night of *The Ringer* was a tremendously exciting affair; as in all good 'thrillers' the identity of the Ringer himself was hidden until the last few minutes of the play when Leslie whipped off his frightful wig and moustache, his make-up as Doctor Lomond, revealing himself as the mysterious crook (*and* showing the audience his usual attractive personality!) At least his identity was hidden from *most* people! I fancy few people know this little chapter in the history of the play. On the night of the dress rehearsal Daddy and Edgar thought it might be a good idea to get Sir James Barrie's reactions to the play; he might have some useful suggestions; so Daddy rang up Barrie and asked him if he'd care to come and see the dress rehearsal. Barrie came. He sat in solitary silence until, as the final curtain fell, Edgar went up to him and asked him what he thought of it. Barrie was full of praise and said, in all sincerity, "What impresses me most is the original and skilful way you take the audience into your confidence so that *they* know from the start who the criminal is: and yet the excitement is sustained throughout the play"!

Poor Edgar was aghast! Though Barrie had no idea that he'd said anything wrong. So uncanny was Barrie's knowledge of stage-craft that he claimed that he knew from the moment when the curtain went up that the first person to sit in a certain chair would be the guilty man. Sure enough shortly after Leslie came on the stage he sat in this chair and Barrie had 'solved' the mystery! Luckily for the author and the management, few members of the audience were quite as quick. . . .

Edgar gave the first of his many fabulous parties after the first night at the Carlton. We sat, I remember, at one long table and I am sure the number of guests ran well into three figures.

That night the General Strike began. A strike which did its best to paralyse the country, a strike to put paid to any play, any book, any form of entertainment whatsoever. Yet not even the General Strike of 1926 put paid to *The Ringer*, which became one of the year's greatest successes, and which was to give us our home in Cornwall.

Once the strike was over, the London Season restarted where it left off. Opera flourished at Covent Garden as always. The Derby and Ascot took place with the same gay spirit as usual, Wimbledon ended with a marvellous men's doubles, the winners being that popular pair Cochet and Brugnon; and with Borotra the singles champion it was a French victory as far as the men were concerned; our own Mrs Godfree beat the enchanting d'Alvarez for the Women's World Championship.

I think that 1926 was the year which was to seal for ever my allegiance to Grand Opera; to whet my appetite in fact and to sow seeds for my foremost and pet extravagance for (I suppose) the rest of my days. I had already been initiated by 'Sommie' Tattersall, that grand old lover of both the race course and the opera house, and in 1928 thanks to Leslie and Gladys Faber I met Eustace and Ursula Blois who took me and my enthusiasm under their wing, and what was even more important, took me often to Covent Garden, of which Eustace was managing director. They were terribly kind to me and, I suppose because I saved my pennies to go weekly and sit in the 'gods', they realised that my visits were the outcome of real love and not because I thought it was the thing to do. Many was the time that Ursula would invite me to her box, or if she had stalls only would ring me up and ask me if I wanted to go. I remember a luncheon à trois with Ursula and Elisabeth Schumann. Mme Schumann spoke very little English and I knew no German at all except 'Ich liebe dich', which I could hardly have murmured. Another invitation from Ursula, which I have always regretted not being able to accept, was to play bridge with Melchior! Just as well, no doubt, as I should have trumped all my partner's aces.

Those were the days when Londoners went mad over Kappel's Isolde and Brünnhilde; Leider and Flagstad were joys yet to come. Melchior sang the Wagnerian tenor rôles throughout and in my humble opinion there has never been a voice to touch his Tristan, Siegmund and Siegfried. Jeritza was another at whose feet most people knelt; she was lovely to look at, had a lovely voice and was a beautiful actress. I fancy 1926 was the last year in which an International Season at Covent Garden sang Massenet's *Manon*. Fanny Heldy—an enchanting personality—sang the part quite beautifully, with Ansseau whose voice was perfect as the Chevalier Des Grieux. I took 'Jim' Wallace—Edgar's wife. It was the first opera of her life and she

loved it. Incidentally how careful one should be when intro-
ducing someone to opera. *Tristan*, to me sacrosanct, would be
the last I would try on a newcomer. *Manon* was good, easy
tunes, and with Heldy as Manon easy to the eye as well. I think
that of all, however, *Traviata* would be my choice as an introduction to someone who obviously needed to go slow. Did
ever any first act hold a greater plethora of well-known and
lovely music?

Russian ballet was also having a tremendously successful
season, I think at the Prince's Theatre. Those however were
still rather the days when it was the smart thing to go to the
ballet. The ordinary Londoners did not rush off in wild enthusiasm in 1926 as they do now; their education in ballet was
limited; only those with some knowledge went, and members
of society who always went to where it was the fashion to go.
My own knowledge and adoration of the ballet has been slowly
developing throughout the years. Lady Diana Cooper took me
to my first, when I still wore plaits down my back and when
she, I think, was still Lady Diana Manners. There was a season
at the Alhambra, and we saw *Petrouchka* and I think *Tricorne*,
and in those days I was too under-educated to appreciate it, and
preferred to look at Lady Diana anyway. Years passed, and then
came a Christmas spent in Monte Carlo, and there indeed
Daphne and I spent as many evenings as we could at the
Théâtre where Diaghilev was giving glorious spectacles like
Scheherazade, Narcisse and *Lac des Cygnes*. Tchernicheva was at
her zenith then, and in 1926 was still, with Lopokova, out-
standing as a ballerina. I saw *Carnaval* that year, *Zéphir et Flore*
and *Aurora's Wedding*; yet it was not until the mid-'thirties,
when 'Bo' Foster took me under her wing, that I began really
to put half the pence on one side to rival opera, and it is only
since the Sadlers Wells-Covent Garden company have come
into being that the scales seem even more weighed down in
favour of ballet.

1926 was, for me, a year of enchanting visits. It had started with my glorious trip to the Riviera with the Towles; in the summer I went to Veuilles-les-Roses with the Hicks family. I can remember the crossing, via Dieppe, to this day, and my utter misery as I lay prone on the floor of the public saloon which was littered by other bodies as well as my own, all of us longing for a speedy End. The trip began badly; for some reason we went—on recommendation—to Le Tréport, which out of season (it was then only early July) seemed the most God-forsaken spot on earth. It only took Seymour one night to make up his mind about *that* place. By next morning, as far as the Hicks family were concerned, Le Tréport had 'had it'. Off we all motored to discover Veuilles-les-Roses, a veritable little paradise, with a stream running through the village, roses growing on and over *all* the little houses, a charming hotel, a decent plage and a comic little casino in which we all won and lost our pittances playing Boule. And there we stayed a fort-night, having a perfect holiday and being joined presently by the Robert Courtneidges. This was the holiday which gave Seymour his name 'Uncle Ted' for me, and which stuck to him for always, where I was concerned. This was the period, surely, during which I grew to know and love him more than I had before. I had known him since I was fourteen, but he had up till then been 'your father' (to Bet), or 'Seymour' at home in my own family. From now on he became my very special Uncle Ted, almost a second father to me, and the most amusing, most exciting, most exacting, most lovable friend anyone could wish for. It was a perfect holiday of peace, happiness and fun.

I had not been back very long from France when I was invited down to the Lonsdales, Fred's family, at Salcombe. The girls were now all grown-up and all three very attractive indeed, as was Leslie, their mother. They had taken for the summer a house in a small bay, with pine trees growing to the water's edge, and here with a vast army of dogs of all breeds I found myself, about to enjoy several weeks of divine hospitality, Riviera-like sunshine and Lonsdalian wit. For even when Fred was not down, the same brand of humour and dialogue could always be counted upon to spring from the lips of members of his family. Fred did appear—and disappear —at intervals, often bringing people with him, people like Michael Arlen, Henry Daniell, Rupert Higgins. Over the household Mrs Fred—Leslie—reigned quietly and humorously. Leslie had a divine sense of humour, and so had the girls. Alsatians, bull-terriers, a Peke and a small something else spread themselves happily about the place (and never fought each other as far as I can remember), and one's days were spent rather as one imagines nowadays are spent those of American millionaires in California: bathing, playing tennis, aquaplaning, picnicking and so on. We were 'good-time-girls', but our pleasures were taken innocently enough, I'll swear.

It was at Salcombe that I met lovely Isla Buckley, then aged sixteen, as Irish to look at as she could be. Enormous blue eyes, dark short hair, a figure like a water-sprite and with the most endearing manners and manner of any sixteen-year-old I have met before or since. Isla and I started a friendship then which has grown with the years. Later she took the name of Isla Bevan, and was one of the most beautiful of all Mr Cochran's Young Ladies before she gravitated into serious parts on the legitimate stage; and now she is Mrs Charles Harvey, lovelier than ever, with a Sally-Veronica who is my god-daughter. Her brother Tony was only fourteen when I knew him first (they were known in Salcombe as 'the little Buckleys'); he was a sweet little boy, one did not visualise him in those days as growing into Anthony Buckley the celebrated photographer. Salcombe was a very attractive place; I have not been there since the war, I wonder whether it is still. It was the attraction of

Salcombe as a place, that prompted Mummie to take us all to Cornwall for a week. She, poor dear, had been glued to London for many months, for she rarely left Daddy when he was acting, and she was pining for a change and breath of air. Moreover at the back of both her and Daddy's minds was the wish to have 'something in the country' for Daphne, who was not strong and who would never be really fit, so doctors said, living in London. Paris was her love, and France, and she would seize any and all excuses to go over there, but she was still only nineteen and naturally our parents being 'fussy' parents wanted her where they could keep their eye on her.

So in the middle of September Mummie and the three of us got into the train at Paddington, Cornwall bound; Looe bound, to be precise. I cannot remember why Looe had been chosen and we certainly could not imagine why when, through-out our first and only night there, the village clock chimed every quarter and kept us all awake in the small commercial hotel to which we had gone. So the next morning a car was procured, and with bags, baggage and the good-will of the understanding proprietors we drove over to Fowey, arriving in Bodinnick. We were immediately enchanted. To quote my diary: "Motored to Fowey which we fell in love with directly. To Bodinnick first, *adorable*. Unfortunately could not get into the Inn there. Saw over perfect little place to be sold. Lunched at Fowey Hotel and have taken awfully nice rooms near there. Motor-boated to Polperro for tea, very nearly sick. *Quite* heaven on earth, no words to describe it. Motored back, perfect scenery."

Within a week the 'perfect little place to be sold' was ours. And thanks for it are due to Edgar and *The Ringer* as I said at the beginning of the chapter, for it made a small fortune for those most concerned, one of whom was my father.

The little house in those days was called Swiss Cottage. There may have been a slight semblance of Swiss châlet architecture about the top storey, but to us Hampstead-dwellers the name was synonymous with suburbia. Swiss Cottage became Ferryside very quickly. It took only six months to transform this more or less uninhabitable shambles by the ferry and water's edge into a small haven of enchantment. Originally a 'yard' and sailmaker's establishment, it was built in three storeys, of which only the top floor had been used as a dwelling-place. The house was built 'against the country', in other words great bulges of cliff form the inside walls of many of the rooms and landing. I think Ferryside is a unique house in a unique setting, and hope I may be pardoned for extolling the home in which I have now lived for so many years. Many people would have given one look at it, in 1926, and said, 'a dream, but an impractical dream', and left it at that. Not so Mummie, who was a splendid doer-up of houses, with great imagination. The long low ground-floor regions, hitherto the boat store—through which ran a stream!—was transformed into a superb living-room, the sail-loft into bedrooms and a bathroom, and the already habitable top floor was also changed beyond recognition, with walls pulled down and rooms enlarged. The house is supposed to be very old, certainly the outer walls bear all the signs of several centuries' buffetings against the prevailing sou'westerly. It looks, I think, a fascinating place to strangers who sail past us, for often one hears comments of approval floating over the water; and most people are kind enough to stand spellbound at their first glimpse of the long room, which takes up the whole of the ground floor (now minus the stream!) with its view right down Fowey harbour and out to the sea beyond.

September '26 was our introduction to Fowey, and after Daddy realised how earnest were all our desires for the cottage, he said 'go ahead', and so began the exciting business of interviewing builders, and a real architect, of buying furniture, and new curtains and chintzes and all the hundred and one things that go to making a new home such an absorbing business.

In the meantime life continued to be pleasant at home at Cannon Hall, with a jolly Christmas spent at Sandwich, followed by a wonderful trip to Switzerland with the Wallaces.

Sandwich had always been a favourite haunt of my parents, ardent golfers both of them, and to the Guildford Hotel we went that Christmas with a crowd of friends including Basil and Kate Loder, the Lonsdales, Gladys (Cooper) and her Joan, Roland (Pertwee), Leslie and Gladys Faber, Bet, Pat Wallace (Edgar's eldest daughter), Heather Thatcher and my uncle 'Coley', Daddy's brother-in-law. Not all of them were there for all the time, but a glorious holiday it was with fun for everyone, and at the end Daphne and I with Pat joined the Wallace party at Caux for winter sports, arriving in time to win a prize at the fancy-dress ball on New Year's Eve!

Edgar, generous as ever, had invited out a fantastic number of people as his guests, and I shall always remember my first morning out there, my first (and still my only) visit to Switzerland in winter-time: the arrival, after a bad night, in the early and still dark hours at Montreux, the buffet breakfast and dawn breaking, the slow trip up the mountain in the funicular and our final arrival at Caux itself in the middle of the morning, with the sun blazing, the mountains a mass of snow; the view from our bedroom balcony breath-taking as we saw for the first time the Lake of Geneva spread below like a far-away blue carpet and Mont Blanc gleaming across it in the distance; and breakfasting again on rolls and honey and coffee out on the balcony in such heat that a thin silk dressing-gown was all the covering needed. Truly a superb place. Of course I had set off to Switzerland with ambitions and enthusiasm; I had visualised myself waltzing on ice, turning telemarks and probably becoming bob-sleigh champion. One morning, possibly two, on skis was enough to damp, in more ways than one, my ideas as far as that sport was concerned. Several bad falls and miserably aching ankles soon told me moreover that I was unlikely to become a champion on the ice, but at least I enjoyed to the full the luge runs which even if very inferior to a 'bob' were exciting enough for me, especially the races and more especially when one nearly went over the tops of the runs. It was probably the most healthy holiday I've ever spent in my life, out in the open air from breakfast until the dusk fell. There was plenty of fun to be had after dark too, with skittles and indoor bowls, and dances every evening. Hosts of new friends to be made, and for me the inevitable 'crush'. He was a charmer, and I wept bitterly the day he left to return to Oxford, and 'it' lasted for a year and a day, if not quite a bit longer.

Edgar was a superb host, and spoilt one completely. We were an enormous party, and he reigned like a king at the top of the table at which we all gathered at lunch and dinner, hanging on his words even there in the same state of absorbed expectation as audiences sat through his plays in London theatres, and his readers had learnt to do at home by their own fireside. His family there consisted of Jim his wife, alas to die at a tragically early age, how attractive she was, and what fun; Pat his eldest daughter, with a brilliant brain and superb sense of humour (and I know of no one readier to make jokes against herself than Pat); Mike (alas, killed in the war) and the little 'Penny'. Mike was a charming little boy of almost ten, and Penny was much younger. I cannot remember Brian, the eldest of them all, on that holiday.

1927 started well. At the end of January Daddy produced *Interference* at the St James's, with Gilbert Miller. This was by Roland Pertwee and Harold Dearden; and had in the cast, beside Daddy, Herbert Marshall, Hilda Moore and Moyna MacGill. The play, though not a 'thriller' in the accepted sense of the word, was in fact an extremely thrilling story, with the suicide (or was it murder? I forget after all this time) of Hilda, and moments of acute tension when Daddy was left alone on the stage with the dead body for what seemed an incredible age. The play was an enormous success and had a wildly enthusiastic reception on the first night, to which we took Gladys, Beverley Nichols, Cecil Beaton and Sir Ian Malcolm in our box.

I rather think that it was about this time that Bart Marshall and Edna Best came into our lives. Edna had rightly all London at her feet by her performance as Tessa in *The Constant Nymph*, a performance of such poignancy as has seldom been bettered by any actress on the English stage. Noel Coward was the original Lewis Dodd; and Cathleen Nesbitt, Florence; that original production of the play, which I remember having seen in the autumn of 1926, will always remain in my memory.

With Bart in *Interference* started that happy friendship with us which, though circumstances and America have separated us, I hope still exists.

I cannot imagine who it was who had the foolishness at this juncture to suggest that *I* should have film tests, but someone did, and I did! I was short, plump, not at all photogenic, certainly not pretty, nor yet quite plain enough to be cast for a 'comic'. Why I even allowed myself to be so deluded I cannot imagine, for I must have wasted much time, my own and that of various studios. And needless to say, nothing came of nothing. It was all bound up with the Laskys, someone had misguidedly admired my hair and eyes—as if either were means to the end as far as a career for films was concerned.

That Easter a great treat came my way. A motor trip through Burgundy into Alsace and back to Paris, with Margaret Miller. The holiday started badly enough with my arrival at Victoria only to discover I had left behind my passport, but I finally arrived in Paris in time to get a few hours' rest before starting off the following day for Fontainebleau, Avalon and finally

5*

Dijon. Beautiful Rita Jolivet came with us. In those days she
was living in Paris, having a job, I rather think, on the *New
York Herald*, and was, as she still is, the embodiment of Gallic
wit, fascination and fun. In my usual impetuous way I immediately fell a prisoner to her charm, and not only her charm
but her superb courage. Rita had lost almost everything in that
first war, and was lucky to be alive, for she was one of the
Lusitania survivors, and had in fact gone down with the ship.
I listened horrified and aghast when I was told the story. No
one would have imagined, listening to Rita's chuckle and her
flow of sparkling conversation, that she had suffered many
horrors. I remember she took us over her old home, a beautiful
château at Vassy, by then overgrown and with an atmosphere
of a ghost-haunted past. But she was gay, with her brilliant
smile, her flashing eyes, her infectious laugh. I remember a
wonderful lunch (or was it dinner?) at the Faisan D'Or where
the spécialité de la maison was capon cooked in wine; and our
visit to the famous Hospice at Beaune, an exquisite place full of
a unique atmosphere entirely its own. It was Easter Day itself
on which we drove through blossom-infested Alsace, a sight I
shall never forget. Miles and miles of—what were they? apple
trees, cherry trees?—and little Grimm's-fairy-tale houses with
high red roofs—higher than the walls of the houses—upon the
tops of which were, built precariously, storks' nests. The
scenery through which we motored, mountains and forests of
the Jura, was some of the most glorious I had ever seen, and
my excitement was intense when we reached the banks of the
Rhine, and I looked across the water at the distant haze which
was the Black Forest, and told myself that at last I was close to
the legendary home of the Nibelungen. We reached Strasbourg
in the evening, a truly fascinating city, with at that time a
markedly German atmosphere, and the buildings, most of
them very old, seemed a setting for a fairy-story. The cathedral
was beautiful, but what I recall most is the famous clock the

chimes of which are heralded by figures, human in size, who carry out their task, by the face of the clock.

After the beauty of Burgundy and Alsace the drive back to Paris through Nancy to Rheims seemed unending, deadly and monotonous. We stayed the night at Rheims, in the then magnificent new Hôtel which like a phoenix had literally sprung into being on the ashes of that devastated city. In 1927, nine years after the '14-'18 war had ended, that part of northern France was still a vast area of devastation, haunted by the ghosts of the fallen. To me, an English girl whose country had been little scathed in that war, the place made a profound impression; surely I said to myself the French will never forget or forgive. The French themselves, thrifty, hard-working and unconquered, had built villages, towns and cities in the destroyed areas. Gleaming white ugly modern architecture bore witness, in the scorching sun of that hot April, to the people's will to work. It was the countryside itself that filled me with horror and gloom, mile upon mile of treeless land, blown-up trunks, land—unlike the rest of France—which looked barren, dead, decayed. Even after nine years there were still visible signs of warfare, a German helmet here, a skeleton there, for we were motoring over the battlefields, and along the celebrated Chemin des Dames where death and blood still seemed to reek about the place, and through the city of Soissons which was a total wreck, desolation abounding everywhere. My relief was great when we reached Compiègne, with its atmosphere of charm, finally Margaret's own flat in the Île de la Cité, where we could hear again the chimes of Notre Dame. As I looked upon a Paris which seemed unaware of that corner of France we had left behind, I hoped that future generations might remember, and ponder and be wise.

A week of Parisian gaiety with Margaret followed. As usual I met a score or more of interesting French and American men and women, writers, film magnates, artists. And as usual one

more exciting young man who took me to one of the most
entrancing places I've ever been to, the Moulin de Jarcy.
Margaret came along as a chaperone, but tactfully took a nap
after lunch instead of sharing our canoe on the river. . . .

The young man *might* have materialised into something
serious—for he did follow me to England—but for two things.
The first was the move to Fowey. The second was my Wireless
Accident.

The move to Fowey took place in early May, and every
other business paled beside it. Mummie and I and Tod undertook this task which, Gargantuan as it seemed spiritually and
backbreaking physically, was finally achieved in three days,
with Viola Tree as our first caller before the week was out.
Daddy was acting in the successful *Interference* and had shown
no untoward hurry to visit Ferryside, for which we were truly
thankful. The *right moment* we felt was of paramount importance; the time would come. Daphne and one of the Cannon
Hall maids arrived, we now ate as well as slept in the house and
before a fortnight had passed had added to the family one more
ball of parti-coloured fluff, a minute and adorable Peke that we
called Chen, and two tiny blue Persian balls of fluff, brothers,
John and Michael. They were born and bred in Lerryn, that
enchanting riverside village as yet—God be praised—untouched and unspoilt by modern vandalism.

At the end of May a matinée performance of *Twelfth Night*
acted by the clan Forbes-Robertson, if I may so call them, was
produced at St James's Theatre, in which for some reason I
appeared as one of the court ladies to Olivia, played by
'Blossom' (Maxine) Forbes-Robertson. The matinée took
place immediately after I returned, with Mummie, from
Fowey. I remember little about it beyond the fact that Esmond
Knight was, like me, one of the few non-Forbes-Robertsons in
the cast, and that at the full-dress rehearsal I cut my hand on a
tin in the theatre, fainting dead away! Jean played Viola and

looked delicious. The matinée went off successfully enough, but that same evening I met with an accident which sent me to bed with greater pain than I have ever suffered before or since. I was carrying a square portable wireless across the drawing-room at Cannon Hall and slipped on the parquet floor, fell, the corner of the wireless running into my side and piercing my kidney. It was not until an hour or two later that this was discovered when I lay in writhing agony in a blood-soaked bath. Our doctor was summoned, followed by a surgeon, then two nurses; and the blessed relief which came from morphia then helped me to sleep and forget. I was very ill, and in bed nearly two weeks, finally arriving downstairs wan and 'of interest' to an inevitable Sunday lunch party, where I was fussed and made much of by darling 'Mary' Tempest and her husband, and Lily and Jack Gilliat.

I cannot remember when exactly it was that Jack and Lily came so much into our circle. My parents must have known them before I did, but I myself recall our first meeting at a big supper party at the Somerset Maughams'—I imagine after one of his first nights. Lily is well named, and when I knew her first was like a lily-of-the-valley. I love to look back on the many happy times I spent in the Gilliats' house in Stanhope Place, with exquisite Lily and her debonair and charming husband. There was another man who exuded charm. He used to enjoy teasing me, was always ragging me about the unsettled state of my heart! Lily was an enchanting and wonderful friend to have, rather like Debussy's music. Alas, that she should have lost not only her beloved Jack but her two brilliant sons so tragically and long before their time. And now the small Virginia, whose dancing-classes I watched and whose parties I peeped at, is Lady Sykes of Sledmere, with children of her own, and I look at my greying hair in the mirror and think 'it was all a long time ago'.

Luckily I have always managed to recover quickly from ills,

operations and accidents, and it was not long before I was on my feet again, forgetting the excruciating pain that I had suffered, and once more haunting the box-office of Covent Garden and the Centre Court of Wimbledon. That was the year in which Grete Stuckgold sang Aida gloriously, and Pertile of the divine voice was Radames, and that greatest of modern contraltos Olszewska, Amneris. Karsavina was the première danseuse. The year that Ljungberg sang Tosca and was to my way of thinking 'divine', with Ansseau as Cavaradossi and Stabile, Scarpia. What a cast! Olszewska also sang Carmen that summer, but although she looked superb I did not think she was really suited to the part. For me, the highlight of that summer was *Turandot*; Ursula Blois took me, and from that year I have never if I could help it, missed it. As a spectacle it is surely more satisfying than anything else to be witnessed on the operatic stage. The music contains some of the best Puccini ever wrote, and *if* the singers are what Puccini hoped for, then one is in for an evening of sheer magic. Florence Easton was my first Turandot, and I am pretty certain that Liù was that incomparable Lotte Schöne, and no one who ever heard *her* Liù will remember anyone else's. How desperately important second rôles in opera are. How one's evening can be ruined for instance by an inadequate Brangane, a second-rate Liù, a wobbling Venus or a reedy Sieglinde.

There was magnificent ballet again too. I saw *Les Biches* for the first time, with I think Nikitina, and was immediately captivated by it; and in the same programme were *Tricorne* and *Neptune*; I saw Lifar in *L'Après-midi d'un Faune* one matinée performance and *Romeo and Juliet, The Cat* and *Biches* again, and the same evening I returned for the evening performance to watch *Le Pas d'Acier, Matelots* and *Fire-bird*, and saw Danilova for the first time, that exquisite ballerina at whose shrine I worshipped for years. No one has ever touched her performance in *Beau Danube* or her can-can in the *Boutique Fantasque*.

1927 saw Helen Wills as holder of the Women's World Championship at Wimbledon—it was a thrilling afternoon; I watched her beat d'Alvarez and then saw Cochet take the championship from Borotra, one of the most exciting matches I had ever seen, and the tournament finished with Tilden and Hunter beating 'Bunny' Austin and Lycett in the men's doubles.

It was in 1927 that Frank Curzon's Call Boy won the Derby. And 1927 was the year in which, on the seventh day of November, I found I had exactly £1 14s. 7d. to last till January 1st! There was nothing to do that time but weep on Daddy's shoulder, which I did. To the tune of nearly one hundred pounds. Do girls still have 'allowances' I wonder? or has the time come when no parent has the wherewithal to 'allow', and do all the Johns and Marys—and Angelas—work for their pennies? Until I was thirty I had one hundred and fifty pounds a year. On it I was supposed to do everything but pay my railway fares. I started in a grand way at eighteen buying clothes where other débutantes bought theirs, and soon found it far too costly a business. I gravitated from South Molton Street and Knightsbridge to Oxford Street, and thence to Shaftesbury Avenue. . . . I prayed for a 'little woman' who did not materialise until once again I was on the upgrade. But you parents who still have something to give your daughters, to help them with, remember—if you live in London (or any big city)—there are many other things than clothes on which girls have to dole out their money. One likes to return hospitality and not only in one's own home, and that means little meals at little restaurants, with very often little drinks, and the bill is *not* little. Hair has always been an expensive item for a woman once she's grown up. In my young day there were no such things as 'perms'; I started with the old-fashioned 'tong', and was overjoyed when after several years of that procedure an honest hairdresser told me my hair waved naturally and it only

needed a set! Cinemas, cigarettes, presents . . . flowers for a bedroom, a visit to a concert . . . £150 is very soon spent. I only
know that I personally was always 'in the soup'. I inherited too
many of my father's extravagant tastes (and I still have them).

At last, as I was about to reach the advanced age of twenty-
four, I began the first of my ventures with what is occasionally
described as Good Works. My sentimental affection for
animals led me—how I cannot remember—into taking on the
hon. secretaryship of the whole Hampstead area of the
R.S.P.C.A. Through no fault of anyone it wasn't in too good
a way and needed reorganising. Hampstead for that purpose
consisted of N.W.3, N.W.8, N.W.6 and parts of N.W.1, and
streets upon streets and roads upon roads had to be canvassed
and collected from. A helpful band of collectors and enthusiastic animal-lovers were culled from the highways and by-
ways, and from the more unfortunate of my personal friends
living in the district. But as it was 'my pidgin' the bulk of
house-to-house collecting fell to me, and for autumns for many
years to come I would spend weeks on my feet doing
methodically streets and roads which took me from Parliament
Hill to Golders Green, from Belsize Park to Kilburn. I had no
car of my own in those days and it needed quite a lot of
organising, but doubtless it was good for both Wendy and
myself. What wasn't so good was when it came to delivering up
all the collections to the treasurer and in my usual careless
fashion finding I was 'out' and having to make good the error!
I was helped greatly in the whole task by a charming bank
manager in one of the Hampstead banks, the hon. treasurer of
the branch, who having several daughters of his own knew
how to deal with me. Every month an Inspector called on me
and gave me numbers of revolting cases of cruelty and neglect,
which went down in a book, and once a year we had a big
meeting and a report was made out by me, which entailed a
great deal of ink-on-the-fingers, sucking of thumbs, puckering

of the forehead, resort to the spectacles and scratching of the head. The first year I took the branch on, my enthusiasm prompted me to organise a bazaar, and have it opened. I rather believe I asked a certain bishop to do it. *Six people came.* We did not repeat the performance.

In February Daddy put on a new play, with a new star. The play was *S.O.S.*, the star, new to London West End lights, none other than Gracie Fields, who although famous on the music-hall stage had not played a straight part hitherto. Daddy had seen her frequently in *Mr Tower of London*, under the manage-ment of her first husband Archie Pitt, and had been convinced of the success she would and could achieve as his leading lady in the new play. And he was right. She was excellent and made a great success. There was a moment when she wanted to buy Ferryside. Many years ago now, but she and Archie Pitt turned up one day, and Gracie did cart-wheels on the lawn (with the village looking on in great astonishment), then rowed herself out to the harbour point, singing at the top of her voice, her long hair flowing to the winds, and returned to the house with a fabulous offer which I'm thankful to say was refused. Daddy adored to hear her sing his favourite songs, old ballads and such-like, and I remember him making her sing over and over again 'Douglas Gordon'. In *S.O.S.* another more-or-less newcomer played the ingénue: lovely Betty Stockfeld who became one of my greatest friends. She played Bart Marshall's daughter, and George Curzon Daddy's son; Gracie played the wife of one of them, a woman as far as I remember no better than she should be. It was an interesting play, good 'theatre', but it did not run for more than about six months.

In our party for the opening was Peter Macdonald, now Member for the Isle of Wight, and it was he who first interested me and introduced me to politics, and soon I was started on my second stage of Good Works. This time I was enrolled as a Young Conservative, under the auspices of Eveleigh Leith, and before I knew what was what I had been bustled off to South-wark to address envelopes for the coming Municipal Election down there. I don't think I enjoyed it very much and being then (as now) extremely impressionable I did not make the best canvasser for the cause when the time came to help with the next General Election. Southwark was not a beauty spot, and did not lend itself as a particularly prepossessing district to capture socialist votes. Squalor was fairly evident and so was poverty in the tenement dwellings the concrete stairs of which I tore up and down, knocking on people's doors, quickly having them banged in my face. When one irate man told me he voted Labour and always would, I remember sighing in sympathy and saying, "Yes, so should I." Which was hardly the answer I was supposed to have given.

About this time London went wild over a new play and a new actor. The play was *Young Woodley*, the actor Frank Lawton. Frances Doble—everyone will remember the story—played the part of the master's wife with whom young Woodley fell in love, Woodley being played by Frank who leapt in a night to the front rank of brilliant young actors. I had known Frank for years, we all had, from the days when we used all to meet at the Actors' Orphanage when Frank was a boy (head boy, I rather think) and Daddy was President. In the famous annual cricket matches, played on a gruelling summer Sunday as a rule, Frank used to captain the Orphanage team against that of Daddy's Actors. Wonderful days those were at Langley, where the Orphanage used to be, run (then) by Anslow Austin and his wife Connie, who had been on the stage herself once upon a time and still seemed to hanker after the symbolic smell of grease paint. What lunches she used to prepare . . . salads, cold salmon, ice-creams, fruit salads . . . and one was waited on by the boys and girls, and afterwards (and before of course) we all sat together watching the cricket of Godfrey Tearle and Owen Nares and little boys of fourteen and fifteen, with as great a thrill as if it was a Test Match. And anyway did not Aubrey Smith play for the Actors annually, giving it a semblance of first-class cricket?

Never was anyone less spoilt by success than Frank, one of the most charming boys I ever knew. We were once guests at the same house and a very funny thing happened. Frank with his sister, and I believe also his brother, missed the last train, and had to spend the night. Our hostess—Eileen Idare—had to lend them all her own most feminine night-attire. To this moment I can conjure up the vision of Frank in pink crêpe-de-chine frills and lace.

In March however I was still trying to do my best in the political field by way of 'helping out'. Our Central Southwark Conservative candidate was at the bottom of a three-cornered poll in the L.C.C. elections, which was my first battle to date. Undaunted however by defeat I was whisked off by Peter Macdonald the day following this débâcle to witness a mass meeting at the Albert Hall which Baldwin addressed. At the time it all struck me as being enormously impressive, but after twenty-two years and 'coat-changing' more than once I can now only think of the then Prime Minister as an extremely benign English gentleman; an old Harrovian (like Daddy!) whom I should have liked one day to have sat next to whilst eating underdone roast beef and talking about the countryside.

High in the political field then was Duff Cooper. He was talked of in certain quarters as a future Prime Minister, so that his presence as guest of Honour at the Actors' Benevolent Fund dinner was rather a coup. The place chosen was the Savoy and my father was in the Chair. The speeches were good. It was at a stage Golfing Dinner (I think) that the guest of Honour was the Prince of Wales and I still have the scrap of paper on which he had jotted notes, which as treasure trove Daddy brought back to me. But that was a For Men Only dinner; on the Duff Cooper occasion women were present, including me, sitting between Eustace Blois and Leslie Faber, and as Roland was also present I imagine the evening went with a swing as far as I was concerned.

A very great and very old friend of the family used to be, and still is I hope, Ronnie Squire. He has a daughter, Jacqueline, who in 1928 was still a very small girl. I met her for the first time that spring, one April afternoon, accompanied by her utterly nonplussed papa *who was trying to buy her some underclothes*. I do not think I have ever witnessed a more pathetic spectacle than this hero of so many Lonsdalian Comedies trying to buy little Jacky drawers in Debenham and Freebody's! He looked rather like the Sapper character he had played in *Bulldog Drummond* who never knew where anything was; gone—certainly—was the panache that one had become accustomed to expect from this Lonsdalian man about town. With sighs of profound relief he greeted me and the task of fitting-out (with many more things than pretty frilly drawers) was given to me. I have always remembered that first meeting with Jacky, who was the sweetest little girl imaginable.

Once again a summer full of gaieties was in full swing, with its train of the Royal Academy Private View, special matinées, opera, Ascot, garden parties, Lord's. . . . For the annual matinée of King George's Pension Fund (for actors and actresses) that year the Terrys en famille headed an all-star cast in *The Scarlet Pimpernel*, a wonderful occasion. As at so many of these big charity performances I sold programmes, which was always fun, but on this particular occasion tiring, as there was not one single seat left, and I stood the whole afternoon before going on to hear the *Walküre* in the gallery! Frieda Leider was the darling of this year's Ring, and truly she was a superb Brünnhilde. Melchior sang in both *Walküre* and *Siegfried*, but Laubenthal was the Siegfried in the same cycle's *Götterdämmerung* and although he looked superb he quite frankly did not compare to Melchior. (But then who ever has?) Ljungberg and Lotte

Lehmann were both singing, and so were Olszewska and Anday, and Heger conducted. Jeanne and I were enthusiastic worshippers of The Ring, and dear Dame May Whitty used to feed us in the long interval, in her charming flat round the corner in Bedford Street.

There is a lot to be said for hearing Wagner from the Covent Garden amphitheatre; the enthusiasm was far greater, *in the old days*, than in the smarter parts of the theatre and criticism occasionally offered a battleground. Possibly the men did wear their hair rather long and look as if they seldom took baths, and the young women's noses shone, and all around one people pretended to read scores in a light that must have made such an undertaking completely impossible; but at least their spirit was genuine and their worship real, and there was none of the wan and precious patronising criticism that one heard going on ad nauseam in the foyer below where a great many of the audience came to be seen rather than to listen. *Tannhäuser* was rather unsatisfying after the grandeur of The Ring, and Ljungberg, though she sang beautifully, was not as good an Elisabeth as she had been a Sieglinde. Tannhäuser was sung by Oehman, Herbert Janssen—one of the best Wagnerian baritones ever heard at Covent Garden—was Wolfram, Ohms Venus. 1928 was one of those rare years when Covent Garden chose to give *Louise*, and a glorious production it was, Jeanne Guyla taking over the name part from Heldy at a moment's notice and an adorable Louise she made. Why is not Charpentier's opera given here more frequently? There was *Samson and Delilah* after a long absence. Georges Thill and Ansseau sang alternately Samson, and I was much impressed with Frozier-Marrot as Delilah. I saw it twice. But probably the highlight of the season to me that year was Pampanini's *Butterfly*. I have heard her often, and have heard many Butterflys, but never shall I forget the shiver that went through my body and the stopping of my heart as—I was sitting high up and uncomfortably in the amphitheatre—I heard for the first time Pampanini's voice in the distance, off-stage, in the first act before she slowly makes her way with her retinue of girls on to the stage before her marriage to Pinkerton. It was a faultless production, and the audience rose as I have only seen them give homage to one other: Flagstad. And, as when I see and hear Flagstad, I myself just forgot where I was and tears poured down my face and I howled like a child.

I suppose there are people who think that giving way to emotion at the opera is too fatuous and too affected for words. ("Great fat prima-donnas! how *can* you cry!") If a prima-donna is the size of an ox but has the voice of one of God's angels, and the music she sings comes straight to one's heart from Heaven I do not think it is so surprising to cry. . . .

Bohème was another opera for me this year, never one of my favourites, strangely enough. But Sheridan was a good Mimi and Pertile, Rudolpho. Bellezza was conducting most of the Italian operas, which also included of course *Turandot*, now an established favourite at Covent Garden in the International seasons. Eva Turner gave a wonderful rendering as the princess, and this year both Pampanini and Sheridan sang Liù. For the first time I saw *Otello*, an opera which has since become a great favourite of mine if sung really well. Miriam Licette sang Desdemona then with Zanelli, but the best *Otello* I remember was in 1939 when Tibbet sang Iago and Martinelli Otello and Norena was the Desdemona.* Just before the war I think. Looking back over the years, with now only my annual rush up for Flagstad, 1928 really seems to have been a bumper. There were that hardy pair *Cavalleria Rusticana* and *Pagliacci* . . . Tom Burke a grand Turiddo, though I personally was just a bit disappointed with Gianinni's Santuzza, but Pertile and Pampanini were superb in the Leoncavallo. He was in glorious voice all the season and never more so than when he was Radames to

* This was written before the Scala's performance in Sept. 1950.

Eva Turner's Aida in which rôle I infinitely preferred her—that year at any rate—to Turandot. Of course the evening at Covent Garden that should have stood out above all others in my memory of the season was that when Chaliapine sang *Boris Godounov*. It has done, but alas! not because of Chaliapine; but because I was overcome by ptomaine poisoning and in the first act alone disappeared nearly half-a-dozen times, was finally given ice to suck and on my last reappearance the cloak-room attendant, with arms akimbo and giving it up as a bad job, exclaimed, "Wot! *Agine?*"

I daresay that readers who do not share with me my love and enthusiasm for opera will find my past attendances at Covent Garden boring. I ask them to bear with me, because I can almost re-live the evenings as I write about them, the likes of which I'll not know again. The glamour of the past has gone . . . those evenings of mighty tiaras and long white gloves . . . men with button-holes . . . cars and liveried chauffeurs . . . myself nine times out of ten peering over the edge of the amphitheatre watching the élite below me, with awe and no real envy, presently to clatter down the flights of stone stairs into Floral Street and beat my retreat through the throngs of people to the stage door of Wyndham's or the St James's to cadge a 'lift' back with Daddy; or just occasionally in my smartest evening dress, opera cloak and long kid gloves rubbing shoulders with the great, if I were with Ursula Blois or Viola or a rich young man enamoured enough of both opera and me to take me to Covent Garden rather than the latest hit in town.

On a hundred and fifty pounds a year one could only aspire to the amphitheatre or the gallery if one wanted to go as often as I did. How strange it is that now when I go to the stalls or grand tier, being better able to afford the luxury, the raiment of my co-audience in the stalls is even poorer and of less respect to the artists than my amphitheatre pals would have worn in pre-war days—and nights. When I listened to the broadcast on the radio of the gala performance of the ballet given in President Auriol's honour *I wept*, and thought of that line from *The Silver King*: "Oh God put back thy universe and give me yesterday."

The 'notice' of *S.O.S.* went up, and Daddy became busy on the production of a play by Arnold Bennett, *The Return Journey*, a Faust-up-to-date play, with Daddy as the rejuvenated modern Faust, Henry Daniell as the Mephistophelian character and Grace Wilson as the girl. Laura Cowie and Bobbie Andrews were also in the cast. It was a strange and as far as I remember neither a very pleasant nor attractive play, and did not run for long. We 'children' (!) did not go up for the first night, remaining in Cornwall for three glorious months without interruption, and it was during the autumn that Daphne saw Menabilly for the first time; Menabilly the centuries-old seat of the Rashleigh family, complete with furniture yet unlived in by its owner. It was a late October afternoon when Daphne and I decided to set out and explore this famous mansion with an almost Sleeping-Beauty-like legend of undergrowth which kept at bay most trespassers and sightseers. Dusk fell and we realised we were lost in a veritable jungle of tropical trees, shrubs and 'bush'. An eerie and most ghost-like atmosphere pervaded these uninhabited acres, and we threshed backwards and forwards, this way and that, falling into holes and over submerged tree-trunks, realising only too well that we knew neither the way to the great house nor yet the way back to Fowey. Owls by now were hooting, and strange night birds emitted shrieks and cries, the unmistakable smell of fox was frequently apparent and the dogs kept at our heels, tails down, all enjoyment vanished. We knew that many people said Menabilly was haunted, and by now *I* was convinced that local superstition had not lied. The moon came out and presently we found ourselves near a cove, which we recognised, and knew to be a long step from home. We were both

dead tired when we reached Bodinnick, and not a little alarmed
by what to me at any rate seemed to have been a terrifying
experience!

Daphne now was determined to find the house and next day
we set out once again by a different way. And found it.
Curiously I remember I was not only disappointed but
frightened by it. It seemed so lonely, so gloomy, so—yes—
haunted. If it had been empty it would not have had that
strange 'of another world' feeling that it gave me then. We
pressed our faces up against the window-panes, gazed at Victorian furniture . . . pictures hanging . . . a rocking-horse . . .
but all was sombre, and one knew that the rocking-horse had
known no child for many a year, and that the house was
mourning her past glory, for it had been one of the greatest in
Cornwall, and carriages drove through the avenues now impassable and in which we had lost ourselves the evening before.
I suppose Daphne was drawn to it even then; she certainly was
by the following spring when she would get up at crack of
dawn and picnic alone amid the beautiful rhododendrons
which surrounded the house in a flame of colour, as Loge's
flames kept guard over the sleeping Brünnhilde. Menabilly—
even an unlived-in almost derelict Menabilly—in the spring
was a very different matter; its past still clung to it, but more
kindly, it seemed to come alive again with the birds that sang
ceaselessly and with the rabbits that played all over the unkempt lawns oblivious of one's presence, knowing this vast
domain to be their home, not ours.

For years Daphne longed for a dream to come true, a dream
whereby *somehow* this house which had taken complete pos-
session of her heart and soul should one day be hers. She told
herself that this would come to pass. Twenty-two years ago I
suppose she must have laid her plans, and twenty-two years ago
she had not yet written her first book.

To-day I sit in Menabilly and realise only too well the whys and wherefores of her love for a house that for reasons of entail can never be completely hers; it has a compelling charm, and a compelling *hold* of one that I have never felt in any other place. There are places more beautiful I know; places with greater historical value; places with grander views and more exquisite gardens. I have been living here three months now, winter months moreover when Menabilly—a cold house—is not at its best, yet subconsciously I find myself thinking 'good' when I don't have to go out, or if I do a strange pleasure fills me when I return, and 'back' I sigh happily. It is the grounds with those bird-infested trees, those gigantic rhododendron woods which seemed so unfriendly twenty-two years ago, which put reins around one as it were. I understand, which I have never done before, why Daphne can never really bear to move beyond the gates. It is almost as if fairies pulled one back, compelling one to remain. And now, since she and her family have lived within its walls, the house seems very happy once again. The sombre gloom which enshrouded it with all its Victorian lares and penates has vanished. Children's voices, a small West Highland's bark and Daphne's smile and love have reassured Menabilly that it is serving a purpose again, and it seems to be giving them the love they give Menabilly.

But as long ago as 1928 the thought of one day living at Menabilly certainly never entered *my* mind, which was too taken up with autumnal rounds of gaiety, autumnal collecting for the R.S.P.C.A., Actors' Orphanage committee meetings (upon which I now served), parties, the theatre, the round of first nights on which Mummie and I went on an average once a week I suppose, concerts, one's friends. One play stands out in my memory of 1928: *Jealousy*, the gripping, cast-of-two play in which Mary Newcomb conquered London with her superb acting. I little realised as I watched her that a few years hence some of my happiest days would be spent with her, and Alex Higginson her husband, in their beautiful Dorset home.

Arnold Bennett's play had not been a success, and early in December Daddy produced and played in *The Play's the Thing* by Molnar. Neither did this piece capture the London public (which never have understood Molnar, admittedly). It was all rather depressing and one began to wonder at the turning tide of fortune.

But Daddy refused to allow a momentary defeat to depress him, what with Christmas coming and the usual big Cannon Hall gathering to celebrate it. We all lunched at Great Fosters, I remember, and tremendously impressed we were by the tapestries and linenfold panelling of this beautiful Elizabethan mansion. Surely Great Fosters must have been one of the pioneer efforts of turning vast private mansions over to hotels? Our own dinner-party ran into the usual number of eighteen or thereabouts, and it must have been this Christmas I think that Bunny Bruce, Nigel's wife, took me to task over my *fat*. She told me I was a disgrace, which I had never realised before. Obviously she believed in the method of being cruel to be kind. I was very fat: I was five feet two inches and I weighed over ten stone ... but 'no one had ever told me'. I suppose it was my fat that kept me jolly when my young men turned me down, and I wouldn't be surprised if it were my fat that had been the cause of the turning down in the first place, come to think of it!

It was now that I made a new and exciting friend: Eileen Idare, one of the grandest and most generous friends anyone— man, woman or child—could wish for.

I should not be surprised if many musical comedies of the past did not owe a great part of their success to the brains and skill of Eileen, for Idare was responsible for the dressing of so many theatrical productions, and Eileen was Idare. Even without a programme one could tell at a glance if the show was one of hers or not, there was an unmistakable stamp about her colour-schemes, her materials, her chic. Her choruses looked as lovely as the Chelsea Flower Show, and surely one cannot pay a higher compliment? She had a knack of blending soft hues in different layers of chiffon which made any theatrical production of hers an absolute joy to the eye.

I knew her—and was to know her—very well, and I have never known anyone in any job work harder than she did. She had genius and it is a thousand pities that her second marriage divorced her from a career in which no one was her master. Eileen was brilliant in a number of ways; as hostess in her Shiplake cottage or in the various houses I knew her in in London she had no equal, her parties had the excitement of a kaleidoscope and alone she was a perfect friend. She never minded what she did and if she was working twenty-four hours she would manufacture a twenty-fifth in which to help a needy or sick friend if help was wanted. She had more joie de vivre and more exotic glamour than anyone I have ever known, and in her early thirties her Hebraic beauty far outshone that of the usual rose-like 'lovelies' to be seen at fashionable restaurants and night clubs every evening of every week.

I had two operations in 1929, a bad one for tonsils and a horrible one a few months later for appendicitis, yet there was never a day in which Eileen did not come round to the nursing home, busy as she was on one theatrical production after another, to see how I was and to bring me flowers, and not only bring them but rearrange the old ones! I look back on my friendship with Eileen Idare full of gratitude and happiness.

To start the new year with an operation hanging over one is not the best of omens and it was not a very happy year for several reasons, but it was a treat to be ill at No. 9 Mandeville Place, run by those three wonderful Gordon sisters with a staff of nurses who alternated between being angels and 'girl friends' willing to gossip and listen to one's miseries. The food was Ritz-like and I cried when I left, and often used to go back and help (hinder I should think!) clean up the 'theatre' after an operation. One hears of so many cases of people being miserable and badly fed and neglected when in hospitals and nursing homes; I only know that even with the horrible pain I had to bear, and later during my second operation a private misery as well, I could not have been amongst kinder and dearer women.

The tonsil business over and done with, I quickly recovered after a lazy convalescence at Fowey and returned in time for Daddy's first night of Audry and Waveney Carten's play *Fame*. If ever a play showed promise of success this did, for it had a wildly enthusiastic reception and was splendidly acted by everyone, and it was a good if melodramatic story. Yet the critics were unkind, and it only lasted three months.

In the meantime, almost immediately after the operation, I left for my first visit to Scotland. Scotland the land that stole my heart. Perhaps it didn't steal it, maybe I just gave it. I only know that I shall never be content till I have my own home in the West Highlands, that a year to me is a wasted year in which I have not crossed the border, and that I would rather have a drop (preferably more than a drop!) of Scottish blood in my veins than any other in the world. And as far as I know I haven't even a drop.

Rita Jolivet, now Mrs 'Jimmy' Bryce Allan, had written inviting me to stay with herself and her husband at Wemyss Bay; I had received her letter during the tonsil crisis, and it was in March that I spent a wonderful fortnight there, a fortnight of perpetual sunshine, and indigo sky and sea; a fortnight gazing across the water towards Arran and Bute; a fortnight of discovering Loch Lomond, the Campsie Fells and—Edinburgh. Even Glasgow in a thick fog was not left out of the itinerary! My escort there was a very serious, very shy young man who took me to the Necropolis of all places! In order to dispel his shyness I volunteered the information that nothing in the world shocked me. To which he replied, with quiet horror in rather clipped Scottish tones: "Not even the rape of a child?"

Once back in London there was work to do in Southwark

again, for the General Election was not far off. This time I was given office work to do and wrote out envelopes by the hundred. Anything was better than saying the wrong thing to the wrong person at the wrong door, I felt. One afternoon after an orgy of such envelope addressing I called at Mandeville Place (I used to drop in once a week regularly to see them all), and after a cup of tea my ex-nurse said to me:

"Come and meet my latest patient, he has also just had his tonsils out."

In my diary this meeting is rather quaintly described in the following way: 'Met a nice young man in bed', which conjures up the vision of both of us tucked up beside each other. He asked me to go and visit him again, and when I did I was given too many glasses of very good sherry and found myself later hugging a lamp-post in the manner of time-worn jokes in *Punch*. It was with great difficulty and many giggles that I navigated the escalator of the Bond Street tube, arriving at Cannon Hall in time for dinner, quiet except for an occasional hiccough. The young man's name was Stafford Bourne; he was in fact Mr B. of B. & H. fame, and for twenty years I can look back on a friendship which has endured steadily and happily through the vicissitudes we have both passed. Stafford was a grand 'chum'. We used to have weekly lunches at the Ivy and once a week we used to go to the theatre, and many were the jolly week-ends I spent in the bosom of his entire family at his mother's lovely country house, Garston Manor, and many the swimming parties I enjoyed in what must be the most beautiful private swimming-bath in London; and now I hope I add Jane's friendship to his, not omitting the affection I feel for two diminutive Bournes that hold their own with any children in the British Isles for sheer charm and attraction.

Just as I was in the midst of my annual orgy of opera I was hauled off to Mandeville Place once again, this time to have my appendix out. It was a hateful business and I wept tears of bitter (and childish) fury when—with dozens of amphitheatre tickets safe in my pocket—I was told that the operating theatre and not Covent Garden would be seeing me for the rest of the season. However I managed *Rosenkavalier*, *Lohengrin* with Fritz Wolff and Lotte Lehmann, The Ring, two performances of *Tristan and Isolde*, *Meistersinger* with lovely Meta Seinemeyer, Schorr and Wolff, AND *Don Giovanni*, so I suppose I had no great right to grumble. Ohms sang most of the great rôles that season very finely. It was an unhappy summer for I had at last found what novelettes are pleased to call Mr Right. But my parents and the world, and (rather naturally) his wife, definitely considered him to be Mr Wrong, and a very bad time was had by all. The General Election of 1929 was very much bound up in that whirlwind and ill-fated love, for we had a superstitious gamble on the issue: if the Conservatives won all would be well for us; if Labour, then all would be over. It was the first time I'd had a vote, and a great deal of my heart went into the ballot box. Politically we were opposed, and used to have wonderful arguments over our beliefs when we met surreptitiously at the zoo or in unknown restaurants, and Ourselves became too disturbing a topic. Anyway a Labour Government was returned, and even if its majority was only a poor one it was a deal bigger than any majority X. and I had.

Until then I had never lied to my family, either about people or about what I did. I was by now twenty-five, of an age when most unmarried daughters have either left home for a flat or a job of their own, or who else come and go without questions asked. I think there can have been very few girls of my age, class and upbringing who got into hot water if they were out later than two a.m., and whose friendships (and possible love affairs) were matters of marked approval and disapproval. I only dwell on the matter of X. in so far that other parents and children who may read this can take warning. Naturally they were grieved to learn that X. and I loved each other, but a little more love and understanding would have been a great deal more help than the Coventry we were sent to, and bitterness and much misery might have been averted. As for myself, I determined never to tell the *unnecessary* truth again. How often do I hear parents exclaim—"My children never tell me things"; the fault, dear parents, lies in the manner you show when you *are* told things. It is no encouragement if you're in love, or even want to go away for a mere week-end with another girl friend —or just a late night 'date'—to find yourself saying 'one, two, three' before screwing up courage enough to inform the household of this stupendous piece of news. To begin with it ruins half the pleasure of participated enjoyment; to hope for "How lovely! *are* you?" and only to receive a cold "Oh", is the perfect fertiliser for any deception-to-come. Disapproval towards the innocent (if silly) goings-on of the young is enough to quell any enthusiastic ardour and spontaneous heart-pourings, and may well be the cause of such eventual lines as these: "What a party! Talk of orgies! everyone in other people's beds."

If titles of plays were anything to go by that year, it is hardly surprising that *Bitter Sweet* and *Journey's End* stood out for me in my scheme of things.

I do not think I have ever loved a show more than I did *Bitter Sweet*; most certainly if I were to choose three to see again out of all the many years' pick *Bitter Sweet* would be one of them. With the original cast, for there was never a Sari to touch Peggy Wood. *Journey's End* I saw with Stafford Bourne and James Gunn, the portrait painter. Surely no more devastating play about war was ever written. And how superbly acted it was.

A young actress who took London by storm that autumn has shown since that she possesses qualities that entitle her to be considered as one of the few great actresses on the English stage to-day. It was in October that I went with Mummie one evening to see Matheson Lang's new play *Jew Süss*, and I jotted in the diary: 'A divine girl in it—Peggy Ashcroft.' No one who ever saw Peggy Ashcroft's Juliet could have left the theatre dry-eyed, and no one who watched her superb performance in *Edward, My Son* could call it less than great.

I get so angry when I read in papers that there is no young talent on the English stage to-day. I do not know Peggy Ashcroft, Pamela Browne, or Vivien Leigh, so that I have no axe to grind in singing their praises; but I am certain there are not to be found in any other country to-day three young actresses to better them.

Daddy in the autumn of 1929 was still looking for a new play and being forced once more to fall back on old favourites. In September he revived again *Dear Brutus*; this time Mary Casson played Margaret, the dream child. She was adorable, and her very real youth brought with it a pathos that Faith Celli's faery genius had somehow hidden. Faith was elfin, Mary Rose-like, sheer Barrie and a class apart; Mary Casson was a real little girl —lost.

It was that Christmas that Daddy once again took over the dual parts he had created twenty-five years before, Captain Hook and Mr Darling in *Peter Pan*. Jean Forbes-Robertson was Peter, Mary Casson Wendy. I had always been told there had been no one to equal him in these characters and now seeing him play them for the first time I realised how right was that view. He was superb! both as the gay debonair father of the three children and the celebrated rascally pirate captain. I watched Mary Casson enviously from our box; how I wished I was Wendy once again. But the stage and I had for-sworn each other or—had we? Suddenly I was given, like the people in *Dear Brutus*, a second chance. Sir Nigel Playfair asked me if I would like to play a small part in an English version of *La Dame aux Camélias*, which was soon to go into rehearsal with Tallulah Bankhead. I was very much tempted, when

once again exactly the same choice presented itself. To act or—
ITALY. Italy won; Italy always wins with me. I wonder in a
match with my heart between Italy and Scotland which the
winner would be. . . . Italy for a holiday; to live in per-
manently? Scotland. Scotland provided it was the West, and
Argyllshire at that.

In January 1930 Daddy, Mummie and I set sail for Capri;
although we did not know it at the time. We were nearly
turned out of the train in our shifts at one of the frontiers for
we had been issued with wrong tickets. In those days handsome
tips squared such contingencies. . . . We were making for Naples,
and someone had thought up the unusual idea of going by
train to Genoa and on by an Italian America-going liner, and
we caught the Conte Grande, a delightful voyage, one I should
like to repeat. Looking across to Naples from Capri was
superb, but as a city we were none of us particularly taken with
it. Willie Clarkson was reputed to have said, "You can 'ave
Rome", and we felt rather like that over her sister city. But
what glory beyond . . . the wonders of Pompeii, the exquisite
charm of Amalfi (where we noticed Osbert Sitwell having
lunch), Positano, Sorrento, Salerno, piazzas where macaroni
lay like vast carpets, spreading in the sun to dry; the horror of
Vesuvius, up which we went in a terrifying funicular during
which black sulphurous smoke belched from the volcano
ceaselessly covering us with dirt—and cold. The British Navy
was in Naples, and we were charmingly entertained in the
flagship H.M.S. Revenge.

But it was Capri that won the day, Capri that captured me as
no one place has ever done quite so violently, so that when I
begged for us to spend our holiday there and not go on to
Sicily, I was listened to and given in to. And from the day we
landed with bags and baggage till we left it scarcely ceased
raining. Too much has been written about Capri to start again
here. Twenty years ago it was unspoilt, and attractive as was

surely no other place in Europe. In spite of all the vows I made
to the contrary I have never returned. Is it that I am frightened
of disillusionment? There were few people there as it was
definitely 'off season', but we made great friends with Francis
Brett Young and his wife, to whom we had been given a letter
of introduction. They could not have been kinder and nicer; I
was thrilled beyond measure, as his *Portrait of Clare* was almost
a bible to me and we soon became friends. I remember a walk
up the Monte Tiberio talking about Wagner; and at twenty-
five I could hardly have found a more entrancing way of spending an afternoon than discussing my idolised *Tristan* with the
author of my favourite book, on my adored island of Capri. . . .
The Brett Youngs took us to San Michele, but Dr Axel Munthe
was away (I met him years later, sat next him at a lunch party,
and was able to eulogise to him on his lovely home): and they
introduced us also to one of the most charming Italians I ever
met, Edwin Cerio—I forget if it was he or his brother in whose
villa were the first white peacocks I was to see; and we used to
climb the olive groves of Anacapri, and drink Cinzanos in
Morgano's, then the fashionable café of Capri. It was a place in
which I could have been perfectly happy entirely alone. Italian
villages have that effect on me, Capri more than most maybe. I
longed to be able to remain behind and to try and write.
Capri. . . . When we left I sat on a heap of old rope in the stern
of the steamer with tears pouring down my face, and there
Daddy found me. I had fallen again terribly in love—this time
with a place, and there was something far from satisfactory in
the knowledge, for you can't even get letters from a mere
island! I went back determined to write a book.

I was now twenty-six and had recently met Edward Holstius,
the first person to suggest seriously to me that I should 'write'.
We talked of perhaps collaborating one day. . . .

Daddy at last found a 'winner' in *Cynara*, in which he played
once again with Gladys and in which also Celia Johnson made

one of her earliest successes. That was the summer I met the other Angela. That was the summer I found Argyll.

Did I know I had a twin with the same name as my own? I was asked one day, when I met this twin's brother at a party. No, I had no idea, I said. Then a meeting must be arranged, said he. One meets many coincidences as one goes through life, but surely few are stranger than the 'twin-ish-ness' which persisted in the lives of Angela Halliday and myself who were twenty-six before we finally met each other: our names were Angela, our birthdays the First of March 1904; our mothers' names were Muriel; our fathers both went to Harrow; we had both lived our early lives (unbeknownst to each other) in Regent's Park, we had both had a Nurse Pearce; eventually her niece and mine were both born on the second day of an Eton v. Harrow match; and we nearly met death together in a motor crash on a holiday Scotland-bound. It was a most exciting business getting to know each other, for we shared many interests and had even more in common than twin sisters. We differed in a small matter—she is six feet, and I am five feet two! Angela was adopted as one of the family before many months were over and has remained so entangled ever since.

It was in July that Faith Celli asked me if I would like to go and stay a week or two with her in the little cottage she had been left on the isle of Seil.

I wonder if there can be anything more glorious than waking up in the Highlands when one has seen one's last glimpse of daylight at Euston. It is one of those 'things' that never fail to give me a frisson of excitement, and a journey that never grows stale. In the old days before the through-to-Oban coach was available one had to abandon the night train and one's sleeper at Stirling, and oh! what a delicious breakfast awaited you on that Glasgow train and you ate it—or tried to—with eyes feasting more on the views out of the window than the feast of real Scotch porridge, baps, honey, butter, coffee, which the railways in pre-war days gave one in lavish quantity. The names, enchanting names, of the tiny wayside stations at which one stops: Crianlarich . . . Luib . . . Balquhidder . . . Achnacloich . . . the superb grandeur of the pass of Brander, the distant view of Loch Earn, and finally the approach to Oban itself, along the shores of Loch Etive, and the distant glimpses of Appin, the mountains of Morven, and Ardgour, and the nearness of Ben Cruachan as, with face pressed to the corridor window, you greedily take in the beauty Argyll is offering you. My tenses will go awry, for time is not when I begin to think of that land of dreams, 'I was', 'I am' are the same to me. I was spell-bound on that first journey, and the drive, sixteen miles of it, to Faith's An Cala became more and more beautiful with every yard we covered. We crossed over a tiny bridge, which she always assured one was the only bridge in the world that spanned the Atlantic. Highland cattle grazing . . . a herd of wild goats . . . tarns by the roadside over which the water rippled in swift waves . . . up a steep hill and then—spread below, like jewels from which to deck a crown, tiny islands gleaming in a sun-speckled sea. The Isles of the Sea . . . and Jura . . . Easdale and Luing . . . Scarba; and across the Firth of Lorne, Mull, strange, aloof, secret like the guardian of untold magic.

Faith's house was a haven of peace and enchantment. It gleamed white, as did all the tiny cottages in the village, giving the place a sunny and happier look than one is accustomed to seeing in that country where most buildings are grey. They looked, from the hillside as one gazed below, like tiny seed-pearls. An Cala and its surroundings soon cast a spell over me, and I knew that that part of the world would make me a willing prisoner for as long as I live. Faith was by herself, with just her faithful Lisa and a dearly loved dog, and we spent long glorious hours tramping on the hills amongst the bog-cotton and whortleberries to the sound of tinkling bells round the necks of sheep and goats, and sometimes we went fishing for lythe and saith, by the light of the midnight sun. . . . And at other times I walked alone, in complete peace. It was there, on Faith's island, one afternoon in solitude, that I found that Peace which Passeth Understanding. If IT comes to one in one's lifetime and one recognises it there is no joy to equal it. It has not the fiery joy of passion, not the glory of happiness which comes to one with great love for another human being; it is a quiet God-given moment of such tranquillity that you can hear the precious stillness of extreme quiet and want nothing else at all. It lasts but a few minutes, but one is near to God in one's heart for having tasted it, having known it.

The hills of Seil behind An Cala had always that strange unearthly *healing* gift. Once, many years later, I was desperately unhappy, and sent Faith an S.O.S. She told me to come, and even as I climbed into the train at Euston I had that feeling, as one has before an operation for pain, that soon I should feel better. In the middle of the night I woke and felt easier—we were even then over the border—and it was as if some anaesthetic were already taking charge of me spiritually. But the hills of Seil, and the views of the Isles, and the sound of distant sheep bells, and the soft-clinging smell of peat-laden air did to one's soul what even no knife can do to the body, it healed without a wound.

Fewer and fewer plays those days seemed to be written which were of any use to my father, and he began 'dabbling' with a film career. And how he loathed it, and made no bones about it. For a man whose life had been spent in directing others in the art of acting, the film technique irked, bored and infuriated him. The early-rising, getting to a studio by seven-thirty a.m., with all the likelihood of remaining idle through-out the entire day without a 'shot' being made, the shouting and yelling in accents and language often foreign to his ears, plunged him into the utmost gloom and despair. The people with whom he came into contact were utterly unlike his 'mates' of the stage, too. No one knew him, he was a 'new boy' and—like those new boy days of his at Bushey in 1918— he hated it all. The English film industry at that time was in its infancy as far as 'great' films were concerned; one still said, with rather a bored sigh, "An English film? Oh let's go to some other place", though men like Alfred Hitchcock were ably pioneering and were to show the world before very long that British films could stand shoulder to shoulder with any. But my father, alas, never lived long enough for that day; nor, do I really believe, would he have ever enjoyed acting in films, nor had the patience it takes to endure the hours, days and weeks of hanging about which seem to be part of the job. He played the lead in Galsworthy's *Escape*, and was with Bergner in *Catherine the Great*, in a small part which did not suit him. In his last few years he waited for another *Dear Brutus*, another *Ware Case*, another *Bulldog Drummond* which never came. So he was forced to produce old plays, which had been successes in the past, revivals of his own and other people's.

Early in 1931 *The Pelican's* production was a case in point, with himself as the Frenchman originally played by Nicholas Hannen, and Gladys in Josephine Victor's old part. She, of course, was divine as the mother who was fighting for her son.

As for myself I had written a book! It had taken me many long weary months, and I had poured heart and soul into it. I was encouraged all through this early effort by Edward (Teddy) Holstius, who with his sweet wife Valerie had become great friends of mine.

The curious thing is that I cannot remember showing it to my family. It went the rounds of many an unknown author's first MS. and returned always with the same kind message: I could write, but the subject was considered too unpleasant. I called it *The Little Less*, and it dealt—but only in part—with a girl's love for another woman, and after the hullaballoo created by *The Well of Loneliness* no publisher was ready to take on another battle for the same cause. I was dreadfully disheartened, put the story aside, and gave up all hope of writing for ten years. *The Little Less* was finally published as my third novel, somewhat whittled down, in 1940 or '41.

I had—or have—always been an easily discouraged person at whatever job I undertake to do, and in 1931 I had not the 'guts' to start again writing, after the months I had taken over *The Little Less*, in spite of three or four publishers writing me personal letters encouraging me to go on. Instead, I shrugged my shoulders, thought "What the hell!" and continued the butterfly existence I enjoyed, music as always playing the greater part and swallowing up a lot of that hundred and fifty pounds allowance. Once more Covent Garden was beckoning me, and once more all too readily I was rushing up and down Floral Street. The Ring of course, and *Tristan*—this year Leider again sang the great rôles, and Lotte Lehmann Sieglinde. *Tristan* was Pistor. Meanwhile off had come *The Pelican* and Daddy was now playing in *The Church Mouse*, a play about which I can remember nothing at all. He produced and organised an all-star matinée of *Bulldog Drummond* early in May in aid of the Harrow mission, at the Palace Theatre, at which I was given the job of organising the selling of the programmes (choosing my girl friends to be sellers of course!). But life alternated for me between Hampstead and Cornwall, and I used to find the choice difficult enough; woods carpeted with bluebells versus *Tristan* . . . rocky coves and a blue sea or *Turandot* (the princess, with Nemeth singing, won that round), drives over the moors in our new (very *old*) Morris, or Chaliapine. . . . Once again my luck was out with this great singer: the last time I had heard him I had been seized with ptomaine poisoning during his *Boris*; this time he was in *Prince Igor*, and as the evening passed I felt dingier and dingier, my eyes could scarcely focus the stage, the opera did not appear to me all that it should have done. Twenty-

Angela aged 1

Daphne 2, Angela 5

Angela aged 6

Angela 9, Jeanne 2, Daphne 6
with their mother about 1912

Jeanne, Angela, Daphne and Gerald du Maurier
outside 24 Cumberland Terrace about 1914

Muriel du Maurier 'Mummy' 1918

Gerald du Maurier 'Daddy'

CANNON
HALL

PROVIDENCE
CORNER

FERRYSIDE

Jeanne, Angela and Daphne in the
conservatory at Cannon Hall

Angela aged 11

Angela as Wendy

Angela always loved dogs - the family got their first Pekinese in 1912

Angela at 18

Angela aged 21

'Flapper'

Angela du Maurier with one of her favourite dogs

four hours later I was in bed with a temperature of 103 degrees, and there I remained for many days to come. It is rather an appalling admission to have to make that I remember Chaliapine less as the greatest bass of all time and the greatest actor on the operatic stage, than as a guest at a dinner-party at which I could not take my eyes off him as he continued to kiss a very beautiful lady's arm. . . . I have the menu, and a drawing made and signed by him.

I cannot help recalling the incident of that short illness, in that one aspect of it shows the amazing change of the times. Because my eyes had given me such pain I rushed off to Sir Richard Cruise, who ordered me some new glasses. They were delivered to me within three days.

I was never one for taking to my bed longer than was necessary—far too many pleasant things might be missed, and as to the unpleasant . . . one did not escape them by having temperatures. There was more opera to go to—Ponselle, for instance, in *La Forza di Destino*, the first engagement I got up for, only to get to the theatre to find she wasn't singing! There was Wimbledon. There was Faith Celli's wedding to Arthur ('Peter') Murray at fine St Ethelburga's Church, and there was another trip with the Hickses; this time to Worbarrow Bay in Dorset, which I believe is now barred to country-loving civilians, and fated to be used as a battleground and not the heavenly spot which the Almighty intended.

It was my first visit to Dorset since as a child I'd gone to Swanage after whooping-cough, and the only memory of *that* holiday is standing on Swanage platform to meet the train in which Nanny and 'baby' and Daphne were, and hearing voices call out "Titanic Disaster! Titanic Disaster!"

The Dorset which Bet loved and wanted to show me, that of Corfe and the Purbeck Hills, of Wareham, and Dorchester and *Tess*, was new to me and once again I fell under the spell of the

6*

West Country, not knowing that in later years I should know the Hardy country much better when, staying often with Mary Newcomb and her husband at Stinsford, I should be in the very centre of it.

By mid-July 1931 I was very excited; for my twin Angela and I were soon to be Scotland-bound, this time in her little car, with Wendy my Peke; we were to enjoy the isles of Skye and Mull, and wander at our leisure through the glens and hills of Argyll. There were cross-roads in Yorkshire, however, which felt differently. Or was it destiny? I only know that at one moment, sitting as her passenger in the tiny M.G. Midget I was reading the map, and then there was NOTHING. I woke, the other side of a hedge. Someone stood over me enquiring if I was alive. "Where's my dog?" I whispered (for which remark I have never *really* been forgiven!) and then once again I knew nothing. All I remembered later was that for the first (and only) time in my life I had gone away without my rosary, which I had remembered as we ate our picnic lunch on the Great North Road.

"My rosary, it's because we didn't bring it," I whispered incoherently at one juncture, which I suppose is the reason I was later asked if I wanted a priest.

No one will ever know why the three of us were not killed. A larger car than ours had come straight across the Great North Road without warning and crashed into us, sending the M.G. turtle. The coachwork of it was smashed to atoms, yet we later learnt that the engine was sufficiently unimpaired for mechanics to drive the car away. I had been thrown right out of the car over the hedge; Angela—conscious throughout and collar-bone badly broken—was in a ditch with Wendy. We were taken in an ambulance to the nearest hospital, given the children's ward to ourselves and treated like queens; Wendy had a child's cot by my bed. The food was of the Mandeville Place variety, and included chicken. Angela cried in pain throughout the night

"I've come to the end of my tether", and for some reason could not be given morphia (she literally never stopped), and Wendy and I never stopped being sick. I was concussed and had badly damaged the vertebrae of my back (undiscovered for some years) and poor Angela's neck was disfigured for life. And there was no question of Skye or Mull *that* year.

We were there for a week, and though at the time I did not know it, Wendy had suffered a misplaced heart in the smash, and on the journey back to London in the train had hysterics, which she had never previously suffered from. We had decided to return to Fowey, which was known to Wendy as Fish-and-Bingo, pronounced Feeshandbingo (because she always came mackerel-ing in the motor boat and knew what fish were, and Bingo was the spaniel-sheep dog belonging to Daphne who lived only there). When I saw poor Penny going down with hysterics I calmed her and asked her whether she would like to go to Feeshandbingo, *or* go to Mr Driver (her vet in Hampstead). Every time I said the name Driver her tail wagged, and no response at all was forthcoming at the thought of Cornwall. So on arrival at King's Cross we hared up to Hampstead and left her, and there it was discovered she had misplaced her heart, *and* got a cut somewhere and had of course been concussed like her mum. We had made as little fuss as possible over the accident because Daddy was having a holiday which I did not want spoilt, and no good could have been gained by a wild rush up to Yorkshire from Cornwall; Angela's sister came, and some of her relations.

VII

Twilight

CORNWALL now began to play a larger and larger part in our lives. It was lovely to have a home in the country where friends could come, and to where we could get away from London without causing too much of a commotion to Cannon Hall and its staff. As long as someone was with Daddy . . . for he never wanted to be away from his beloved London for long, and we generally took it in turns with Mummie, the others spending long weeks and months at Fowey once summer had started.

It was in 1932, I think, that Angela and I went out to Lago di Garda for the first time. We went to visit Micky Jacob and arrived at Desenzano, to be met by Gladys Faber with the news that Micky was desperately ill in the hospital there. It was naturally a great disappointment to me, but every other day I used to take the little steamer over the lake from Sirmione where we were staying and visit her in the big hospital in Desenzano in which soft-footed nuns padded through the corridors in silence. It was my first visit to Garda, and every time I go out there—and I must have been six or seven times by now —I am astonished that a place so beautiful should be so singularly unspoilt by tourists and sightseers. It is the largest and I think probably the most beautiful of all the Italian lakes and is the least known except to the Italians themselves and pre-war Germans and Austrians who were inclined to appear in hordes from the north.

Angela and I were entranced by Sirmione, and we fell in love with a tiny baby called Melena. She was a year old then, and now she still writes to me, and I suppose the time is not far ahead when I shall get a heavily embossed card announcing her betrothal. It was July, and the heat was sweltering and mosquitos murderous. But Sirmione's bathing is as good as any I know, as anyone will agree who has lain in the really warm, sulphurous water lapping over flat rocks which stretch from beneath the olive groves of Catullus far out into the lake. September is the loveliest time to visit Garda, when the oleander trees (which are to Lago di Garda what azaleas are to Como) are in bloom; but at all times of the year the grandeur of Monte Baldo, the vast expanse of blue water which from some angles gives the appearance of a sea rather than a lake, the flat-roofed villages perched high on the hills, the lakeside villages sparkling like gems in the sunlight—Salò . . . Gardone . . . Malcesine . . . Limone . . . Maderna . . . Riva—the surrounding mountains studded with olive groves and sentinel-like cypress trees, make it one of the most beautiful districts in Italy.

Angela and I were alone in the annexe of a hotel: one night we awoke to the banging of windows and the clanging of doors, and a noise like something from the Bible. It was a lake storm, of whose fury we were in total ignorance, and the sound of a 'mighty rushing wind' terrified us, though not as much as presently stealthy footsteps on the staircase did. I think our hair stood on end in our fear! It was but one of the hotel staff come to see if damage was being done.

Before the war Lake Garda's little steamers did a heavy and lucrative traffic, one could be sure of a boat at any time of the day, but now it is a very different matter. There are only about four left, and as the lake is something like forty miles in length it gives each steamer but two trips daily, and I am bound to say that for a holiday there nowadays a car is badly needed, for there are so many places both on the lake and within its reach that beckon one.

It was the following year that we thought we would try our luck once again in Scotland. This time we were even more ambitious; we planned a caravan holiday. Angela and myself in one, and Jeanne and Mary Fox (Hilda Hanbury's eldest daughter) in another, and Skye was our objective. We took the high road and they took the low road, and the meeting place was to be the shores of Loch Lomond. Eventually two very dilapidated caravans did meet. Ours was towed behind a small Standard, theirs behind a really tiny Morris. Both collected from dumps, if that is the word (and believe me it was), from 'somewhere in Scotland'. The second night out, by a disused quarry under Ben Nevis, in a Second Deluge, was enough to prove to poor Jeanne and Mary that they'd 'had it'. Their caravan was a lake in the morning, and after chaotic consultations it was decided to abandon it, and they would try their luck at inns, cottages, hotels and farms.

Our own caravan was not all that to write home about. The new road through Glencoe was still in the making, which meant one drove in bottom gear on a road which Bonnie Prince Charlie must have given orders to remain untouched. When we stopped, tired, hot, weary and hungry to prepare our evening meal we discovered that the jolting on the road had produced unspeakable chaos. Everything was on the floor: loose coffee, shoes, macaroni, Lux (burst open), tomatoes, pyjamas, saucepans, candles, boot polish, *eggs*!

It was not a holiday conducive to improving the temper. Moreover Angela's height was about six inches more than the inside of the caravan and she had to live, when inside, in a continual stoop. Even the superb drive through Glengarry and Clunie and on to Dornie ferry left one unmoved except to swear, and the three-hour queue both at Dornie and Kyle of Lochalsh were Last Straws. The others fared somewhat better as they found a hotel the first night, and eventually after our joint searching over the whole of Skye (or so it seemed) got 'rooms' in Portree, whilst we in the caravan out-spanned on a lonely stretch of moorland on the Staffin Road beside a crofter's cottage and two Highland calves. Mosquitos, midges and red ants were so appalling that I cried. We were forced to remain for hours in the evening inside the caravan, in all the August heat, or be eaten alive. Food was no easy problem either; the inhabitants appeared to live from tins. Our stores from the Edinburgh Cooper's diminished all too quickly, and fresh vegetables, fresh meat—and even fish—seemed almost unobtainable. On looking back I can see it was like a post-war period minus the ration book. One cabbage a week and we flew a flag in joy. The others joined us for most meals—Angela and I did the cooking—and presently a young man and his tent appeared in the party. I shall never forget the night of 'the worst thunder-storm the Highlands have known for forty years'. The young man begged to sleep with us and he bedded down on the two-feet-wide floor between the bunks. I think his tent had collapsed or blown away. The peals of thunder, forked lightning and almost atomic energy loosened by the heavens worsened, and suddenly the still small voice of Angela sang out: "Stanley, I'm sorry, but you *must* go outside for a minute." . . .

Those were certainly the days before women wore slacks to the extent that they do now; they were certainly not known in Skye. When I went to a house (a farm-house) in Uig one day, wearing a mac over some shorts, the door was opened by a woman who looked at me grimly and said: "Men shall not don the apparel of women, nor women the apparel of men," with which she closed the door and refused to have anything more to do with me.

Mary and Angela had gone North with superb rods, in high hopes of getting some fishing. Of course everywhere was private and not a trout graced the plate of one of us. (We sent urgent telegrams home for sardines.) But there was a lot of enjoyment to be had, the ice-cold baths under a waterfall every morning for instance; Jeanne's and my all-day climb of a mountain (and the silent black looks we received on our return from Angela and Mary, both of whom had made out telegrams to be sent to our bereaved parents . . .), the peat-laden air of Skye and invigorating health we all felt . . . and finally the cool linen sheets on the Bryce-Allans' beds at Ballikinrain Castle where we stayed after thankfully saying good-bye to the caravan.

I want to go to Skye again, to Skye in some degree of comfort. I want to explore Lochs Scavaig and Coruisk which we never got to, and see Dunvegan Castle. I want to walk further from Sligachan than I managed eighteen years ago when blistered feet put an end to what should have been the walk to end walks. (It was, but not as the expression would have it mean!) The Red Cuillins and the Black Cuillins—I badly want to see them again, to find out whether I've been wrong all these years; for I have maintained for so long now that Skye is beautiful but grim and foreboding, that there is not found that beatitude which is found on Mull—Mull with her silver birches, oaks and rowans; Mull with her larches and fir trees; Mull whose Ben More, Sgurr Dearg, Ben Buie and Dun da Ghaoithe are every bit as fine as the Cuillins but so much kinder; Mull with her Duart and Lochbuie; her fairy glens and glades through Torosay and Ardura. And whose Great Glen in its own serene beauty is one more road to the Isles.

It was the treelessness of Skye that gave me that strange unfriendly feeling, the treelessness and the barren severity of the Black Cuillins themselves. To me Skye and Mull are the Bad and Good Fairy—or is it that Skye was just bewitched for me? or, like the Princess Turandot, asked me questions which I could not answer.

It was while I was in Italy staying with Angela that we heard the news that Daphne had married.

It had all come about in a romantic way. It must have been in the autumn of 1931, during *The Ware Case* tour, when we were all spending more time than usual at Fowey that we first *saw* 'Tommy' ('Boy') Browning. He kept whizzing up and down the river in Ygdrasil, his motor-cruiser-boat, on which he was spending what seemed to be a very lonely holiday. I think it was Angela and I who actually *spotted* him first, in the local post office, and duly reported to Ferryside. We were very much intrigued, and all took it in turns to watch his activities on the river through Daddy's binoculars. We didn't know who he was, but I think we tumbled to the fact that he was in the Brigade of Guards. We called him 'Harold Alexander', although he bears no resemblance to the field-marshal, but at that moment Angela and I thought he did. Months passed before Daphne met him, and then the occasion was once again at Fowey. It seemed he had originally read her novel *The Loving Spirit*, and had wanted to explore the neighbourhood which had inspired her to write that first book of hers. Fate or a good fairy played into their hands, for Tommy's late father, 'Freddie' Browning, had known Daddy well, so the conventional matter of calling on Daphne who was living alone was simplified. After that things moved quickly! Both he and Daphne had a horror of publicity and large gatherings, and Mummie who had visions of her daughter looking glamorous in white satin, trailing up the aisle of the Guards' Chapel on Daddy's arm, was doomed to disappointment. Both announced that it was to be a very quiet wedding or none at all. They even waited until I was safely in Italy and Jeanne in Wales. And then one morning in July 1932 at the frightful hour of eight o'clock two motor boats caught the tide; Tommy and his best man, George Hunkin the boatbuilder of Bodinnick, in one, and Daphne, Daddy, Mummie and our cousin Geoffrey Millar in the other; and after a steep climb from Pont Creek to the old parish church of Lanteglos they were married. I received an account of the wedding, out at Sirmione, from Mummie. "Daphne looked very sweet in her blue serge which I pressed the evening before." Poor Mummie! And it seemed they went off after a very ordinary breakfast of sausages and bacon in Ygdrasil for their honeymoon. Tommy was a major in those days and must have been stationed in London, because a little Queen Anne house belonging to Cannon Hall, which was then free, was done up for them as a wedding present from Daddy and Mummie, and renamed Cannon Hall Cottage.

The Loving Spirit had had a success, and it is still the best-loved of Daphne's books by some people. For myself I preferred her second, *I'll Never Be Young Again*, which I remember shocked a great many members of our father's club ("for a young girl to be so outspoken and knowledgeable in the matter of sex" . . . that was the type of criticism this charming novel in Hemingway style evoked). Curiously enough Daphne's third book *The Progress of Julius* is singularly badly remembered, and that indeed was a brilliant affair. But by 1933 she had other things to think about as well as books to write and her career as a writer. She had a husband in the Army and a small daughter, Tessa, who was born on the second day of the Eton and Harrow match, Daphne having been present on the first! Whilst she was making her way into the world Etonian Tommy and Harrovian Gerald watched the remainder of the match; their thoughts, I cannot help feeling, at Hampstead. Tessa of course was christened at Lanteglos where Tommy and Daphne had been married. She was an adorable baby and a most amusing little girl, and it never ceases to sadden me that Daddy never knew his grandchildren beyond the first few months of Tessa. Like many men of his generation he wasn't much of a hand with tiny babies, unlike the young fathers of to-day who can bathe and even change nappies! He was wonderful with children when they began to grow, and he certainly would have delighted in Tessa's sophisticated ways. Like me, she went early to theatres and we took her, aged two and a half, to *Peter Pan*, which she adored, and also to a pantomime where she gave, all unconsciously, the perfect criticism: after a very dull song by a none-too-good comedian, she yawned and said, "Why doesn't that thing come down again?"—the thing being the curtain.

My father had not had a theatre of his own for the last few years, although he was acting under his own management. It was a change, and an unhappy change, compared to the old Wyndham's and St James's days. It was like living in furnished houses. One never felt really at home, and consequently even his productions had not the easy intimate value about them that those of the past had had. I don't think I was growing away from the theatre, I am sure I was not, but I find it far easier to remember the plays and the casts and the subsequent friendships from his plays of my childhood and early grown-up days, than *Diplomacy* at the Prince's, *The Church Mouse* at the Apollo, and others. *Diplomacy* however did bring some friendships which remained on a permanent footing. Joyce Kennedy, who played Zika, was a dear friend until she died, and her husband 'Nap' de Rouet has remained in the fold. We saw a lot of them during the last few happy Cannon Hall years. And Eric Portman (the Count Orloff) and Basil Rathbone (Julian) have become *our* friends now.

Van Druten's *Behold We Live*—at the St James's once again— was a desperately depressing affair, but beautifully played by my father and Gertrude Lawrence. He returned for a short time to Wyndham's for Edgar Wallace's last play, *The Green Pack*, in which Joan Maude played the girl.

Only a few years before he died Daddy went on tour throughout the country with *The Ware Case* with Cecily Byrne in Marie Löhr's old part. This was the first tour he had made since he was a young man and it was a big success.

I cannot remember ever becoming acquainted with the film industry once Daddy had started acting for it, though in the past we had exciting enough meetings with stars, himself as great a fan as we girls. I was pretty young when Rudolph Valentino was at the height of his fame, and not only in awe of him but, like millions of women the world over, thought he was just IT. One had lost one's head in *The Four Horsemen of the Apocalypse*, and mentally one had 'lost all' after *The Sheik* (I speak for myself!). Therefore to be summoned to Wyndham's Theatre dressing-room to meet the man face-to-face was well-nigh heaven at twenty. I just sat tongue-tied and became rather silly. He was charming and unspoilt, and both he and his beautiful wife seemed as excited to meet my father as we were to meet him. My self-confidence and self-esteem went up in leaps and bounds when he actually knew me for the second time at a first night the following week! It must have been about then that Alice Terry, with her glorious red hair, came to London and lunched at the Savoy with us all, very simply and sweetly, and came on to a cinema with us afterwards! What a lovely actress she was in those far-away silent-film days. John Barrymore of course was a friend from the past, and although he had greater charm, wit and glamour than any of them, we knew him so well that he was Jack and one had forgotten the Barrymore. Once he gave us all flowers when he went away, and told Daddy that he would marry Jeanne (then aged about twelve) when she grew up! I never wanted to look at anyone else in the room—even the loveliest of women—when Jack was present. He was Byron . . . dressed rather like him too. His hair grew long, yet it was neither affected, unsightly nor effeminate, and he would stand (and he had the best figure I've ever seen) in a stance peculiar only to him—and my father, oddly enough—and say very funny things in that low halting voice. . . . I see him now in a pink shirt (sounds bad, it wasn't!), beautifully cut suit, but what I remember most was the cleft in his chin.

Another exciting occasion was when Gary Cooper came to lunch. Mummie, poor dear, was in bed with 'flu, and Daddy pretended that a very dreary childhood friend of his, and his wife, were coming to lunch. So bored was I that not only did I put on a thoroughly unbecoming jumper, but I did not even powder my nose. At one-fifteen a breathless parlourmaid (looking like a ghost) ushered into the drawing-room "Mr Gary Cooper", and *he* walked in, with a friend. That was an occasion when my heart stood still. I had no idea that my father had even met him, and to be faced like this (plus one's shiny nose) was too much. As Mummie was in bed it fell to me to be hostess and have him sit on my right. It is to be hoped I behaved with the right decorum and savoir faire, but I would certainly have preferred to have sat at the other end of the table and gazed! He talked about big game hunting nearly all the time and was very nice, so easy and unspoilt, and he was then very definitely the Number One favourite on both sides of the Atlantic.

Distinguished strangers of the theatre and film world were nearly always taken to see my father and nearly always he entertained them, often at Cannon Hall. Sometimes, as in the case of Gary Cooper, we rejoiced if it was to be Cannon Hall with us, rather than the Carlton, without; but certain people filled us (when very young) with embarrassment. Sacha Guitry and Yvonne Printemps were a couple that made us swallow first before coming in to say our how-d'you-do's, for we knew that French would be expected of us (by Daddy if not by the Guitrys) and we would become stupidly tongue-tied. (I kept for years a green bobble that fell off Yvonne Printemps' hat.) One grew more used to the great as one got older, it's true. As a teen-ager I used to be very embarrassed by those two kindliest of women, Elsie and 'Momma' Janis. I cannot think why! Daddy used to tease me in front of people, too. I remember at the age of fourteen or fifteen having lunch with him and Lily Elsie (whom I worshipped) and when she gave me a roll he must needs say I would probably sleep with it under my pillow. That kind of thing is apt to make the young either very shy, tongue-tied and blush, or give birth to unbecoming over-ripe repartee. We all were of the first variety. But let me hasten to add that his teasings were never meant to hurt, there were no pricks behind the fun.

Daddy rejoiced in Daphne's success as a writer, though alas she had only published three novels before he died. He adored *The Loving Spirit*, was, as far as I remember, a trifle shocked by *I'll Never Be Young Again* and was utterly absorbed by *The Progress of Julius*. Her great successes were to come later. He would have loved *Rebecca* and I think *The Parasites*, but I think the period novels would have appealed to him less, although he was ever a worshipper of Dumas, Harrison Ainsworth—and his own contemporary, Jeffery Farnol. Of one thing I am most certain, he would have given highest praise and his blessing to *Gerald*, which would never have been written, I am sure, if Daphne had not discussed such an idea with him at some time. It came in for a great deal of adverse criticism from old friends who thought daughters should have old-fashioned filial ideas about parents, and who obviously 'hadn't a clue', as the saying is, to Daphne's and Daddy's relationship. And its most bitter detractors I find are people (mostly men) who never knew Gerald.

I am sad that I too had not started to write in earnest in those early days, for certainly we received every encouragement from him to write, to act, to sing, to paint. When he criticised he was fair; he did not think we were good because we were his children, when we were mediocre he told us. But if we were good at anything it gave him enormous pleasure, and no expense was ever spared to help us further a possible talent. As a child Jeanne had shown great promise as a tennis player; she was sent to the best pros and she became an extremely good player, able to hold her own as a girl playing with three good men. But Jeanne had too many interests, and flitted from the tennis court to the piano, from the piano to the paint box, and even from the paint box to the violin for a brief interlude, and became a most proficient Jack (or Jill) of too many trades; and now that she has sunk All at last (including Miss Muffet) to the sacrifice of the paint box one wonders if she will become at long last master. As a young girl her black-and-white drawings showed definite inherited talent from our grandfather, but she had not started to paint in full earnest during Daddy's lifetime.

His knowledge of Daphne's ability as a writer came more from the many short stories published before her first novel than the books she wrote while he was alive.

As to myself, singing had been my 'thing', and long before I had become such a devotee to grand opera I had announced that my intention and ambition was to sing in opera. By the time I was Covent Garden's most enthusiastic patron I had hardly any voice left. I had started at sixteen with Mme Saint-André, who had given me thoroughly enjoyable lessons, and she did not over-train me and she pronounced me to be a contralto, which she was herself. Paris and Ritter-Ciampi had other ideas. Then came periods of nothing and then both Olga Lynn and Mark Raphael took me in hand and did their best, but by then I think the damage was done, and I had no ambition left. I adored my lessons with both 'Oggie' and Mark, but I wanted Covent Garden or nothing (which was silly). I gradually grew into a mezzo-soprano, and now I can sing the psalms lyrically in a country church, and what was my 'beautiful lower register' (I quote!) is nil, and I certainly would not offer my services on the platform for a W.I. gathering. I used to adore singing German lieder, and Italian songs, and the exquisite chansons of Duparc and Fauré; I never sang much English. But I am grateful for whatever knowledge I accumulated because I have learnt enough to appreciate and realise the good and bad points in others. I may be wrong, but I think myself that only when one has learnt an art or a trade can one

appreciate it in full in someone else. Which is the reason probably that I adore the ballet (I used to dance very well) and the
opera; and the reason I so much prefer listening to the piano
than to any other instrument. I would rather listen to a really
gifted amateur pianist in my own drawing-room than to
Menuhin at the Albert Hall. As to my singing in the long dim
distant past . . . what I loathed more than anything was "Darling, go and sing something", and then either I would have to
stand quaking and croaking whilst Jeanne played for me, or I
myself would try to accompany myself with generally dire
results as my songs inevitably had difficult accompaniments
and I could never manage both well! But my lessons . . . how I
enjoyed them. I used to go to Oggie. But Mark used to come to
Hampstead. Oggie made even exercises wildly exciting and
romantic. At a much later date Olive Rubens tried again, but
she was of the school that wanted me back at the beginning, and
it was no use my saying, "Olive darling, I want to sing Brangane", because it was quite obvious really that all I would have
been good for was in the back row in an oratorio!

If only, if only, if only. . . . I wonder how many people echo
these two words when they're well past 'forty year'. If only at
twenty one had the sense one has at forty! And yet again, if
only one had been less flighty. . . . I often think that in spite of
the colossal hard work, I should have enjoyed musical comedy!
I could have sung, I could have danced—but I couldn't have
looked!!! (And I should have hated to have been the Funny
Woman, even if I had brought the house down!)

The trouble with us was that we were never *made* to do
things. If we hated something we were allowed to give it up. I
in particular, being very idle, was never told that I *must* do
such-and-such a thing.

"I shouldn't then, darling" was the line. After I'd gone on
the stage I should have been made to stick to it; then if I had
been a failure there would have been time enough for my tran-

sient gadding. I do not blame my parents, they over-indulged us, that was all. There never were sisters who wished so arduously to eat cake and have it. One's ambitions change of course. Mine of Brangane has ceased. Even the desire to travel widely is beginning to look hopeless as an ambition. This is hardly the time and the place to say what I feel about 'How I Would Like to Write a Best Seller' (I am still wary of brickbats!). My ambition now is a cottage in the Western Highlands, where I could look at the mountains and feel at peace; and write the books—and even plays—which dart in and out of my mind waiting to ripen.

So during these last few years I gradually turned from ambitions, and even my interests underwent a change. London receded, and Cornwall saw me more and more often. Extravagant yearnings for Covent Garden lay fallow; if I found myself at Ferryside in the early summer I stayed and did not tear back for The Ring; I was beginning to realise that one could enjoy life a little cheaper west of the Tamar.

Bet had joined the British Red Cross in London and now prevailed upon me to do the same. She had a flair for nursing, I had not! Moreover I found exams and practical work exceedingly difficult. Mine was not the mentality that ever discovered the way to make up a hospital bed in the correct style, nor which splints to use for what fractures, and my bandaging was deplorable. I looked a perfect fright in V.A.D. uniform (mistakenly imagined by countless débutantes to be attractive. Not it!). My life was haunted by the fear that one day I should have to be on duty in a tent at Olympia or the Derby, and cope with fainting females being sick. With reprehensible ability I got out of all the things I should have done, such as serving my time in military hospitals, hop-fields and other fields of peace-time action. It was as much as I could cope with doling out spoonfuls of cod-liver oil to small children in a clinic (*without having*

to wash the spoon), and smearing yellow ointment on to disgusting cases of heads and hands covered with impetigo. Yet I
enjoyed the clinic days, for I loved the extremely grubby little
urchins who came for treatment, and sometimes cried. I used to
cry too in the children's hospital where I spent many afternoons; some of the tiny inmates were ineffably pathetic and
although I never got used to bed-pans and dirty beds I loved the
hours I spent there. There was the canteen too, run in the out-
patient department of a very famous London hospital. That was
the cause of turning me into a rabid socialist for quite a long
time. The conditions of the poor filled me with unspeakable
pity, and I was foolish enough to imagine that only a Labour
government could put these conditions right.

For some time now I, with Angela, had served on a Unionist
committee in a London constituency which had neighbour-
hoods of the richest and the poorest; we worked in the poorest,
in women's clubs. Our member was a rich man with a
fabulously wealthy wife, and their affection (?) for their less
better-off constituents was patronising to say the least of it. One
afternoon such behaviour led me eventually to vote Labour in
the election that eventually came. A winter Christmas party
was to be held for the women—and their children—of a great
many 'wards'. The Member and his wife were to be present,
and the great attraction was (supposed) to be the Member's
children's presence. It wasn't a very nice day, it was cold, it may
have snowed, there may have been a fog. The fact remained
that scores and scores of poor women had come from far and
wide to the centre of this large area bringing their children by
'bus and on foot. The Member and his wife (both exquisitely
arrayed) arrived (in an opulent car) minus their own progeny.
"*Nanny* thought it was *too* cold and foggy for the boys. I cannot tell you *how* disappointed they are to miss it," milady told
the company in tones of patronising honeyed sweetness.

If the woman had only been human enough to have told the

mothers that *she* was afraid her children would catch cold (not that they would have); but her "Nanny thought" has rankled all these years. There wasn't a woman in the gathering who had ever known the services of a nurse, let alone a nanny. . . .

And so it was that hospital work and the tactless remark of an M.P.'s wife altered my views considerably; until 1945, when after six years of war, and five glorious years of one man's leadership, I changed my tune once more.

There were compensations for being a V.A.D. in peace-time: one could go and see festivities such as royal weddings for instance, and by carrying trays of hot coffee to stands where people had paid many guineas for seats, one could (by risking pneumonia and rheumatic fever, for one wore indoor uniform *outside*) watch the Duke of Kent and Princess Marina bowl down past one, for nothing. Which I did—to the detriment of my health, as down I went on the clinic floor the following day in such pain and in such a faint that I only narrowly escaped rheumatic fever.

The Red Cross was very particular about the facial make-up of their V.A.D's. I shall always remember my lips being scrubbed with methylated, before some V.I.P. arrived for an important inspection.

"Good gracious, du Maurier, who do you think you are? In the chorus? Come here, and let me take that stuff off at once." I am sure that soldiers, especially wounded ones, would infinitely prefer their V.A.D's enhanced and not au naturel.

In the weeks at Fowey which had followed the motor smash, Daddy and Angela insisted on teaching Jeanne and me how to play bridge. They succeeded up to a point, and often during the winter evenings when he had no play running we would have very happy evenings with Daddy and some crony of his. He too now began to spend more time at home, and even more time at Fowey. The summer before he died we so nearly sold

Ferryside to Bart and Edna, who adored the place and came frequently to stay with us. In fact everything was settled; and then apparently one day—it was almost as if he had had a premonition—my father told my mother that he had a feeling the sale would be a great mistake. It was off. The Marshalls were bitterly upset at the time. And yet how right his feeling had been: for soon after the Marshalls had parted company, and we had no father. And Ferryside, though we knew it not at the time, was to become our only home.

For some time my father had not felt really well. He saw this doctor and that, and nobody seemed to imagine anything was really wrong, and then suddenly like a bombshell came the news that he was to have an operation. Even then none of us were told how serious that operation was to be. And when it was over, they said it was successful, and one wondered—as one looked at his pale haggard face—what an unsuccessful operation led one to look for on a patient's face. He died on April 11th, on the thirty-first anniversary of his wedding day.

When one writes to other people letters of condolence, one invariably uses some well worn cliché—"no letter of mine can help", or words to that effect. Yet, the sympathy of countless friends and even acquaintances, *did* help me.

That day was the saddest and most horrible I had ever known. One had other people's sorrows to bear as well as one's own, my mother's most of all. The endless answering of telephones, and speaking to the Press, fell to me, but three things helped to make that time bearable. It is at such moments that one discovers who cares . . . both for one, and for the departed dead.

I shall remember always belovèd Marie Tempest appearing early in the morning after the news had been made public, and just sitting holding my hand in the dining-room. Mary had always been devoted to Daddy, and to Mummie and to me. There are few people who have the love *and courage* to face a house of mourning; but Mary had and did, and her true and enduring affection for us was never more fully appreciated than by me on that day. She was right in all she said and left unsaid, in all she did and left undone.

And then came six lilies to me from the sister of my dear dead X. Those two people, above all others, have my gratitude for that day for always.

When Daddy lay in the Lady Chapel of the Hampstead Parish Church, surrounded by more flowers than I would have believed possible, it made one happy and gave one peace. There was more beauty around him than he had known for a long time, and he would have appreciated the rather theatrical and macabre entry to the church itself late at night, when his bier was taken in, in utter darkness except for the candles which preceded it, with only Billy, my cousin Geoffrey and myself there. He had been born in Church Row, he had returned, and was ready to sleep eternally with his beloved ones in the place he loved so well.

VIII

The Years of Providence

At the bottom of Cannon Hall, adjoining our garden, were two Queen Anne cottages. They belonged to the property: one had always been called Holly something (and was renamed Cannon Hall Cottage when the Brownings moved into it), its neighbour was, I think, Providence Cottage.

Soon after Daddy died, my brother-in-law was moved from London to another Command, and was therefore giving up Cannon Hall Cottage. Their next-door neighbours also left. So what was more natural than to convert the two, and live in them ourselves. Cannon Hall was sold, and 'Providence Corner' came into being; and for the next five years my mother, Jeanne and myself alternated between there and Fowey. It was a horrible wrench parting from Cannon Hall, but it was inevitable. Even had we been Rockefellers I do not think we should have wanted to remain, for the house just breathed my father, and his spirit would certainly have lingered there, yet leaving it a mere shell for the people left behind. I personally have not the love for big houses that so many people have, and much prefer the atmosphere in a cottage. I had always been very proud of Cannon Hall and admired it for its stately beauty, but Providence Corner stole my heart from the moment it became our home, and it was a real grief to me when we parted with it recently.

The years, though few, at Providence were very happy ones, and not spent in abject poverty as rumour once had it. I heard quite by chance that it was said that "Gerald du Maurier's

widow was living in a workman's cottage, wasn't it awful?"...
So maybe that was the reason which prompted Sir Malcolm
Sargent, sitting next me at a supper party Irene Ravensdale
gave for Jascha Heifetz, to ask me, "Are you all right for
money?" which was nice of him but rather bewildering! There
never was a sweeter little house, and my white panelled bedroom looked on to a golden laburnum and a white chestnut
tree in early summer, and there were 'Pink Pearls' clustering
behind, and apple trees too; but Cornwall and country-life
beckoned us more and more, and we began to spend whole
summers there with but an odd week or so at Hampstead (for
those were the days when it was still possible to keep two
homes going).

It was July when I went out to Naomi Jacob, to stay with her
in the little house she then lived in at Sirmione. I was feeling
bruised with sorrow, my own and my family's, and it was like
blessèd balm to get away to that land of blue skies and sweltering sun, and above all the tonic-like quality of Micky's
affection and solicitude. She had other friends, British friends,
staying in the village and very soon I began to feel strengthened
in mind and body.

It was during this holiday that I made my first visit to Venice.
Two men friends of Micky's whom I knew slightly were there,
and I thought it would be a good plan to join them. Off I set,
in a third-class wooden-seated compartment, my rail companions smelling strongly of garlic and new wine, and I eventually arrived, feeling extremely hot, a little bewildered
with my limited knowledge of Italian. I sat for ages on what I
took to be a steamer, outside the station, only to realise as time
went by and I did not, that I was remaining over long on the
landing-stage, a very ready target for the tongues and wit of
rather undesirable Italians hanging around me! I was only in
Venice a couple of days then, but it was enough to make one
realise two things. Firstly that it was the fairest city on earth,

unutterably beautiful and still unspoilt even with steamers on the Grand Canal. Secondly that one needed to be a millionaire by choice, but failing that the possessor of a very handsome income, to stay there. Strange that a city which can boast of no vehicular traffic at all can still remain, in my memory, as the noisiest place I've ever been to in my life. All night long it seemed I was kept awake by the tramp, tramp, tramp of the hundreds and thousands of pattering feet which passed beneath my window and by the shrill tones of Italian voices. The heat in July was very great and we spent most of one of the days out on the Lido, which was singularly unattractive I thought, the water a thick heavy café-au-lait in colour, and definitely not as one had imagined the Adriatic.

My return to Lago di Garda was most amusing. I travelled with a gangster. He was a friend of Al Capone's! Of course he may have been pulling my leg, but I don't believe he was. There were several of us in our red plush upholstered carriage, and none of us spoke the same language. I for some reason became interpreter, translating, surely very badly, the different tongues, and looking, in my cotton frock and shady hat with sunburned nose complete, the epitome of an English nursery governess on holiday. (Which reminds me: I once took Jeanne to a children's party at rather a grand house when I was about seventeen; I wore a dark blue serge coat and skirt, was plump and rather shy, and was quite obviously mistaken by the butler for the nursemaid; the nurses were far too high and mighty to bother with me, and I was not welcomed by the children, and sat in dreary solitude for several hours, unable to share the joke with anyone till I got home.)

Returning from Italy, after my few weeks with Micky, I ran out of money by the time I reached Paris. I had eight francs, French ones, to see me through the rest of an eight-hour day, *and I was very hungry*. Changing from the sublimity of my Simplon Orient sleeper at the Gare de Lyon to the ridicule of this situation of poverty I was just able to buy two ham rolls. I shared the Paris-Calais compartment with a young Adonis, and we talked. He was British but looked like a Scandinavian god. He went off to enjoy one of those luncheons over which the French railway companies excel, and I devoured my rolls. At Calais I realised it was to be a porter's fury or my own dislocated arm, for my suit-case was no featherweight. Adonis disappeared, I braved a porter who finally spat at me and threw the case on the deck, with every epithet he could conjure. Luckily it was a calm day and I was able to sit out, where eventually Adonis rediscovered me, suggesting we travel on together. This at any rate solved the Dover porter for me! Once in the train, however, comfortably installed in a Pullman, "Wouldn't I like tea?" Wouldn't I? . . . my tummy was now rumbling in hunger and vied with the engine for noise. I then explained my misfortune. He was most charming, and said it didn't matter at all, for of course he meant to pay. Every time he looked out of the window I reached for another sandwich, and what disappeared off the plates in Penge Tunnel I hate to think.

Bet was very much to the fore these days, and her parents used to present her with cottages to play with and housekeep in. There was a lovely week spent in the mountains of Capel Curig with her; and it seemed an odd change when she gave up 'Mountains' (as it was called) for a converted railway carriage at Shoreham. However, we had many week-ends of amusement in this curious place which never ceased to remind me of an area reclaimed from a cyclone. . . . Bet was trying in the Welsh days to learn cooking; Aunt Ella was not blessed with the best digestion in the world, nor had the place any local Fortnums. I remember I was known to have a bottle of sodamints, and after one luncheon Ella looked at me rather wistfully and said "Could I have three?" The Hickses were fond of making and keeping jokes and sayings. "Could I have three" has gone down into their annals, as has one of mine of the same vintage, "Water is very filling", which was my (supposedly tactful?) contribution to a lunch not altogether what Bet had planned.

Ivy St Helier was with us on one of the Shoreham week-ends, and I shall always remember her look of horror—"Betty —darling—it's margarine"—when in those days of plenty Bet had pillaged marge instead of the best butter from her Welbeck Street home.

One's old friends clung to one and one clung to them. Amongst these were Jill and Laurence Olivier. 'Larry' was not then at the height of fame which he so richly deserves to have won, and was then married to Jill Esmond. I spent many happy evenings with them, and week-ends too at Apple Porch, Maidenhead, which belonged to Eva Moore (Jill's mother and my godmother), and I shall always remember the Christmas party to which they invited me at their wonderful Cheyne Walk house. Innumerable people were there, though I remember most vividly Peggy Ashcroft, and—I think—Vivien Leigh, and everyone was given a superlative present, myself the entire set of Rachmaninoff's *Isle of the Dead* records. The Oliviers used to go out of their way then—and I expect Larry does still —to give people just exactly what they want; he and Jill made wonderful hosts in those far-away days, and their house was a happy one to go to and play in.

As I have said, one clings to old friends, but now I began to meet and make exciting friends of my own. Hitherto they had for the most part been culled from my childhood and from Daddy's plays and productions. But now, and in spite of the fact Daddy was no longer with us, I began to discover for myself people belonging to the profession who were to be my own friends. I was to be Angela, and not merely Gerald's daughter (nor, as yet, 'only the sister'!). It was in December 1934, only a few weeks after our arrival at Providence Corner, that I took myself alone to the Old Vic to see *Saint Joan*, a play I adored, with Mary Newcomb whom I admired tremendously, in the part created by Sybil Thorndike. I had known Mary slightly for some time but this visit to the Old Vic, where she was the season's star, was the prelude to a friendship that has lasted now many years, one that for me at any rate has given much joy and happiness. Mary and her husband Alex Higginson were then busying themselves with the move from Cattistock to Stinsford, and I think I must have been one of the first of their friends to visit them at their exquisite home in the centre of Hardy's Wessex. It is Stinsford that is the setting of *Under the Greenwood Tree*, and in the little churchyard which adjoins the house his heart is buried.

There began for me then a time of very great happiness, for no two people could have proved dearer friends, and my frequent visits soon made me look on Stinsford as a second home. At first I found it somewhat difficult accustoming myself to an environment so different to any I had known before. Alex was the Master of the Cattistock, and the conversation was very much centred around horse, hound, point-to-points, kennels and all forms of country-life of which I was totally ignorant. Mary, as the wife of an M.F.H., took a tremendous interest too, yet I never remember feeling out of it, and as time went by I realised that one's ignorance was not of world-shattering importance. I do not think I have ever known a garden lovelier than that of Stinsford in rose-time; nor when the arum lilies were out in the long monk's pond which lies at the bottom of the herbaceous borders brimming over with delphiniums. Wistaria and a heavy-scented wax magnolia climb the medieval grey walls by Mary's window, there is a lawn with the soft smooth texture of a billiard table and a massive walnut tree under which we would drink champagne cocktails in pleasant languor in those far-off days of peace. Happy warm summer days in Dorset . . . with bees humming, and the sound of a lark high in the sky above the lush meadows beyond. I was to know Stinsford at all seasons: in the winter, gay with hunt balls; in the early autumn, when I lazed abed in a high haunted room covered in antique Chinese wallpaper while Mary would be out cubbing; and in the spring when narcissi, daffodils, tulips and wallflowers made one wonder whether after all the youth of each year was not perhaps the best. Yet it is of the summers that I remember Stinsford's beauty and glory most. I remember too the astonishment I felt the first time I encountered Alex's summoning of his servants at the dinner-table with his hunting horn. . . . I remember also with what pleasure I used to view each course served on different priceless plates—so much more exciting than the same conventional service throughout dinner; it made all the difference to one's interest in the dinner (in the same way as a play is of more interest—to the eye at any rate— with changes of scene). The three of us used to play six-pack bezique by the hour. Yes, they were jolly happy carefree days for which I am grateful.

1935 was the dawn of the Higginsons into my life. It was also the year which brought me the friendship of two more people whom I had often admired on the stage and had never met, in spite of the fact we lived but five minutes away from each other: Gwen Ffrangcon Davies and Marda Vanne. We met at last, through 'Lena' Ramsden, and long walks on the Heath now ensued, the inmates of Holly Place with their pug, Snuffles, I with Wendy, and sometimes Mummie's Belinda (a present from Fred Lonsdale), and Lena with her French bull-dog. Holly Place and Tagley, that entrancing cottage in the wilds of Essex . . . what memories they evoke. Gwen once sent Marda and me alone there for a week, we were to do the cook-ing between us. . . . In spite of my Buckingham Palace Road cooking classes I had forgotten one does not chuck butter ad lib. into frying bacon, and my omelettes (at which I rather fancied myself) forever broke. We survived and so did our friendship.

So these new Gerald-less days passed. And our life, and mine in particular, now centred round Providence and one's friends there, with an ever-growing exodus to Cornwall; and visits to Dorset, and to Faith in Scotland, and trips abroad, recurring with frequency. Faith and An Cala had long become an annual pleasure, and whether one was in need of the balm healing salve of the soul, or mere fun with Faith as we climbed her hills (picking up basketfuls of sheep droppings which she held to be more precious than gold for the lovely garden she was making) I was filled with the real joy of living every time I stepped aboard that crimson painted train with the magic words Stirling–Perth–Inverness–Oban on white boards above the carriages.

Phyllis Terry was responsible for my meeting with Lena Ramsden, and Lena in turn with Gwen and Marda, and two more people whose advent caused great joy: the late William Nicholson, and Marguerite Steen. Lena gave better parties in her Primrose Hill studio than anyone I know. Apart from the vast quantities of superb 'eats' and drinks, there was always an embarras de richesse in the way of talent, and you never knew who was going to spring up next to entertain with wit, song and dance. For there would be Davy Burnaby, Nellie Brier-cliffe, Marie and Pat Burke; John Gielgud; Gordon Daviot, Gwen and Marda; Phyllis Terry; William Nicholson; George Howe, Philip Leaver, Marguerite Steen, 'Peggy' Webster, Martita Hunt; the piano played far into the night, voices sang, voices declaimed; and Lena's presence whether in Primrose Hill, Stockport or Newmarket guaranteed a good time being had by all. It was at such a party that I first met Marguerite and William, which led in its turn to my visits to Apple Tree Yard where William had his famous studio, and he would welcome one wearing a regency waistcoat, white trousers, an immaculate bow tie and with that Puck-like Lob-like enigmatic smile upon his face; and he could be serious or ribald in such quick-change time that it was difficult to adjust one's own rather dull-witted medium to his brilliance. I often think of William Nicholson as having been the really only great man I have known at all well. I treasure my recollections of evenings spent in his company as one treasures heirlooms in a casket. His was indeed a precious spirit, and the amazing thing about him was his eternal youth which forever kept at bay the awe which one should have felt in his presence. I suppose one of the most wonderful afternoons I have ever spent was at Apple Tree when with strange humility he showed Jeanne and myself picture after picture as though we were Duveens or Kenneth Clarks. It certainly ill-becomes me in my abysmal ignorance to speak of painting, but to my idea his work alone of this century stands worthily beside the masters of the past.

It was at Apple Tree on a Twelfth Night party that I was to make yet another new friend, beautiful red-haired Brigit Patmore, Brigit of the soft bewitching voice and aquamarine eyes, who was ultimately the reason for me writing again. It was Mary Newcomb, Marda and Brigit Patmore between them who made me read poetry to a far greater degree than I had hitherto done; Mary introduced me to Walt Whitman, for which I am in her debt for ever, Marda to Shakespeare's Sonnets, and Brigit to far more poets than I could here enumerate. Between them I found myself devouring poetry, and for the first time in my life neglecting fiction; I started compiling an anthology to which even now I add when I discover as I think a poem worthy, and one day—who knows—some philanthropic publisher may take it to his heart.

1936 had only just begun when great sorrow swept the country, and I can hear those quiet still words coming over the wireless even now: "The King's life is drawing peacefully to its close. . . ."

The end of an epoch indeed. The man, the King, the real father of his people, whose voice had brought him into the homes of countless millions, had said "God be with you" for the last time, and we instead echoed his wish.

Daphne and I watched the great funeral procession from the balcony of St James's Palace. It was tremendously impressive—so much scarlet down below us worn by the troops lining the streets, and the unrelieved black of the mourning civilians, and the hushed quiet throughout the long hours of waiting for the cortège, and when it came, the gun carriage . . . with field-marshal's helmet and baton . . . his sons following . . . the new King. . . .

In 1936 I bought my first car. This is a red-letter day for any-one, whether it be a Rolls Royce or as in my case a Morris eight! It was bright green with a sloping back—for it was a two-seater—and I realised capital to achieve it. (I have been realising it ever since, but no new car can be seen as tangible evidence.) I had not had it a fortnight when a police car crashed into it and ruined its first beauty. . . . And no sooner had I got it back when we repaired en famille to Majorca.

It was my twin Angela who suggested the Majorcan holiday, and Mummie, Billy, Jeanne and I, and Jill Olivier (who was expecting a baby in three months' time) set off aboard a Bibby liner from Liverpool.

Nobody really enjoyed that holiday barring myself! The hotel was rather inferior and so was the weather; the wind made the blinds rattle unceasingly in a deafening manner; and the lavatories all smelt. But for me there was charm in the myriad cactus bushes to be seen far and wide, and the gleaming white houses of the villagers. Cala Radjada, Sóller, Valde-mosa . . . and Palma was a city of enchantment. Life in our village rather centred round a certain café, and the inmates and habituées might have been drawn from the type of novel one does not leave lying about in the schoolroom. (As I have remarked, I enjoyed the holiday.) Jeanne and I shared a room;

it had a balcony; one night we heard steps outside, the door
rattled and a man's voice—in French—demanded admittance.
Shaking with terror I called to him that if he did not go immediately I would wake my husband. He went! It was in Majorca
that I regret to admit I had my worst blind. A new-made
friend and I dined unwisely and far too well. I began the
evening with several apricot brandies, we continued the meal
with octopus and much wine, and after three Chartreuses we
walked (?) into the cold night air. . . . Poor Jeanne.

"You're drunk!" she said in tones of outraged disgust. I
could not contradict her. Next day was Labour Day, when no
one did a stitch of work, and the hotel staff disappeared in its
entirety, and I disappeared in bed. Mummie was told that
octopus did not agree with her eldest daughter. If I were asked
what I recollect most about Majorca I would reply the jugs
and jugs full of neat orange-juice, pressed for one as one
waited. The best drink in the world. (So why bother with
Chartreuse?)

We returned to England in May, docking one early dawn at
Plymouth, surely the loveliest of all English ports at which to
arrive.

For me wonderful evenings at Covent Garden were in store,
opera with Flagstad (her first season over here), followed by
Russian ballet, the likes of which we are now rather inclined to
forget. I had arrived back too late to hear The Ring in its
entirety, but shall never forget the impression made on me by
Kirsten Flagstad as Brünnhilde the first time I heard her in
Götterdämmerung with Melchior, and then later as Isolde. It
would be churlish to forget the Isoldes and Brünnhildes of
Leider and Austral, both magnificent singers and both in their
day unsurpassed; but Flagstad has the added quality, the power,
which makes one cry. There is something phenomenal about
her; she was a great singer before the war, and now after her
years of suffering I find it impossible to watch her Isolde (or

even write about it) without tears pouring down my face. Melba's voice had the clarion quality of pure gold, it seemed perfection, yet *it did not touch*. I think perhaps its very perfection was due to the fact that it lacked human warmth. Rosetta Pampanini's 'Butterfly'—and in slightly less degree Lotte Schöne's Liù (and Elizabeth Schwartzkopf's recorded singing of 'O my belovèd father')—have been to me the acme of perfection of combined singing and acting. But to witness nowadays Flagstad's Isolde is to watch a fellow human being's intense suffering over love and death; there are moments when her performance becomes almost unbearable in its poignant greatness. With Ivor Novello I watched her in 1949 give her hundred and fiftieth performance of the part; it was an evening that I shall never forget—and how bitterly I regretted my inadequacy, when Ivor took me round to her dressing-room afterwards, that could not give expression to the worship due to her great art. To quote Whitman—

For in any roof'd room of a house I emerge not, nor in company,
And in libraries I lie as one dumb, a gawk, or unborn, or dead.

But to return to the brave days when I was—a lot more than twenty-one. Back to the year 1936 in fact, with Sir Thomas Beecham with baton in hand for the Wagner evenings, and Malcolm Sargent conducting Delprat in *Louise*; and ballet with Toumanova, Baronova, Riabouchinska; Danilova, Zorina; Jasinsky, Lichine, Massine; Petroff, Lazovsky; Grigorieva, Verchinina . . . evenings of sublime glory with Tchaikovsky's *Presages*, the Brahms *Choreartium*, *Spectre de la Rose*, *Beau Danube*, *Boutique*—Rimsky-Korsakov's *Soleil de Nuit* . . . *Sylphides* danced by a corps de ballet in which every dancer was worthy to be a prima ballerina . . . indeed they were the good old days. In the autumn the Dresden State Opera had a short season at Covent Garden. I saw only *Don Juan*, but a superb cast it was, with Marta Fuchs as Donna Anna, Teschemacher

7*

as Donna Elvira, Cebotari the Zerlina and Schöffler as Don Juan; Bohm conducting. What feasts of music London gave us in those days when the Queen's Hall stood proudly in our midst; Sir Thomas Beecham's Sunday concerts at Covent Garden, the Courtauld-Sargents, and visiting orchestras such as the Berlin Philharmonic with Furtwangler, the Concertgebouw of Amsterdam, Richard Strauss himself conducting that of the Dresden State Opera. What days and evenings of delight those were for the choosing: Barbirolli conducting the R.P.O. with Horowitz playing the 'Emperor' and Rachmaninoff's Third Concerto; Mengelberg conducting *Heldenleben*, and Myra Hess playing the Brahms second; the beloved Rachmaninoff himself; recitals by poor Grace Moore, and Kirsten Flagstad. Perhaps there is still all that and heaven too, and it is I the country bumpkin who is unaware of the splendour. Many are dead, some have been politically 'liquidated', and I for one mourn the departed Queen's Hall which, with Covent Garden, gave me my happiest memories of the musical past.

The Bad Old Days of owning two houses; living one's life to the full in London (but always remembering to take the dogs for their walk on the Heath directly one was up and dressed, and still tip-toeing into Mummie's bedroom no later than two a.m. with a hushed "I'm back"), and in some ways living it even more fully in Cornwall because one felt spiritually refreshed by the blue seas and wild bracken-clad cliffs of Lantivet, the blackthorn glory of Pont, the what Victoria Sackville-West would call 'through-leavery' and really through leaves— fallen nutty beech leaves—of Lerryn and Ethy and Lanhydrock and Boconnoc; climbs up hills beyond Menabilly to the Gribbin, wandering amidst squelchy bogland across the moors—Brown Willy, Rough Tor, Jamaica Inn . . . Dosmary, Golitha . . . aquaplaning behind the Cora-Anne (named after the Ringer's heroine!) . . . bathing naked in unseen unknown coves . . . friends to stay with one and showing them one's favourite haunts further afield, St Mawes, Kynance, Polperro, Blisland, and those precious churches St Neot, St Winnow, St Just-in-Roseland. If there were real fairy godmothers at my baptism, the gift for which I am most profoundly thankful is that of the power of supreme appreciation and enjoyment which I have always had and shall never—I think—lose. The power to enjoy with enthusiasm . . . Flagstad's Isolde, the view from Torosay, blue delphiniums, an underdone steak, a small Pekinese . . . 'ripeness is all'. The ripeness of one's appreciation, one's zest for what to one is Life. Oh! how I pity from the bottom of my heart the shoulder-shrugging youth of to-day with their couldn't-care-less don't-mind-if-I-do mentality.

For six years by now I had gone to Faith, and every year I used to look across the water to a tall dark far-distant Shangri-La and say—

"Take me to Mull."

And every year Faith would promise that one day she would, and then, in 1936, on the first evening of my visit she announced—

"We are going to Mull. I'm going to take you to Torosay, to meet Olive Guthrie."

Faith and I caught the steamer—I suppose it was the 'Lochinvar'—from Oban, and arrived at Craignure. To me it is (unless rough!) the loveliest crossing in the world. Oban Bay—island-studded by Lismore, Kerrera and rocky islets, and beyond the Firth of Lorne the Holy Isles, Scarba, the Paps of Jura . . . up Loch Linnhe to Ardgour, Morven, Ben Nevis; the tiny 'out-posted' light-houses gleam white, the Ladies Rock, the grey rocks and the Sound of Mull is reached. There is Duart on your left, a thousand years old and more, lived in still by the McLean Chief; and towering behind are the deer-forested slopes of Dun-da-Ghaoithe and Sgurr Dearg. Nestling in a tiny bay lies Torosay, the castle, and its gracious châtelaine was Olive.

Olive, who when she greeted us with cups of coffee (which was the ever-ready-welcome for a boat arrival at two-thirty p.m.), was wearing a very old tweed coat, an equally old (man's) tweed hat (from which poked honey-coloured curls), her cigarette (which she was never without) in a holder, and she spoke in a voice that fascinated me from that first moment of meeting. It was a low voice, an amused voice, a voice with a constant chuckle behind it; as I grew to know her I would beg for her stories—and what a legion she had, and never was there a better raconteuse—for the sheer joy of listening to her voice. Her voice and her hands were what I loved most, at first, about her. She told me how as a tiny girl she had played with Daddy at children's parties, and this was not surprising for her father, the late Sir John Leslie, one of the last pre-Raphaelite painters, would naturally have been a friend of my grandfather, who I know had had an immense admiration for Olive's beautiful mother, Lady Constance Leslie. It was easy to realise that Olive was Irish, there was never a moment when she was not reminding one of the fact. "In my country" she would say, given any opportunity, and continue with some statement that she hoped would put to shame a Sassenach. Yet Irish as she was, I never in my life met a more truly Cosmopolitan person: she had travelled everywhere, met everyone and seemed related to the rest. Faith and I were only there three days, but they were days crammed full of amusing anecdote, a drive to Lochbuie, wanderings in the castle grounds, a climb up the hill from which that loveliest of all views from the Dogs' Graves is embraced, bridge in the evening, and one's eyes feasted on rare objets d'art and lovely pictures. The cabinets chock-full of Fabergé works of art, pictures by Sargent, and de Laszlo, and Sir John Leslie . . . Poynter's life-size portrait of Olive as a young wife, with flaming hair, gowned in white satin seated on an emerald-green upholstered chair. . . . A library with books of every description, rare editions which I was to discover later, and which kept me enthralled for hours on wet days (and Mull certainly could boast her quota on that score). I suppose I was to know the Torosay library better than any room anywhere—I could even now, I think, paint a picture of it blindfold; the view from the large window across the gardens, out to the snipe-bog, the bay, Duart and the distant hills of Argyll . . . Poynter's water-colour of Duart in the gold-mounted golden frame hanging on a wall beneath which Sargent's drawing of Murray Guthrie stood on a small table (the larger original was in the drawing-room with the de Laszlos of Lady Constance Leslie and Pat Guthrie) . . . Dolly Lennox-Robinson's oil painting of Loch Linnhe, a very true portrayal and now one of my dearest possessions. . . . Well-worn shabby green leather arm-chairs more comfortable than any of these modern beauties; the round writing-table in the window, shared by Olive and any guest, although Olive invariably wrote on her knee, sitting by the fire, in the deepest and comfiest chair, while the ash from her cigarette grew, grew, grew till it fell but left her utterly unperturbed and unconcerned. I can see Olive sitting in that chair as I write, wearing some sort of a shooting jacket and Edwardian patent-leather shoes with buckles and louis heels . . . her little black Pekinese at her feet. . . .

But in 1936 one knew nought of what was to come. We were all interested and immersed in a war that had suddenly sprung into being in Spain, and I for one was impatient for news of Angela, who was out in Majorca. Presently a letter came—

"I don't know if you will ever get this but I'm taking every precaution that you will! Everything is all right in this village but things are censored and papers don't get through. I have written to the British Consul in Palma asking when and how I can leave the island. I shall go as soon as I can, whether it will be by British battleship or liner one doesn't know. *Would* you send Daddy a P.C. and say everything is O.K. and that I cabled him two days ago, I doubt if he got it. I can't afford to write to anyone else as we have no money at all—anybody! . . ."

Every form of stamp and cipher had been employed on the envelope and about ten days later another letter, postmarked Marseilles, arrived—"After days of uncertainty we are at last going to leave the island in a body in H.M.S. Repulse at four a.m. to-morrow for Marseilles. The order came to-day for all foreigners to run. They haven't *got* to but this is the last chance of getting off the island. A few Germans and X. and X. and X. are staying. I was going alone in a Dutch boat. I am tired of the discomfort and small boys in blue shirts popping out at one at every corner. Six people were killed in Palma yesterday. X. and X. had an awful time, people falling all around them and then to-day three hundred soldiers *here* to shoot down an aeroplane which never came. They left anti-aircraft guns in ——'s garden. We have to get special permission to go into Palma and shall be stopped eight or nine times by armed guards en route. I hear they are going to bomb Palma again to-morrow. We make a bee line for Toreno where we board the battleship. About sixty people are going from here. . . . I long to know what you've read in the papers. We haven't seen one for nearly three weeks. . . . Not *one* of us has a brass farthing to pay our bills with here or our fares home. The consul at Marseilles will have a busy time. P.S. Imagine me with two thousand sailors!!!"

One has forgotten there were British people to be evacuated from Spain. One has almost forgotten the Spanish war; if Hitler's war had not come about we should have remembered it in far greater detail. Relatively too few people were involved, apart from the Spanish themselves, to bother now about the horrors which to the Spanish—whichever side—must have been appalling. And as Angela stood on board H.M.S. Repulse watching the firing of Palma (unfortunately I have no letter describing that) she was all too acutely aware of her position then and there, little dreaming that before five years were through she would be writing graphic descriptions to me of the raids on London where she drove an ambulance throughout the Battles of Britain and London. In Great Britain the ordinary people, the people who did not know Spain or Spaniards, went on with life as usual. They read the reports in their newspapers, shuddered with horror as accounts from both sides became public, thought how dreadful war was and continued with the glorious Twelfth, the rounds of race meetings, football matches, the 'little season', concerts, the Dresden opera's visit.

Lena Ramsden invited me to Newmarket where I watched the Cesarewitch, and was driven back to London by the late Tom Walls in a pale blue Rolls Royce; Lena, who had a little earlier given a party which lasted three days, the 'last act' of which took place in Fortnum and Mason's gift department where every guest was given a present.

Early the following year Daphne returned from Egypt where she had been for some time, for the birth of her second child. Tessa was three and a half and had been told about the expected arrival. She was always full of quaint and unexpected remarks, which would doubtless have shocked one's grandparents. One of her best I always thought was at the age of two and a half, when in Egypt my brother-in-law's soldier servant complained of a 'hangover' in her hearing.

"Oh, poor so-and-so," she said, "have you got a hangover? That's what Piffy has."

One imagines from thenceforth the men's mess bandied it about that the Colonel's sister-in-law was an inebriate! And all because one morning when she came into my bedroom, aged two, I had said, "Run along, darling, I don't feel well."

"Why don't you feel well?"

(Sleepily) "I've got a hangover."

Perhaps it was the sort of word for a child to cotton on to and remember.

After Daphne's baby was born a Kind Lady in a shop congratulated Tessa, and asked if the fairies had brought her a new sister; she looked up very scornfully and said, "Of course not. It was in Mummie's tummy."

Flavia was born a fortnight too soon, a fact for which I was to blame. The accouchement was all planned to take place in a flat in Queen Anne's Mansions, whither I took myself to keep Daphne company for two weeks till the nurse came. We moved in on April the first and on the second I took her for a drive which I had been in the custom of doing for some weeks, forgetting as I bumped and jolted along the roads in my tiny car that bumps and jolts are not all that good for expectant mothers. At tea-time on April the second Mummie with a friend arrived to take Daphne to a film, to be told by Daphne, in no consternation, that she thought the "baby had begun". The doctor was summoned, and after a great fuss and search the nurse was run to earth, and at ten o'clock that night the telephone rang at Providence Corner and we were told, "Another girl". Daphne had wanted six little boys. Flavia looked like a little red radish for the first week, she wasn't as pretty a new-born babe as Tessa, but at three years old what a dream . . . with eyes like periwinkles and corkscrew curls, and terribly terribly feminine. She is my godchild and now at thirteen looks like Peter Pan, while the tom-boyish Tessa has become a young lady of Fashion.

1937 was Coronation year. I did not go to the ceremony. I was made an 'improper proposal' to the effect that if I spent the night (in a rather questionable hotel) with somebody he would take me to see the Coronation procession. I turned it over and at the last moment funked the idea. For the life of me I cannot think why. Even now I am inclined to believe I turned this handsome offer down more because of the early rising it would have entailed than any reflection on my so-called good name! I listened to the service in Cornwall; I was glued to the radio for hours. I did not regret the un-slept-in bed, and was convinced as I listened that I was much more in the Abbey alone in Cornwall than I would have been in a crowded stand in Piccadilly.

It was not long before I was back in London, and to my annual target; Sir Thomas Beecham once more ruling the theatre, and after an absence of many years *Parsifal* was given with Kerstin Thorborg as Kundry and Torsten Ralf as Parsifal. Once again Flagstad and Melchior sang together in *Tristan und Isolde*, and it was this year too, as I have previously mentioned, that I heard the finest performance of *Otello*, with Martinelli, Lawrence Tibbett and Norena; and for the first and alas only time in my life I visited Glyndbourne. I was staying with Brigit and Derek Patmore at Fairlight and Brigit and I motored over on a rainy, foggy night, thereby missing much of the fascination of the evening, which made wandering in the Elizabethan grounds between the acts impossible; we saw an enchanting performance of *Così fan Tutte* with Ina Souez, Helletsgruber, Eisinger and Baccaloni singing, and Busch conducting. What a deliciously intime quality there was about the whole evening's entertainment; one felt like an eighteenth-century lady of some Court for whom the giving of the opera was an entirely private affair.

Once again de Basil's Ballet Company appeared in full splendour in London in July, and I remember seeing ballets that were new to me, *Francesca da Rimini* with Tchernicheva, Borodin's *Pavillon* with Baronova, Riabouchinska and Lichine; *Symphonie Fantastique*, *Danses Slaves et Cziganes*, *Cimarosiana* and all the old favourites as well, and the Royal Philharmonic Orchestra was engaged.

It was difficult sometimes to choose the signpost: London or Fowey.

Gladys came to stay with us, with Philip Merrivale whom she had married. He reminded me more of my father than any

other man I have ever known. It wasn't actually a facial resemblance, and certainly in mind and ideas they were poles apart,
but there was something . . . his was a personality of very great
charm and he had a sense of humour which, if at times somewhat mordant, was nevertheless delightful.

It was late in the summer and my suit-case was almost packed
for An Cala when I received out of the blue an invitation from
Olive Guthrie to go on to Mull from the Murrays. I had
written to her I believe once since my short visit the previous
year, and was astounded that she remembered me. But, as she
afterwards confessed, she needed help with her rhododendrons!!
It was the end of September, or early October, when I reached
Mull; Olive's daughter 'Bobs' de Klee was there and a few
other people, and I was given a very grand bedroom known as
the Ambassador's Room. What a strange new life I was
initiated into . . . duck shooting in the dusk, stalking (which
very soon had me winded before I'd climbed half a mile),
scraping mussels off rocks for the evening dinner's moules
marinières, sawing rhododendron branches by the hour: and
daily one became more fascinated by Olive's wit, and the
general charm and the enveloping tendrils of Mull slowly
closed around me. The wild beauty of Mull in October is
indescribable, the birches have turned golden and oaks and
beeches a fiery red, there are rowan trees bright with scarlet
fruit at every turn, and as dusk fades into night and you stand
on the doorstep of your home there comes the low thrilling
sound of the stags' roar in the forest, to me the most exciting
noise on earth. Then the full moon, the 'hunter's moon',
appears in the sky and from Torosay you can pick out clearly
by its light the outline of distant peaks, and across the gleaming
bay the untouched stately walls of Duart, the oldest inhabited
castle in the land. All is still . . . then perhaps a heron calls . . . it
is cold, and you shiver and turn to go inside to a peat fire, but
once again you hear that grunt, the lion-like roar from the

forest, hinds are being fought for, life on the mountainside is primeval, savage, real.

I left Mull after a fortnight for I was to spend a little time in Edinburgh with Bet and her husband, 'Jock' Stuart, in their house at Murrayfield. Bet had married the previous April; I had helped her to choose the wedding march to which she went up the aisle on Seymour's arm—the Nimrod variation from the *Enigma*—and they had spent the earlier part of their honeymoon at Ferryside. 'Jock', or Donald as his name really was, was in the Gordon Highlanders, and Bet took to Army life as a duck to water, which perhaps was natural as Seymour had come from a family which boasted of soldiers. Donald was one of the dearest of men—reserved as most Scots are—but I think we soon established a brother-and-sister relationship which isn't always easy to achieve with the husbands of one's friends.

Next to Venice I think I would call Edinburgh the fairest city that I've seen. To me its beauty lies perhaps more in the knowledge of its history, of its antiquity, of its austere lines of medieval architecture, than in the picture-postcard surface beauty which continental cities can offer with such a plethora of colour and exciting fascination. It is coldly grey like all Scottish cities and yet so is Paris, the old Paris and the île de la Cité; and one feels that Mary Stuart would have borne her life more easily if only the sun had shone with greater frequency, and if only the inhabitants had smiled. The cold of Edinburgh was to me worse than anything I have felt before or since. I lay awake one night with such an attack of neuralgia that at one moment I believed I must have meningitis. I forget how many aspirins and Cachets Fèvres I took but it ran into double figures as the night wore on.

The following February, 1938, I returned to Scotland. To Mull. This time snow covered the hills and mountains, but orchids filled the bowls in the library, the room in which we

ate, lived, played bezique, read. It was a fortnight of azure skies
and brilliant sunshine, and the air glistened with Swiss-like cold.
There were snowdrops in little carpets everywhere and when
we left, Olive for Greece and I for a foreign hospital recommended to me, I felt that I should never leave the island
whole, that my heart would remain—perhaps in some corrie,
perhaps on some little cairn—somewhere on Mull.

For weeks I had been suffering agonies of pain. Mummie and
Jeanne were in Italy, Daphne and her family in their Hampshire
home, and after I had seen Olive off to Athens I went into the
hospital where I underwent so many unpleasant tortures
that I lost nearly a stone in under a week. I have never been
so miserable in my life. The nurses spoke nothing but German
of which I knew only one or two inapplicable lines from
Tristan! It was the week of the Anschlüss and the whole
hospital seemed to ring with Hitler's voice bellowing from
Vienna via the hospital wirelesses. After I had been told to
swallow many yards of rubber tubing I hoped the verdict
would be cancer and that I should die. I began to have
suspicions as to the type of human beings running the hospital,
so much did they seem to enjoy the revolting treatment they
forced on me; but in all fairness one must admit it was a fine
hospital most excellently run and appointed. The verdict when
reached was a blank one. With all the X-rays and indignities
and examinations they could not discover what was wrong.

Soon after my unpleasant few days with Hitler's minions I
was on my way to Portofino to join Mummie and Jeanne. Mary
Fox came with me and we nearly overslept ourselves in our
wagons-lits, waking in the morning to brilliant sunshine, Genoa
past and Santa-Margherita only twenty minutes away.

It is very difficult to know what places have seemed most
beautiful, most attractive, most—gemütlich—to one. I have
already eulogised over Capri—over Mull—but Portofino is
definitely 'in the first three', and probably if I were given the

chance, suddenly, of a holiday in any of them, Portofino would be the choice if I could have the same house again. We had rented the Harrisons' villa, the Casa Signorile, and a more entrancing house to find anywhere would hardly be possible. It stands high, overlooking the bay and near the Castello (famed by 'Elizabeth's' writing of her *Enchanted April* there). I arrived, still weak after hospital treatment, and was horrified to discover that the only method of approach to the little house was after a climb of steps which, if my memory is correct, were over three hundred. (There may have been only ninety, but too many for me at that moment!) For nearly a week I did not go down into the village, and what did it matter, as the villa stood in grounds of twelve acres of its own; a pine-clad peninsula, the sea views from which were almost unbeatable. The two Italian maids did everything for one even to the extent of bringing lunch to any part of the garden! Why is Italian cream cheese—fat, onion-shaped or looking like a well-filled pillow—the best in the world? Especially if eaten with new crusty bread and local wine! The little casa had once I believe been converted from a farm-house, and it combined English comfort with Italian atmosphere, and was one of the most adorable places I have ever known.

One funks returning to a place one has once visited and loved; which is doubtless why I've returned to neither Capri nor Portofino. My disappointment on viewing Malcesine (on Lago di Garda) in 1948 after an absence of over fifteen years was shattering. I had treasured its memory for many years with Capri and Portofino for sheer charm and atmosphere. The war had dealt unkindly with my enchanted lakeside village . . . it looked shabby, unkempt and neglected, and there were still visible signs of 'occupation' which none of the other villages on the lake still bore. Only the ancient stronghold of the Scaligeri bore total oblivion to time and modern warfare. From its grey spring-flowered ruined walls all was as still and beautiful as it had been for centuries. But they tell me—the mysterious They who are responsible for rumours from Peru to Timbuctoo—that Capri is Americanised to a degree that I would scarcely recognise, and that Portofino's war was so horrible that houses are still thought to be haunted by the tortured, for according to Them the Gestapo had a gruelling headquarters there, and bloodstains testify truths we would rather forget.

But the loveliness of Portofino in March and April, when the wistaria made one realise that one does not know such a flower in England, and when Portofino Sopra was still in existence—for I understand that appalling fire damage has burned away the heavily wooded district almost to extinction—will ever be one of my jewelled memories, with the Casa Signorile the pearl. Somehow Santa-Margherita disappointed, it seemed both a little tawdry and pretentious, and Rapallo was too smart altogether. It was here, in 1938, that we enjoyed more than one pleasant meal with the Max Beerbohms in their charming home.

I left my family after some weeks of blissful quiet and recuperation, to join Olive Guthrie in Venice on her return from Athens. I arrived very late, and she met me in a gondola, and quietly, in the light of a full moon, we slowly drifted down the side canals to the hotel.

"To-morrow I shall take you to call on the Collione," she said. My heart sank. I knew the fascination interesting foreigners had for Olive.

"Must you? I hardly speak a word of Italian," I answered.

The canals echoed her roars of laughter. My ignorance was profound. The Collione was one of the most famous statues in Venice. . . . What a week we had, but in some ways we had chosen badly, for it was Holy Week and the treasures of all the churches were either hidden in heavy purple or had been put away altogether. I went alone to High Mass at San Marco on Easter Day; beautiful it was, what one could hear of it, but the

crowds were so fantastic that I stood for two hours, heard tink-
lings of bells and far-away chanting, and saw nothing. The
Cathedral with its gold mosaics was staggering in its beauty
when seen alone in peace and quiet, but I still would definitely
give the palm to the Milan duomo, whose glass must be
unrivalled in the world; and for sheer atmosphere I have yet to
find anything more lovely than Chartres Cathedral on an afternoon when vespers are being sung. The French, for all their 'no
church of state' have a far more monastic approach to their
services and churches than the over-ornate theatricality found
in Italy.

Meals in different hotels and cafés . . . especially drinks at
Florian's and dinners at the Fenice; canal after canal in gon-
dolas; shop after shop looking at curios, and presents, and pictures; visits to churches, museums . . . how can one recapture a
week in Venice in a few pages? But Venice has its disappoint-
ments; to me the lack of any tree (but for a clump of cypresses
in a cemetery) and the ensuing lack of any birds except the
everlasting pigeons, spoilt it, or at any rate lessened its compelling fascination.

We went on from Venice to exquisite little San Vigilio on
Lago di Garda, surely one of the most romantic tiny places in
existence, with its minute balconied albergo, its little harbour
just about big enough to hold one Gardonese vessel (orange-
sailed and carrying a cargo of wine vats), its tiny church and the
olive groves which creep to the water's edge. But then the Lago
di Garda abounds in jewels, and whilst San Vigilio is known,
my most adored Bezzuglio is not. . . .

Paris next, Paris in May with the chestnuts in flower and
lilac out, and an Embassy car at Olive's disposal and theatres . . .
exquisite food . . . exciting shops . . . and finally London, and as
if to round off a very perfect holiday one of the most enthralling
evenings at Covent Garden I shall ever remember, a rare
occasion: *Electra*, sung superbly by Pauly, Thorborg and

Janssen, and Sir Thomas conducting. It was an evening of brilliance from the moment the curtain rose until the end of the performance.

That summer I divided my time between Cornwall and Mull, but it is September I remember most vividly, September warm with a haze over Lantivet Bay and the golden corn waist-high as one skirted it daily to climb down the cliff to an isolated bathe; September and—Munich.

Even now, these many years later, I remember the Munich crisis with far greater clarity than the days of horror which actually preceded the ultimate declaration of war. And I remember Wendy and myself in a railway carriage speeding to Mull, from Lostwithiel to Glasgow (without a change in those days), and the sublime news of the hoped-for 'peace in our time' reached me as we got to Bristol.

I am no politician, and my heart has ever bled for the cruel lashings made by ignorant people and fanatics against Neville Chamberlain during that fateful period. It is curious, moreover, that great numbers of people who pronounced themselves ready to fight for Czechoslovakia in 1938 were still in mufti in 1940. It is true that a public servant, or any public figure for that matter, must be ready for the pillory, however horrible, but one does sometimes 'see red' when honest men are blamed for keeping their countries out of war when they, and they alone, know the strength of their own armaments and armed forces.

So Munich came and—dissolved. And the hastily dug trenches in London's squares and parks remained. Gas masks; were we then already issued with them? But we went ahead happily, blithely, like the dancers before Waterloo eve, to our parties, our race-meetings, our concerts; we applauded Mengelberg and thoroughly appreciated his handling of *Tristan* excerpts, Franck's *Psyche*, a Tchaikovsky symphony. And Richard Strauss . . . a Nazi? Who says so? Heil! for such music as: *Also Sprach Zarathustra, Heldenleben, Tod und Verklärung.*

In February 1939 my first book was published, and that and my first trip to Ireland were more interesting to me, I fear, than the growing unrest of Europe.

The Perplexed Heart gained a fair amount of publicity and kind criticism on the whole; the former because our name seems to attract attention willy-nilly, *and* I was Daphne's sister. . . . This was the book which prompted a reader to write me a letter beginning, "As the mother of sons I must protest. . . ." Michael Joseph published it and I owe much of its success to him and his brutal blue pencilling. Evening after evening I used to go to his house and together we took line by line, scratching this, deleting that, until I was so despondent and miserable that I asked him why he bothered to publish the damn thing at all. He said he believed I would one day write a good book. . . . It was Brigit Patmore whose belief in early days had encouraged me once again to try to write, and I dedicated the effort to her.

I went to stay with the Leslies at Glaslough. Ever since I had known Olive Guthrie she had never tired of extolling the beauties of the home in which she had been brought up, and which she loved more than any place on earth I believe. Her brother, Sir John Leslie, and his wife Leonie (Winston Churchill's aunt, sister of Lady Randolph Churchill) were my host and hostess and two people were never kinder to the girl I then was, nor—and I do mean this as a sincere compliment— was I ever aware of the age barrier between us. Sir John was deaf, but it did not seem to matter, he entered into everything, and Lady Leslie was certainly a wonderful woman, with a brilliant wit and a cosmopolitan chic, and panache if one may use that expression about a woman. I was there for nearly a month, and the February sunshine made it difficult to realise I was in Ireland and not some Mediterranean land. The lake over which the house looked, with the woods beyond, was a magnificent view to look at each morning from one's bedroom window. Olive herself was at her happiest there I think, with two people she adored, in the country she adored, and amongst a people she adored.

There were several shoots whilst I was there; Olive herself was a good shot both with gun and rifle, and the days would be spent healthily, and our evenings quietly playing cards or enjoying music. I was taken to many interesting houses, but I have nowhere seen trees to touch those of the domaines of Caledon and Glaslough. I also went to Inniskillen, where I remember many superb portraits centuries old, and to Rossmore. Perhaps my three peaceful weeks at Glaslough were a fitting apéritif for the remaining week I was to spend in Dublin, where it seemed I was fêted daily from morn to midnight! We stayed at the Shelborne and I returned to London with my head buzzing from my gaieties. Alas, the one man in all Ireland who I had wanted to meet above any, and who Olive had promised that I would, had died either during my visit to Glaslough or just before: Yeats. It was a bitter disappointment that I had come to Ireland too late for that privilege.

I was taken to a Sunday tea-party at the famous Sarah Purser's; I was shown over the Rotunda by no less a man than Bethel Solomons himself. I met—had tea at his house—President Cosgrave; I was taken to the Dáil and heard de Valera and Dillon speak—we had tea afterwards with that most charming of men, Desmond Fitzgerald. There was a dinner at the celebrated Kildare Street Club, there was at least one famous stud to which I was taken (and in those days I fear I was not as impressed as I would be now!) and there were visits to the Abbey Theatre with Lennox Robinson and dinner at Jammet's afterwards, and visits to the Robinsons' house at Dalkey, and to the Nolans too, in their house in one of the beautiful Georgian squares. Last and never least the kindness showered on me by that very dear friend of Olive's, Mrs McNeil, 'Jo', the widow of the late viceroy. Truly it is a visit to look back upon, and makes one realise how incredibly generous and hospitable the Irish are.

England however was exciting enough for me to return to, for I was suddenly in the news with my *Perplexed Heart* and— let's face it—enjoying the fact. There were definitely two schools of thought about it where readers were concerned, the shocked and those who were not shocked, and the former— amongst my friends anyway—were those whose own lives were not all that impeccable! There are many people who maintain that a first novel is invariably autobiographical, and people began to wonder which of the rather shady characters in this book was me! And it so happened that although this was the first of my books to be published, it was not the first I had written. . . .

1939 . . . and truly an Eve of Waterloo spirit. The visit of the President of France, M. Lebrun, being the most colourful and spectacular of the many excitements. This I watched from Carlton House Terrace, next door to the German Embassy, and did I or did I not watch Herr Ribbentrop?

Mull . . . Cornwall . . . London. . . . Time marched on, and always Hitler's men were marching with it. Good Friday— surely it was on Good Friday that Albania was invaded? And one by one, as like a game of chess, pawns fell, castles were captured, knights went by the board . . . the encircling move-ment became even more deadly and we still went to Covent Garden and Wimbledon, and Richmond horse show and Henley and Ascot and Lord's. And Olive came to us at Fowey, and when Mummie and Jeanne left for the Buckingham Palace Garden Party, she and I went for a motor tour in the West, little dreaming that within two months the great fear would be a Fait Accompli.

I suppose it is the sign of a Small Mind that really great Happenings are invariably wrapped up for me personally in smaller 'unimportant' things. War that September was expected. But for me Wendy's death was not. My little constant companion of nearly fourteen years left me within that first week of the declaration. The vet said it was a form of meningitis, and she suddenly seemed to lose her reason and became *queer*. I remember spending days which alternated between filling sandbags (most unnecessary), helping a farm getting in the harvest (and being fed better than I have before or since) and nursing Wendy. And then she died, and I could bear it all no longer. Mine had been the hand that started her final sleep—with overdoses of luminal—and I could not bear anything or anyone and I drove away. To Scotland. To Mull. Yes, I was an escapist just then; not from the war, but my own misery. I got into the car one Monday morning at nine-thirty, and drove Emma Trechman to Gloucestershire, and dropped her; on across the border to Lockerbie—over three hundred miles—on the Tuesday, and touched down at Torosay by tea-time Wednesday, having seen the first balloon barrage at Paisley on the way, nearly eight hundred miles in two and a half days. There were, of course, Guthrie grandchildren and others there of various ages, sex and degree, and it must have been then that I met my 'husband', aged eleven, a most adorable person—and most beautiful. I don't know how or why we became 'hubby' and 'wifey', but I remember being greatly touched when he was overheard telling somebody that "Angela was about eighteen" (I was the same age as his mother).

Daphne wrote: "I am so distressed to hear about darling Wendy. But she was looking very frail when we were down at Fowey, and I felt she wasn't going to live much longer. Fourteen is a terrific age for a peke. And if Armageddon has really started, the poor little thing is better out of it. But it is wretched for you, and everyone will miss her so much. We are still here

(Hythe) hanging on, and I rush to the lav. whenever the post arrives in case there is a letter from the War Office ordering Tommy off. I think the Expeditionary Force goes this week. I can't bear to think of it. All our friends, John Prescott, Jack Whitaker, everyone I can think of. Tommy I'm sure would rather have gone with all of them than perhaps have to go in a month or so with other regiments none of which he'd know. . . . I've let myself in for being Gas Decontaminator!! We have a First Aid Post at the school for wounded women and children with a Gas Decontamination Centre attached to it. They asked for volunteers and I felt as Commandant's wife I ought to make an effort! Actually all it entails is leaping off to this place if there is a raid and dressing in oilskins and sea boots from top to toe, and smothering 'casualties' with bleaching powder! As there is never likely to be a Gas Raid it just means the acute boredom of leaving one's comfortable bed whenever there if a warning and sitting about in a draughty sort of work-house with a trio of stalwart V.A.D's. . . . It is heavenly here and I'm sure we should have loved it but for all this. I still have a queer feeling something will stop it, but I don't know what unless it's a miracle. My soul quails when I see our bellicose statements about 'fighting to the last ditch': it's so simple for all the damn politicians, and they probably get a kick out of playing 'power politics'. I've been reading Winston's *Aftermath of the World Crisis* and I must say it makes one depressed to read what went on *after* the Armistice. Apparently we continued the Blockade until 1919, and made not the slightest effort to help the German people. I quite realise everyone was very bitter, but I bet all that sowed the seed for Nazi-ism to-day. And yet as Eden said in his speech last night, the Germans have now done this aggression *five times* in eighty years, which makes me rather despair of them ever being a peaceable sort of people. They seem to enjoy having bloody leaders. How is the 'Muse'? I don't feel like 'musing' myself. I don't think I could lose myself in a fictitious story whilst living in such uncertainty. I fluctuate between insanely deciding to join the W.A.A.F. (!) if Tommy goes abroad, or trekking for a Pacific Island and never mentioning war. I feel anything between would be hopeless."

Not long afterwards she wrote again: "... I get a lot of light relief out of our First Aid Post. We have incredible 'gas practices' every week, when dressed up in hampering oilskins, hoods and macs and we have to undress pretended casualties. The thing is almost impossible and one visualises the real thing, probably tearing off women's clothes, with they themselves unconscious! Last week a *maniac* came to lecture us, and with a face devoid of any humour went into fearful details of gas possibilities. She talked in a very high-pitched voice, using large gestures and said 'At all costs do not let gas vapour penetrate the nooks and crannies of your body'. . . . She then whipped out lots of little phials from her attaché case all filled with gas, and rammed them under our noses, muttering savagely 'It's like curry, isn't it?' with a wild gleam in her eye. The final straw was a demonstration of how to pull an unconscious person out of a gas-filled room. Instead of dragging 'em by the heels, she made a V.A.D. lie down, and proceeded to straddle herself on top of her, clasping the V.A.D's arms round her neck and heaving violently dragged her along the floor beneath her by pressure of her knees!!! It was the most indecent thing I've ever seen in my life!! All the while with a fearful grim face, which I've tried to draw and can't! . . . I hear Fowey has become a munition dump and Mummie is building a shelter!"

I remained in Mull for two months, finishing my second book, *The Spinning Wheel*, which had Mull (under a disguised name) as its background, and then started the trek south, dropping Olive at Glasgow (Ireland bound) while in slow stages I drove back to Cornwall. Littleborough to Isla and her small family, Stow-on-the-Wold to Bet and her baby—Donald was already in Palestine—on to Angela on Dartmoor and finally to Fowey where for the time being all there was to be done was helping in a Canteen, where I at least met and made one friend for life by giving him two lumps of sugar in his daily cup of tea.

My brother-in-law was Commandant of the Small Arms School at Hythe still, and he and Daphne had moved into the Commandant's house just before the declaration of war and had done it up most charmingly. Mummie and I spent a few days there with them just before the first war-time Christmas; and spent as well (though I did not know it) my last days and nights at Providence. Black-out in London seemed infinitely more sinister than in the country, where darkness prevails anyway, and I remember how strange I felt when I spent some evenings at Michael Joseph's house after dinner, going over *The Spinning Wheel* and returning through Swiss Cottage without realising where I was; I who prided myself that I knew my native city backwards.

IX

War Years

THE war had begun in September. Cornwall was then thought to be a beautifully safe place and evacuees arrived by the thousand. Fowey had at that time a smallish quota, and I am thankful to say (unkind as it may sound) that Ferryside was not commandeered for such purposes. I am frank enough to admit we filled it with our own friends. Soldiers began to fill the town and for some months, until it was taken over by N.A.A.F.I., I helped in the locally run Service canteen several times a week. For the first six months the war was more or less negligible. I do not believe that even Hamm was being bombed in the early days of 1940, and I dashed up to Scotland for three weeks in February where Olive Guthrie was up to the eyes in work for Merchant Seamen at the Oban base. A merchantman was torpedoed while I was there and I shall always remember the pathetic little crowd of rescued Lascars shivering and hoping to die as they lay like bewildered animals in the quarters allotted them. Oban was then a base for sea-planes (flying boats actually). I had my birthday on Mull—something I had never imagined possible in war-time—and when I left the West Coast it was with the feeling that the Hebrides knew a great deal more about war, with merchantmen sinkings, U-boats, convoys, than we did in the south.

In April *Rebecca* was produced in London, and Mummie, Jeanne and I all went up from Fowey for the first night. The enormous success of the book had taken place just before the Munich crisis. (Mr Chamberlain, so his daughter told me afterwards, took a copy of the book with him to lighten his worries as he flew to Berchtesgaden; which makes me—and I'm sure Daphne—very proud.) The play opened with pre-war splendour as far as the audience was concerned, and it was beautifully acted by Celia Johnson and Owen Nares. I remember it was the last time I saw Mary Tempest, looking quite exquisite in a white satin picture frock, her hair honey-coloured and her face unlined and more full of fascination than any débutante's. I talked to her at the Savoy at supper afterwards; she was like a very delicious fairy, or a piece of porcelain without price.

Yes, it was April, and although I left London in comparative peace for a quick visit to Cambridge I returned to find 'Norway Invaded' staring me in the face from placards on Liverpool Street Station. Then things began to move swiftly, horrifyingly. In May I drove from Fowey to Stinsford for Whitsun and, in company with Mary and Alex, listened with tears running down my face to Neville Chamberlain broadcasting his farewell to the nation as Prime Minister, and I drove home feeling bewildered and sad, little realising that it would be nine years before I was to see Stinsford again.

Although Kent was likely to become a target for any form or warfare Daphne wrote: ". . . This is a good place in the summer, anyway for the children and they seem so happy that I see no point in suddenly upheaving yet awhile. The kitchen-garden too, bursting soon with produce! But of course if raids start I should shift. I feel for the next month or so the Germans will be pretty occupied with Holland and Belgium. What hell it all is. . . ."

But things moved more quickly than everyone bargained for, and in June she sent the children down to us. I can still see Flavia aged two—or was she three?—in a blue sunbonnet with corkscrew curls, the epitome of sugar and spice . . . and one evening lying in her bed with tears running down from those periwinkle blue eyes—silently. They came to a cottage in the

village and ate with us. On Tessa's birthday bombs dropped in
the garden beyond ours and in the harbour, and so a cottage
was taken further afield for them to move to, but they never
went to it and it was eventually claimed for evacuees who
ruined what had been a perfect gem. Then came Dunkirk.
Daphne wrote again: "I quite see the force of Fowey getting
tricky if Germany begins to get more bases along the French
coast, and if there are heaps of Quislings rampant in the place
a sort of 'Norway' landing might be effected. I think for the
time being though it should be all right, and I shouldn't like to
think of them rather isolated elsewhere unless some of you or
I were with them. They seem so happy in their cottage in
Bodinnick, anyway for the present. . . . Tommy says his
Brigade may be ordered to France at any moment so I have got
to be prepared for this. If so I would probably come down to
Ferryside if you could have me, and then we would have to
make plans for the future. . . . We have heard various reports
about how people were killed. Jackie Lloyd, Dermot Paken-
ham and Christopher Jefferies were all killed one after another
by a *bloody* sniper. Poor Patrick Ellison had to walk *a mile* with
a piece of shell having gone right through his back to his chest
and it's a mercy he's alive. Then his hopsital ship was bombed
all the time. Handsome Naps Brinckman, you know who I
mean, has been wounded in both legs and was captured by the
Germans. He is now presumably a prisoner. Awful for his wife.
The people who are wounded and home are lucky, I think, as
they will not be fit to go again for a few months. . . . Are you
writing? I find I can't get down to it, it all seems so pointless at
the present time. I had a silly letter from —— saying New
York had prospects of getting vast sums for the serialisation of
my next novel, and couldn't I give them *some idea* of what it'd
be and when, etc. So I wrote a rather thick letter back, saying
as the New York office was many thousands of miles away
they perhaps did not realise that this country was faced with the

biggest crisis in history and almost certain invasion, that I was busy writing letters for the Grenadier Relief Committee, my husband was going abroad at any moment and that 'vast sums for the next novel' seemed a little beside the point——! The sordid commercial outlook of people *still*, makes me quite sick."

I was on my way to Mull in June, soon after Dunkirk had been evacuated, and the trains seethed with troops so weary, so pitiable that one felt ashamed of one's own conditions. I went via Bristol and Birmingham and Glasgow, and the war for the first time showed one living victims.

I went to Mull for what was to be a month; I remained nine. Even now I find it difficult to explain away such behaviour. The Battle of Britain was being fought for part of that time and all too eagerly I listened to my family's pleas of "stay where you are", trying not to hear the still small voice of my conscience, which kept telling me how feebly I was pulling my weight by gardening all day long at Torosay and helping with the children. Olive had plenty of work on hand in Oban, and had also organised an amazing amount of work to be done for her Merchant Navy Depot from Ireland.

By July Tommy was stationed in Hertfordshire and Daphne had been allowed to join him. They were wonderfully lucky for they found billets in a charming house with people who ultimately became great friends. She wrote me: " . . . We are still most happy and comfortable with the X's, who are heavenly; you know how bored I am staying with people as a rule, but this is quite different. But I feel if the invasion does not come off we might look for a house in September and have the children. I am rather worried about them in Fowey, after the bombs, and feel they would be better with Tommy's mother, or even at Nanny's home which is only about ten miles from here, and which would mean one could see them. But I do feel we should all be together soon if we can, and near to some

school for Tessa, which she does so love. . . . I am quite prepared to see us all interned because of our name! Specially if the
Pétain government turn nasty and madly ally with Germany,
which I should think quite possible. I'd much rather they all
went Red! But by every sign they are quelling all attempts of
the poor people and workers to protest. I think that Laval and
crew are real blackguards and are just intending to 'get in' with
the Germans as much as they can, and have a sort of Fascist
dictatorship. They'll get all the big business men and those
bloody silly royalists, and everybody else will be kept down.
'To the tumbrils' I say! I've done no 'private' writing of my
own, but Heinemann are bringing out this sixpenny booklet
some time on 'morale' the material of which was supplied by
my despised Groupy friends, and which I have re-written for
them. I have done the introduction too, and epilogue. All the
royalties to go to Soldiers' Families Association. . . . The time
has struck I feel for my curious news which I have been keeping
from everyone all these months, in *sole hopes* of stopping worry
and anxiety. I have now written to Mummie, as I felt I should
tell her; another baby, which you once funnily enough asked
in a letter, which I did not comment upon. Been 'like that' for
months! Event due, ironically enough, about Armistice Day!
I have made no plans beyond warning Miss —— (*her gynaecolo-
gist*) and Sister, and am prepared to give birth anywhere, from
a Military Hospital to an Air Raid Dug Out. But knowing how
poor Mummie fusses about us I decided not to say anything as
it didn't seem fair to tell you or Jeanne and not her. . . . I have
implored her not to worry. I am very well and Miss —— says
I am so normal that if I was alone with Sister somewhere I'd be
all right! Only you know how tricky it is actually to make
'plans'. I might be parked somewhere in September where I
can have it if necessary. If London is standing, and there is no
invasion, I could take a flat as before and have Sister. But this
may be imposs. Anyway, I feel it's rather a case of 'sufficient

unto the day' and I feel sure I shall know what to do nearer the time. Tommy funnily enough, instead of being worried or bored, is rather pleased. I suppose he thinks it might be a son, but one must not hope too much. . . . I'm hoping Mummie will understand it was *sheer* saving her from worry that stopped me telling her before. . . . If she should write to you about it, do put my point and back me up. . . ."

And in September she wrote, still from Hertfordshire: " . . . All goes well here and no alarms of great magnitude. We seem to be getting off pretty lightly. Think this bit of Herts must be in a quiet pocket. Actually about twenty Nazi planes flew over us on their way to Luton, eight miles away, the other afternoon, but one knew they were out for bigger fry than one solitary house in fields, so we were more intrigued than frightened. It really was rather an exquisite sight, so remote and unreal, those silvery creatures like birds humming above us at about twenty thousand feet, whilst above them circled their own protective fighters. We also had one of those dreary lone raiders over us on Monday night which dropped about four bombs in a field near. I was awake and heard the drone of the plane and then four heavy thuds and was only aware of vast irritation and said to myself 'Damn that man, I hope he hasn't hit the cows'. But I expect a really nasty raid in a crowded area, with corpses around, would be hell. . . . The cook is stopping as Nanny's sister can't come. I'm advertising for a nursery maid. But the most disheartening thing is that Tommy and the Brigade are probably having to move to the East Coast. It would be in a Defence Area of course and I should not be able to go, and anyway must park myself somewhere with the children. . . . If it weren't for the children and having the baby I should stay on here as I'm fond of the ——s. . . . I was up in London last week between raids to see Miss —— and have my hair done; Miss —— can't leave the London area, so I have to find someone down here. She knows a good lady doctor in the district, so I shall try and get her. I only thought of that important Lane Roberts because he vaguely lives in Herts I was told! But he is more for 'difficult' cases, twins and babies upside down, and anyway I'd much rather have a woman as long as she allows me to have plenty of gas and oxygen. Tessa knows, by-the-way! She guessed because of my smocks. Said shrewdly to Nanny 'It strikes me we are going to have another sister.' And would take no denial. So when I saw her last week, we had quite a girl-friend chat about it. 'I'm very glad,' she said, 'but better not tell Flavia, she might ask awkward questions'!! Flavia actually is looking heavenly, her hair tied in red bows, and oozing sex appeal. I feel she is going to have frightful emotions in her 'teens'! Lord! How I hope for Christian, but bet it will be a girl. (Gloria is the girl's name—don't giggle! —Tommy's choice. I shall always think of the mattress.) . . . I'm feeling pretty fat, with two months still to go, but thank heaven am not fat all over, or square, and don't lurch. Like I was with the others but a bit more so. . . ."

There will be readers, I can imagine, who will say, "Extraordinary, revealing these intimate letters." I do so in order to show that Daphne was living the life of any ordinary soldier's wife, and took war and having a baby during a possible invasion in her stride. Although she was then the celebrated author of *Rebecca* she had for the time certainly forgotten its existence. There was one fear, and one thought uppermost with her, and one that was shared by countless millions of other wives everywhere—when would her husband go overseas?

One felt curiously isolated in Mull, for all the strings of convoys that passed up the Sound daily, for we were a very secret area. I had a green identity card, one's letters were heavily censored and a great deal more went on than one heard about. Here indeed I was nearly expelled because of my French name. The local policeman turned up one day and I had very great difficulty in persuading him that I was no spy; he had of course no notion of Daddy, and I quoted my uncle Guy's record (as a commanding officer fallen in the '14-'18 war) and Tommy's position in the current war, and the fact that my books were being sold in the Oban library. (Daphne and *Rebecca* cut no ice with him!)

It was in August that I opened the paper and saw quite casually that my poor Bet had lost her husband in Palestine. I was stunned. I read it in the *Glasgow Herald*, as the letter from Aunt Ella had been delayed in which she broke the news. All I realised was that Bet and the baby were alone in Jerusalem and that Donald was dead. It was many weeks before I heard more, for communication with civilians in the Middle East took months, except by cable. Eventually she was evacuated to Cairo, and from there once again to South Africa where her parents were able to join her, and where Seymour worked himself nearly to death for the Allied Cause, leaving his E.N.S.A. work to do what he could with Ella in Africa, thereby enabling them all to be together. Life must have been very hard for them for the next few years, and people at home who seemed to think that they and others like them were living in clover are very much mistaken. Money was at a minimum quota and I have often wondered how Bet managed to bring up her small son, move house continually and do daily Censorship as well.

In Fowey Jeanne was working on the land. She had started with some training with a farmer, and by the autumn had taken on a large piece of land, two miles from Ferryside, which she proposed turning to market-gardening. As with everything that she takes up she was completely thorough in her garden. Art and even music were banished for the duration and literature took the form of catalogue upon catalogue of seeds, plants, implements and manures. By the autumn however it was decided to move from Bodinnick across the river to Fowey itself. Mummie had been far from well for some time, and the doctor had thought that the slight isolation of Ferryside had preyed on her nerves, and that she would feel more 'in the world' in Fowey. Billy had been living with the family for several months now, and she too seemed to think that Mummie would benefit from the change. In Scotland I found it an extraordinary proposition and wrote hurriedly, and with heat I fancy, on the subject, from what can be assumed from Jeanne's answer:

" . . . I'm trying to be unbiassed, but your letter rather gave the impression of what *you* wanted to do, and where *you* want to be when you come back without realising much that 'even the weariest river would like to wander somewhere safe to sea'—which sounds as good a parable as any in The Book, and by which I mean even I who love this place have had enough to wish for fresh faces if not fresh fields. So that when you say to Mummie what a curious thing for us to go to the Esplanade I must reply that Life *is* curious these days—it is curious that Mummie who once cared so much about changing for dinner doesn't any longer, that she carves only for herself and doesn't mind my hacking the joint under her eyes, curious that I am concerned more for it to rain for my Cabbage Plants than to fill the Tanks for Baths, that I have to peruse prices and lists of seeds in lieu of Tubes of paint, that one doesn't get shoes cleaned unless done by oneself; in fact Let us Pray for the Whole State of Christ's Church Militant here in Ferryside. Incidentally I took Syb (*Billy*) to St Faith's yesterday. I don't know—it's funny—what Church does to me these days, but any set form of service or gathering makes me feel completely like Simon Thingummy, 'Woe unto ye'. Any *gathering* of people, to Praise and Magnify can only give to me an impression of Poseur Righteousness; it's not that I am agnostic, and a Mohammedan gathering would seem just as useless. I feel more than ever that the Kingdom of God is within one—I should like to have a discussion about it all. Of course one can say

nothing to Syb, as she can see no point but the Catholic's*. . . .
I wonder what my Brush will portray when it's given a chance
again, either I shall be John, or the village schoolmistress, but
'tis no use my starting things and then not having time to finish,
I must give whole concentration to things I've discovered, and
as you remember in my Hampstead studio it was the whole day
or nothing. By the way the Military Hospital here has V.A.D's
. . . why don't you write and ask for details? I am rather sad that
you will apparently weed for hours the Passing Glory of
Torosay and don't consider you can be of import in what may
yet prove to be the Suttons of Cornwall. 'You don't—(sniff)—
mind what you do for Olive'; in spite of Hudson's plea for
more food. Not that I want to persuade you into gardening if
you loathe it but as I say, you don't mind spending hours 'mid
the flowers. . . . It's been very wild weather again—my poor
greens have all had to be staked and I've been like Lob practically kissing each sprout. Write again soon, and my saluta-
tions to OL ——."

Never knowing whether Ferryside would be commandeered
or not—a Damocletian sword always hanging over the family's
head—they finally took matters into their own hands and
moved across the water to a small partly furnished house in the
Esplanade, in a row, and from here Jeanne (and later I) trekked
daily the now three miles to Pont to work on the Matterhorn-
like slopes of the two-acre ground which she tilled manfully
with any help she could find. The younger Fox girl helped till
she was drafted to a farm, and although it was work that was
unspectacular from many points of view, and work which
incidentally proved ruinous to both our insides, it was Digging
for Victory with a vengeance. Two acres of hitherto virgin soil
and ground all to be fenced, all to be tilled, all to be manured,
with every form of pest and handicap therein. No water handy
except what could be caught in tubs, no lane nearer than at the

* Jeanne was herself received into the Church in 1948.

8*

foot of the hill, many hundreds of yards below, rabbits galore—
and even bullocks were known from time to time to break
through the top hedges—and when we needed manure we
either climbed up a hundred feet to fetch the cartload of tipped
farm manure box-load by box-load, or walked the hundreds of
yards down the footpath to the river where we proceeded to
take seaweed by the boat-full and then making the scores of
journeys up again, carrying it in the ricksha contraption of
Heath Robinson design we eventually engineered.

In November 1940 Daphne's longed-for son was born, and a
week later she wrote to me from the house which she had
rented in Hertfordshire: "I've not written before because one
does feel so slack the first week, and unable to cope. I wrote to
Mummie who got fussed because she thought I sounded
'depressed' and made Jeanne ring up to enquire, but you know
how it is, one *is* tired afterwards and to write a laugh on every
page is impossible! Also Tommy had just left. . . . Am thrilled
to have the 'creature'. 'One's son' at last! He's an absurd little
thing and rather like Tessa was, but not pathetic like Flavia.
Rather a clever shrewd little face. Very fair hair at the moment
and his eyes *might* possibly be green. Actually of course like
every other baby! His birth was a most hurried affair. I'd felt
'back-achy' all Sunday (Sister arrived Saturday) and decided
to go to bed for tea, and at six he was born! Suddenly those
violent pains started when I'd swallowed my tea (like people in
books!) and luckily Sister had everything ready. She shoved a
gas and oxygen contraption into my hands to work myself,
which needless to say was useless, and the doctor was sent for
and had barely approached the bedside before I felt the most
violent explosion and Christian *shot out* of me, like someone
taking a header, and *yelling* as he did so! I felt the whole thing.
And though part of me was groaning, the rest was saying 'Ah!
well, so *that's* how it happens, is it?' And then I heard Sister
say 'Oh! good, won't they be thrilled' and I realised it was a

boy. The next few days were tiring because with a third baby (and I think a second too) one gets awful 'after pains', which tire one so. He weighed six and three-quarter pounds by-the-way, a bit more than the girls. They are thrilled with him and Tommy very pleased, though that was a bit overshadowed by his having to go off. . . . Can you come when Sister has gone? . . . Your wire to Angela said 'Daphne has a sow'!! His names by-the-way are Christian Frederick du Maurier Browning (Tommy thinks C. F. du M. B. will look rather distinguished at school!). But personally I think he looks like Pius! The family sound to be settling down all right in the Esplanade. I am still planless."

My own life was now a curiously split one mentally. Part of me was naturally with the various members of my family, but most of me was in Mull where for what it was worth I gardened with Olive alone in the grounds which had in the past boasted eight or ten men, and now had one and a boy. Winter was setting in and it was bitterly cold because naturally wartime restrictions made many fires and central heating—and even baths—impossible. We used to wrap rugs round ourselves in the dining-room in the evenings, and I remember quite well going to sleep under four blankets, an eiderdown, a fur rug, four hot-water bottles, wearing flannel pyjamas, a cardigan and a woollen rug! Cold it may have been but an exquisite dry cold, with snow on the mountains and the frost on the trees snow-thick. Olive's eldest grandson, David James, arrived—bearded—off his M.T.B. for Christmas Day, his twenty-first birthday, and on Boxing Day with most of his relations home on leave a shoot was organised. My 'husband' then about eleven was already extremely adept with his ·22 (would it have been?) and used to bring back rabbits for 'the pot'.

In Cornwall too the winter was a bitterly cold one, and Jeanne wrote of polar conditions and ice-floes in the harbour.

No one was occupying Ferryside, whose pipes burst and the "kitchen was awash and water like a cascade down the stairs aping Niagara". People were having to fetch water from streams, for indoor use. She wrote in January (1941) excitedly of a new radio station she had discovered "about 1300, in the evenings. Coming from Algiers I think, run alternately in French (so presumably 'free') and I should imagine Arabic! A stream of incredible sounding words straight from the Pyramids!" . . . "I'm afraid this dreadful frost will play havoc with lots of my green stuff—I've rolled every damn pea seed in red-lead and paraffin and still the mice come. Am engaged at the moment in 'breaking up' that bit where the chicken-run was, as all their old droppings will have worked ecstatic benefit with the earth, but it's a Herculean little task as it's covered in sawn-down age-old tree roots and stumps, and getting 'em up with a pick-axe is like dragging up unending Cancerous growths all entwined, in fact I daresay brought on my nausea and pains, but there's great satisfaction in doing it. I had thought of putting tomatoes there, do rabbits like 'em d'you suppose, as I don't want to net it. I'm going to grow a mort of French beans as they apparently like Pont, also onions. I am trying to draw up my plans for lists of seeds now, but it's awfully difficult to look so far ahead, specially when one's inexperienced. I loved your little book on manures, wish you could send some more."

Also spracht not Zarathustra but Jeanne du Maurier, whose conversation and letters in former days would have dealt with possibly French Impressionism . . . concerts she was attending, and current art shows . . . religion . . . people. . . . But she was running true to form; her heart for the duration lay in Pont, along with manures, tomato plants, cabbages, and as a garden it was a truly magnificent effort, and fed many.

I did not, alas, manage to get to Daphne, for the children went down with measles and there was veritable chaos in the house, for their Nanny also suffered from maladies. " . . . I cope with the measles patients," wrote Daphne, "while Nanny, still pretty dicky, attends to Christian, but as she is apt to faint at any moment I have to be on hand to cope with her too! Turning into a miracle of efficiency! But it's a nuisance, as one spends one's time rushing about with bed-pans, brewing little drinks, then mixing bottles for Christian and changing napkins, and if one has a *moment* to spare one dashes to the typewriter to scribble a page of *Frenchman's Creek*. . . . I'm afraid your visit will *have* to be put aside, everything is so disorganised. . . ."

Flavia became very ill indeed and one wonders how under the circumstances Daphne got on at all with a book. In early February she wrote again: "Poor Flavia has been *terribly* ill with measles. It was really the most awful worrying time. Of all bloody diseases . . . and this year it's more virulent than ever. A grim ghastly rash like plague, and a hacking cough and a raging fever. And when the fever went down instead of her lying quietly she got all mentally excited, and I was terrified it was going to her brain. She wailed in the most awful way and fought and screamed. God! I thought the pain of having children was over when one gave birth to them but I see now it's only the beginning. Well, when the excitement wore down she was completely exhausted, and just slept and slept. She still does this but is definitely on the upward grade. Tessa is all right again, but Nanny was all 'out' again this week-end, so I have had to do Christian too. He is angelic and couldn't be easier, but it's the actual time involved that is so tiring—that late feed at night, one is never in bed till eleven-thirty and then up again at six—and you know how I worship sleep—I'm sure it's all very good discipline for me, so indolent by nature, but I do long for it all to be over. . . . Can you possibly delay your journey south a bit longer? but if the evacuee twins get it the *cook* will have to look after them and more chaos will ensue! . . ."

In the meantime, in Cornwall, Ferryside had been requisitioned by the Navy, and although everything had to be moved lock, stock and barrel it was some months before personnel moved in. Jeanne wrote: " . . . It's all cleared, a poor sad shell of former happiness. The Big Room you could never imagine to be what it was—it looks like a large dairy or something. No news as to when the creatures move in, there is even talk of it being a hospital. None of the requisitioned houses are yet occupied. . . ." The servant problem was already becoming acute, and—"We had one answer to our advert," she wrote later. "Sounded nice on the phone and was engaged. Arrived and looked like a brothel-keeper. Whilst she had tea in the kitchen Syb rang up the late employer to get her character as she looked so peculiar and he said she was a frightful woman, filthy, and though they were left with no one they much preferred it to having her, he suspected she drank, was a ghastly cook. . . . It was decided to get rid of her then and there, and a room was got for her somewhere. Her last words were 'Is it licensed?'! Actually she went quite peaceably thank goodness —then. Syb next went down some time later into the kitchen, found her there—thought she was dreaming—and she'd come back for her teeth!!! . . . The car for Pont is essential; from here it's desperate without one—without sheer ruination of health. And as I'm for ever being told to 'go slow' I should achieve nothing by the time I got there from here on m' feet, and would never have strength to struggle back if I did achieve much when I got there. When the hut arrives one can probably spend even more time there, for there will be a brave lot to do directly. Am putting in a hundredweight of early new potatoes after all . . . another reason I hope you will work with one is that you can work on your own without me. I say without, because Doctor——has been a bit anti me going very much lately, though the weather has been too bad anyway mostly, to do any good; but I felt incredibly rotten last week, for no apparent reason.

Couldn't sleep, and bad cough but am better now. You would soon get into the way of it." This was the letter in which she wrote a rather heartbroken account of damage done by bullocks—and " . . . God, what I'd give for m' warm studio, filled with the smell of paint, a kettle singing on the stove, and lights glaring through the uncurtained skylight."

At last, at the end of February, I made my way south, and arrived back on my thirty-seventh birthday to the little house in the Esplanade.

It was clean, spick-and-span, and most of the rooms faced the harbour. My own looked into a shop in the back street, which was something of an anti-climax coming from Mull views and years of Ferryside's river view, but it got the sun at the end of the day which was the only time I was in it, cleaning the caked mud off my boots, and then it was quite amusing to sit in the window and watch the passers-by. But it is no use my pretending I could ever be even *content*—let alone happy—in a street. I hate to see other people's houses even in the distance and at close range they give me an almost claustrophobic misery. As I grow older this condition is getting much worse, and instead of yearning for people and houses round me which many women do as middle and old age approach, I yearn more and more for isolation and a house buried in woods or on top of a mountain or in the middle of a moor. London is different, though even there I can only bear living in a street for a comparatively short time. And although the house in the Esplanade was in every way the most cheerful little place you could imagine, I felt as if I was living in a cage and was truly thankful for the long days spent at Pont, overtired and over-sweated as one was. And it was remarkably true what Jeanne had written : there was a tremendous satisfaction in seeing the result of our labour growing before our eyes. I, who had never taken interest in a kitchen garden and vegetables and who had been willing to give 'my all' for delphiniums, lilies and other beautiful but unnecessary luxuries, derived as much pleasure now from cabbages, peas, beans, potatoes, tomatoes, endives and almost every vegetable in the catalogue. There was, too, beneficial rest to one's mind if not one's body, the heavy digging necessary to convert land, and in trenching. But I cannot pretend that working in rain, carting manure, deep bending and squatting for hours on one's haunches appealed either to my mind or my 'innards', nor did I find particular enjoyment in the stains and revolting conditions to hands (which have never recovered) or to feet whose arches finally collapsed and have never again felt comfortable in pretty high-heeled shoes. But bad weather apart the life was healthy and, in corduroy breeches in winter or bared to the waist and in chemise and pants in the scorching summers, there was even enjoyment to be got from it all. It meant the complete cessation of any mental work, of course, and although I frequently found marvellous plots racing through my brain as hour after hour I would be digging, or planting or sowing, one was far, far, too tired by the end of the day even to jot down mere 'scaffolding' in a note-book. For apart from the actual manual work in the gardens there was the delivering of all the stuff as well. And laden with colossal baskets over our arms, looking like peculiar peasants, we called at our clients' houses 'after hours'. This then was the work that earned for one anonymous letters of abuse for living at home in supposed comfort and doing 'damn all' for the war effort, an effort I still maintain which ruined the stomachs of both Jeanne and myself, for the fact of the matter was that we carried continually weights far too heavy, as girls on farms were also doing.

In the spring of 1941 however, or early summer, *The Little Less*—the book I had written twelve years (?) before—was published; I was under a vague contract for three books in three years, and although this one had been previously turned down, now that I was considered established Michael Joseph brought it out. I had worked on it during the months at Torosay 'bowdlerising' it somewhat and cutting it. I forget what sort of press it got, but like the other two it was published in America, again by Doubleday. But it was now of course hopeless for me to say I would or could write anything further. Daphne, still in Hertfordshire with friends, wrote of continued bouts of illness, and an amusing criticism of the book: "We are all more or less disease-bound again. Tessa over her cold, but Nanny was in bed a week with a sort of 'flu and now Flavia and Christian both have chest colds. It really is endless, but I suppose one must be thankful not to be bombed or living somewhere dreary. . . . Christian is heaven, and so sweet with his cough, like a tiny grown-up person and has his own little cough mixture. We are keeping him very warm and not washing him. Flavia has been running a temperature. What a household, but enlivened by a crate of records . . . and *The Little Less* which we have all been perusing (with the exception of Nanny). X. like all fundamentally 'innocent and pure' women, expressed disapproval but nevertheless lapped it up with gusto, while Y. a cryptic smile on his face has been positively gloating. . . . My new-found 'discovery' about you, as a writer, is that I believe you should write short stories. *The Little Less*, like your first, is so much more a series of episodes than a continuous novel. . . . I do wish you would write a funny book, you so obviously can. For future reference for rural descriptions (typical maddening sort of criticism!) will you remember that all birds stop singing in July, and the nightingale has yet to be born that will give tongue under a harvest or September moon! . . . However I had a bit of fun out of the book and think some other people will have the same. . . . I feel it's only a matter of time before I'm asked 'Does Angela know a lot of queer people?'! . . ."

I cannot remember what sort of a 'fan mail' the book produced on the whole, but it made me a 'pen-friend' which has lasted a very long number of years; the original letter, moreover, was one of abuse for the book.

Daphne's *Frenchman's Creek* came out when we were living in the Esplanade. I adored this, which was just the sort of 'escapist' literature one longed for when very tired. " . . . I was awfully pleased that you liked *F.C.*," she wrote me; "I had not thought it was your cup of tea really as it is more or less pure Jeffery Farnol and rather fantastic, so I am most impressed that you should read it through at a sitting. I think the critics will say 'Miss du Maurier has written an impossible story about a lady and a pirate which no doubt her admirers will enjoy' sort of thing, sweeping it aside. About length, Gollancz wanted it short. . . . I am feeling pretty weak as Christian had me awake at six again this morning. My God, ammunitions for me every time. Blessed are the barren. He is completely demoralised under my care, wakes every morning between six and seven, dirty, and screams until I let him come to bed with me when he promptly assaults me. I'm covered with bruises and scratches. He's 'teething' and the slightest thing makes him touchy and I have to pander to his every little whim. His great amusement is to spit out every mouthful of food when I feed him and then roar with laughter. His one passion is an old cow called Norah and when all else fails I say 'let's go and find old Norah', and off we go and gaze at her. In fact Norah is my only hope. I feel the making of Bren guns would really be quite soothing—one could mechanically go on and on putting things in slots and *thinking*, but with babies you can't take your mind off them for a moment. However no doubt I shall survive! The 'girls' are enjoying themselves with Tommy's mother."

By 1941 the Battle of London was raging and one lived in daily dread for those dear up in London, in the real front line of the war. Billy was back at Golders Green, sleeping—or trying to—every night in the Anderson shelter, one's many friends were there, forced to be by the nature of their work, and Angela was more in the thick of it than most, being an ambulance driver in the Paddington district. Of many letters I kept three, because I felt that they were so graphic in their descriptions of those dreadful days and nights. A very great friend of hers had been killed in the big block of Chelsea flats when she wrote the following in April:

"Have just heard that G. has been found in St Luke's Hospital with a fractured skull, lacerated brain, and paralysed, they think she won't survive the night. X. went and identified her. . . . —— was killed by the same bomb, and a girl living with G. escaped with facial injuries. Their flat on the seventh floor was completely untouched. In the basement they got the bomb. I have *never* seen such devastation anywhere. Poor old G. couldn't get a flat at Nell Gwynne and only came to London four days ago. Never as long as I live will I forget that raid. It was hell let loose for seven hours without a second's lull. J. and I stayed in this flat till we felt we must go somewhere else although neither of us really were frightened. I think it was beyond that. So we joined a couple of men in the shelter in the mews and then heard the scream of a landing bomb. At least we knew we shouldn't be hit from shrapnel. The fires made the whole place like daylight and when the raid died down we walked miles round the streets. We looked in at our Ambulance Station, but every ambulance went out two or three times all over London. . . . I didn't have to go on duty till eight in the morning, had a lot of work to do, and never stopped from eight to two. There is such a fearful lot to do when a lot of ambulances go out and we were sending out reliefs to the people who had been standing by incidents for six or seven hours. Ebury Street is nearly flat, Jermyn Street and Green Street are a shambles, but on the whole I am surprised to see so much untouched. From the noise one thought every building in London had gone. The crashing of glass made things sound worse and there is very little glass left in London now. The part of Cranmer Court that was left hasn't a window-pane left in any window. But it's quite staggering how the next morning everything goes on just the same, except for closed streets and 'buses going along the most unlikely roads. Maples I believe was burnt out, Selfridges had an oil bomb and is partially destroyed and Waring and Gillow was hit, but I haven't been around much in the West End. . . ."

Then about a week later, in April, she wrote: "Grosvenor Square got badly hit, No. 20 (those new flats), and the corner part of Stafford's (*Bourne*) flat blown away. All round South Audley Street, Alford Street (Seymour Court gone altogether), Jermyn Street and Bury Street are just a shambles. Park Street and all those side turnings have all had some kind of bomb. Dunhills is a shell and Fortnum and Mason hit but opened again yesterday. Simpsons and the Apéritif and all along there got hell. . . ." And in May: "By the grace of God I am still here. I suppose it was the most appalling night almost anyone ever spent. It started at eleven p.m. and J. and I were happily in bed. We tried to stick it out once again but it got too hot and we went to the Mews shelter and played bridge until that became a farce and by then incendiaries were pouring all around us, so we seized bags of sand from various doorsteps and dealt with them. Fires were raging everywhere and H.E.'s screaming round us. As we got back to the shelter there was a God Almighty crash and tons of stuff and glass seemed to pour on to the roof. I went out to see what had gone and a crater about twenty feet deep and wide had appeared in the road by Albion Street P.O. where two minutes before J. and I had been. A pub and some shops were hit and an ambulance already standing by but some people weren't got out. Somers Crescent lost about four houses and Radnor Mews. There is no glass anywhere except on the pavements. The window of the room I was to have gone to on Wednesday has been blown in—but anyway my tenant won't come here as there is no gas or water. Druces is a crumpled mass of twisted iron and most of Baker Street is still burning. At a block of flats in Bayswater Road there was a huge fire raging and no fire-engine at all. I think every engine and ambulance in London must have gone out. Some of ours went out four times each. This district has got it well and truly at last. Poor J. has gone on duty at eight this morning, and as we never closed our eyes at all all night, and she was violently sick before going, I can't think she'll be much good to-day. . . . I don't think one's nerves could stand many raids like last night's, and until I'm rung up for I shall try and get some sleep."

Owing to a burglary in which a great many papers, etc, of mine were scattered and mislaid, I lost letters which I bitterly regret. There were others from Angela telling of the night she was on duty driving her ambulance through one of the very worst of all the raids when a large store was bombed and scores of people drowned. Another I remember in which she was out at night (on duty) with fires hemming her in on all sides.

When one remembers those days and nights and what the people of London and other cities went through, one begins to wonder why all personnel were not given decorations; one wonders at the miracle of a standing London to-day, and the even greater miracle of the nerves of the people who lived amidst it all and did not waver.

In the meantime all we could do was to continue with the work one hoped was being of use, and spending evenings knitting. I had now mastered the art of sock-making and helmets and sent as many as often as I could up to the Oban Merchant Navy depot. War Weapons Weeks began, and I was very astonished to be asked to open one in a village in North Cornwall. It was a Sunday (or a Saturday perhaps) and I harangued a vast crowd from a tumbril-like farm-cart. It was my first effort in public speaking and I felt called upon to give what practically amounted to a sermon! It raised an amazing amount of money and called forth much amusement from Daphne who wrote to know: "How goes the Hot-Gospeller? and when is the next bye-election? . . . Like you, I have a 'thing' against War Weapons because I have awful visions of bombs being hurled down upon the innocent and I don't know what I should find to say in their favour at a Weapons Week, but still, without them we perish, I suppose. Do you realise the war is getting nearer and nearer to the original Armageddon? It's a hill top near the pipe line in Syria. . . . Personally I maintain that all those prophecies referred to the original fall of Jerusalem, and to old Roman tyrants like Nero and Co. and have absolutely nothing to do with this war or the last or any other English concern. . . ."

Daphne was better. She had been very ill. Too many children's ills and worries had finally been her undoing and she had collapsed with pneumonia from which she made slow recovery. I had had an amusing letter from her, typical of the Daphne known to me and not the general public: "Am beginning to feel not quite such a Lydia Languish as I did, though my day is as quiet as ever. Sleep till ten a.m. (as I take ages getting off at night even with a drug) and then get downstairs about twelve-thirty! Awful—like the worst sort of jaded actress! then lunch, and rest on the sofa all the afternoon or in my chair in the garden. Tea, and a short walk with a spy-glass (birds) afterwards. . . . Side by side with my new 'thing' about music, by-the-way, is a new-found discovery of 'wine'!! I who ne'er tasted a drop. But Tommy left a lot of claret behind and I can't tell you what 'gutz' I find it! Something called Château al Tour and Château something else, and a very good Burgundy. I have a theory that as one reaches the mid-thirties one suddenly matures, and things like food and drink that used to mean nothing suddenly become significant. I have terrible hankerings after France sometimes, and little restaurants, and the smell of them, and in a sort of frenzy I sent for *Peter Ibbetson* and it has given me worse nostalgia than ever for Paris, which probably one will never see again. How is *The Little Less* going? I never saw a notice because I suppose they finally appeared when I was in bed. Can't remember anything now of what actually happened at that time but have an uneasy feeling I may have said all sorts of indiscreet things in delirium and shall be blackmailed for years to come! Will you ask the chemist if they have any Pond's cold cream or anybody's make of skin food, because I can't get any here, and to be without these things is the end. The children are blooming (may it last). . . . I'm not coping at all and don't lift a finger to help or anything! Awful reaction after a glut of coping. Do read Hemingway's *For Whom the Bell Tolls*, so vital and alive and rather terrible. Best descriptions of love I've ever read in any book barring *Lady Chatterley's Lover* but not offensive in any way. Thank Bird (*Jeanne*) for her priceless letter. I wish she'd take to the pen and make the third ('Sisters Brontë'). It seems you are not entirely thorough with your hoe! How about her making me a birthday cake? (and with my new vice for wine anything in the drink line would be welcome!) I must rouse, it's nearly twelve and I'm still in bed. Sordid! . . ."

By the end of the summer I asked permission to go up to Mull to write. I knew that before long my age-group would be called and then it would be utterly impossible to write a line until the war, which looked like going on for ever, finished. Mummie, and who shall blame her, thought it was the thin end of the wedge, and that I meant to hare off once more for —possibly the duration. With Jeanne's permission however I went up to Mull, setting myself the time-limit of two months to write the whole of *Treveryan*, which I had mentally stacked by in readiness.

I worked harder on *Treveryan* than I had on the others, harder that is to say at the time of writing. I put in eight hours a day for two months and I finished it. It is an impossible thing for a 'creator' (whether of art, or literature—or any other force) to have to set themselves a time-limit, but I knew I had to.

Even *my* War effort was supposedly of more use to the country
than my efforts to further literature! Mull was the perfect centre
for writing. I had always found it so. Olive and the children left
me in complete peace, seeing me at meals, and in the evenings.
Sometimes I wrote—if fine—on the small balcony with its view
of terraced gardens, the bay, Duart, and Cruachan in the distance, and later when it was cold (or if it rained) in the dust-
sheet-shrouded drawing-room.

I yearned more than ever for the time when the little house of
all my dreams should be mine. Achnacroish. The small farm
now empty and disused, which lay below the little cairn, just
inside the deer-fenced forest, ten minutes up the hill from
Torosay, alone in the glory of its highland solitude. Here, I
knew, I would one day do good work. And to Achnacroish I
daily made my way, for even if one is pledged to an eight-hour
routine one must get exercise. I had bought it for the traditional
'song' from Olive's eldest daughter; my tenants were sheep,
and no house ever had such surroundings—nor such love spent
on it from an owner who also was doomed to stillborn hopes
and plans. Only a track led to it, only sheep and deer came near
to it. I had fallen in love with Achnacroish at first sight, in the
days when it was occupied. It stood completely alone on the
hill, with good bothies and buildings round it, nestling in trees,
an ideal home for such as I. It was as near an earthly Paradise as
I shall ever find; and there were absolutely no conveniences of
any sort at all. When it was empty no one appeared to want it
and I bought the feu, and even my bank-manager was so
interested he was persuaded to let me 'sell out'. The excitement
I went through interviewing builders, and looking through
catalogues of ranges, stoves, W.C.'s and sinks! . . . It did not
worry me in the slightest that, by fair means or foul, water
would have to be brought from a burn, that no road passed
within a quarter of a mile, that the approach in fact was in-
accessible except by the deer-pony track, that week by week,

month by month, a further pane of window smashed, that another tile came off the roof, that the floors began to sink. . . . I just realised that it was *my* house on Mull, that it had four rooms, and with out-buildings all sorts of ambitious ideas might materialise; and that the golden eagle hovered above and stags came within fifty yards, that oaks and rowans and birches would turn orange and gold for me in the autumn, and that I could walk in unsurpassed beauty for ever.

And then the first blow fell. No sooner had my 'Achnacroish Account' come into being than a law was brought in restricting individuals from spending more than an infinitesimal amount on property, which ruled my dreams out of existence. Instead of the painters and builders and carpenters the sorry scene was a mere replica of the last act of Tchekov's *Cherry Orchard* as one by one the boards were nailed to the windows.

But day by day, week by week, month by month and year by year I waited.

When I returned in November to Fowey I tackled Pont again with fresh zest. It was from now on that the South-West began to come into the raid zone. Plymouth was bombed, and the damage done was as bad as any in the kingdom. The raids of course could be heard all too clearly from Fowey—and seen too. The Fowey siren was barely a hundred yards from my bedroom window and I confess that I used to listen to it sweating, as it wailed through the night, inevitably making a duet with the throb of plane engines . . . ours? theirs? One knew one was so pitifully and inadequately protected, and as a port we were a useful target for Nazi planes who had found the barrage of Plymouth unattractive but were averse to returning with their bombs unloaded. The little house in the Esplanade would shake as the bombs fell in Plymouth twenty miles away and sometimes a low-flying acrobat would skim down the harbour to the voice of short ack-ack reports off little ships, and I used to lie in my white bed reading and trying not to listen to my heart.

Ferryside had been requisitioned by the Navy as H.Q. for officers—our side of the river in fact had been pretty well requisitioned as a whole; W.R.N.S. filled one building, men another and I could not help but be amused when Jeanne and I found ourselves selling veg. at our own back door to the complete ignorance of its inmates. But for all the eighteen months or whatever it was H.M.N. had Ferryside, they used it for not more I should think than three, and yet how difficult it was to return. Mummie was better in health by the time we were allowed to go back, which we did in May '42. Little damage had been done on the whole, little compared to the holocausts of outrage I have seen in the homes of many people, but sufficient to have it done up (permits, etc), and the joy was great when we found ourselves back again. The difference to the 'wear and tear' to Jeanne and myself was certainly marked, for the trek to Pont could be done in ten minutes compared with half an hour—or more if by ill luck one missed a ferry. But now once again the Powers turned nasty, deciding that Jeanne must work the garden alone. So I found a job on a farm. It was pleasant enough, and the farmer and his wife could not have been nicer and kinder, but I found the work very tiring, especially in the rainy weather. It was a small farm and as I was terrified of cows I wasn't of much use really. I started always by cleaning out the cow houses. This, at first, made me retch. I can't think why. But no silver-cleaning butler or footman could have taken more pride in their dining-room table than I did in the spotlessness of my cow houses. But the carrying of the water was desperately heavy, pails and pails of it. There was a colossal field of potatoes which I lifted—a job desperate on back *and* feet, as it was on a hillside; and then there were hedge-paring jobs at which I was very bad, and all sorts of seemingly useless things like ridding fields of thistle or charlock. All was well in fine weather, but in the rain, when I ate my lunch under hedgerows, it was 'not so hot' and always I worked in com-

plete solitude throughout the day, once the cowsheds were
finished, which I found lonely, for Jeanne and I worked well
together and I missed our breaks for the occasional cigarette
and ribaldry. I rowed myself to the farm daily, which was very
pleasant: it used to take about twenty minutes each way. Sometimes friends would come and eat a picnic lunch with me; my
own lunch never varied, I can't remember now what I ate but
I do know that bread and dripping played a great part. At the
work on the farm and at Pont I found smoking a complete
necessity; I could not have got through the days without it, and
now the very smell of a cigarette makes me feel sick.

I worked on the farm for four months when my inside began
to go back on me again—the same horrible pains that I had
suffered in the past, and also my heart had a way of missing
beats and behaving oddly. I was told I must stop all work for a
bit and have a rest. So after a year's absence I tore up to Mull
once again for a month of heaven-sent rest and it was when I
was there that Jeanne wrote and said that the War Agricultural
Committee had decided that she certainly was entitled to help,
and that when I was better I could rejoin her. This was splendid
hearing, for gardening, hard as it was, did not entail quite the
same heavy work as farming, and although I was not a good
gardener I was better at the job than I was as a farm labourer.
Moreover we were our own masters which cannot be denied
makes for happier work. There was a great deal that was
enjoyable about Pont work, *except in real winter*. And I defy
anyone to get any 'kick' out of fingers and toes so numbed and
frosted that tears tell their tale; when feet get caked and clogged
inches thick with mud, and one's oilskins or mackintoshes must
be changed several times, and one's fingers are living icicles. I
never minded the heat. In sand-shoes, sunbonnet and milanese
underclothes I've worked coolie-wise and enjoyed it, though
there have been times when flies sticking to one's sweat can
be trying. But hundreds of tomato plants, and thousands of

corn-cobs, and row upon row of beans, peas, onions and
carrots make up for a lot of bodily weariness; there was great
satisfaction to be got out of two acres of food tilled, sown
and picked entirely by ourselves. At one time Madeline
Seymour came down to Fowey, taking a flat and helping
tremendously hard. Indeed she was invaluable.

The war went on and on and on. One listened to the nine
o'clock news, one blacked-out every particle of light, one's ears
cocked to the sound of 'planes . . . and like a see-saw battles
went sometimes with us, sometimes against. One's diaries,
mine at least, seemed dull and humdrum with endless boring
jottings about work and Pont, and then suddenly an occasional
ray 'Stalingrad Relieved', 'Tunis Victory', or horrible entries
like 'Sikorski and Victor Cazalet killed', 'Leslie Howard
killed'.

I went to London for a week in March ('43), where Olive
joined me and we riotously went to theatres every day, the one
and greatest 'high-spot' being a concert at the Cambridge
Theatre at which Moura Lympany played Rachmaninoff's 3rd
Concerto. It was the most superb performance of this—and I'd
heard both Horowitz and Moiseiwitsch—that I have ever heard.
It was the first time I had heard her, and both Olive and I were
pulp by the end. That anyone—any girl so young too—should
have quite such power staggered both of us. I am convinced
there is no one to touch Moura Lympany in Rachmaninoff's
works to-day; she is a superb artist.

A very dear and beloved friend of Olive's was the late King
George of Greece. I had met him before the war, and now we
met again. We lunched but in tragic circumstances. For just
before we were to meet H.M. came the news that David James
was missing. It naturally had a saddening effect on what should
have been a festive occasion, for Olive who adored her grandson was desperately upset and shocked. (It was not for many
weeks that the news came through that he had been picked up

and was a prisoner. His life as a P.O.W. and his escape has since been brilliantly and absorbingly written by him.) I saw the King several times; we were all dining together during one of the many noisy raids, in a restaurant where the plates and dishes and dancing out-noised the guns. He was a very fine man and the stories of his own grim experiences in Greece and Crete, which Olive dragged out of him, were brutal and yet told with such simplicity that it was very difficult to realise it was a monarch sitting beside one. I had been invited to go with Olive to Greece but the war had prevented it, and now again the King invited me to go with her as his guest at Claridge's for her remaining week. In fact he had surmised that it was all settled and seemed most surprised when I said that I must get back to cope with thousands of onions. It was the first time, he said, that he had been out-rivalled by an onion. But the onion won the day. I did not like to say (as I was thinking) that it was the first and probably the last time a king *and* Claridge's would come my way. And I've bitterly regretted my conscientiousness ever since.

May was appalling in Cornwall, with gales blowing so hard that ferries did not run and even snow fell, as it had in '34 when Daddy died. All through the summer we worked hard and with lighter hearts as dawn at last seemed to break. First with the invasion of Sicily and then the news of Mussolini's resignation and obvious fall from grace. Dig, dig, dig . . . plant, plant, plant . . . weed, weed, weed . . . pick, pick, pick . . . . And always in the summer the water shortage would become acute and baths out of the question just when one longed above everything to lie in the evening in a deep hot bath, with Pont earth seeping from one. But the harbour luckily flowed beneath Ferryside and there was always the sea to soak tired feet and bodies in. In the autumn I made my annual dash Mull-wards; this time a mere fortnight had to suffice, and it was this time I think that enemy planes swooped over Torosay and dropped their bombs on ships at anchor off Oban—a convoy—killing some valuable horses which were being sent overseas. The well-known *crump crump* of fallen bombs sounded singularly out of place in the stillness of the night.

I was still having trouble with my 'tummy' and saw a new specialist before Christmas. Colitis, he said; it wasn't, but no matter, and he put me on a diet that was to drive me and Ferryside out of our minds for many months to come. Doctors, I have discovered, do not recognise war when it comes to ordering diets and putting people on to régimes. They have never heard of rationing. . . .

It was late in '43 when at last Fowey was well and properly invaded. By America. They arrived in their hundreds, the flower of American youth, on a wet November day. All wearing galoshes.

One has heard so much adverse criticism about 'occupying forces' that I want to say here and now that a nicer crowd than the American Navy in Fowey would be hard to find. Jealousy was, I think, at the root of the 'spiky' unfriendliness and unfavourable comments which Americans over here in the war received. This was not altogether surprising, for their men were so much better paid than ours, their canteens so infinitely better fed, that even girls who were not natural gold-diggers found glamour in the G.I.'s pockets even if the men themselves sometimes proved different to what was expected. I saw very little of the American army, nothing at all of the American air force, but I did see at very close quarters the manners, manner and behaviour of much of their navy from 1943 until the end of the war, and in Fowey cases of drunkenness and bad behaviour were at a minimum. Officers and men alike were generous to a degree, worked efficiently and quickly, and all did their best to behave as charmingly and pleasantly as possible in circumstances which were anything but attractive. It was said later that the little town of Fowey did more for its size than anywhere in the South to welcome these homesick new-to-war men and boys. And if this is so, it is somewhat of a tribute, for their presence was bitterly resented at the beginning by quite a number of people who admittedly were inconvenienced (to put it mildly) by having property confiscated, seized, commandeered; by being evicted for the duration and/or having any number of American personnel billeted on them. Damage done was often bad, though I do not suppose worse than by any other occupying force—and in fact I have been told by those who knew that our own forces 'occupied' Italy in a more shaming and shameful degree than any other including the Germans.

We were called upon almost the first night of arrival by the C.O. and his second-in-command who turned out to be none other than the husband of Gertrude Lawrence. These two, 'Larry' Snell and Richard Aldrich, were to become great friends of ours, but in those early days our one desire was to form and cement a friendliness in the town between the two 'peoples', a kind of Atlantic Charter in a real but minor way. Really splendid and invaluable help and friendship was given by certain people and it was not long before genuine affection could be felt and realised between the Americans and ourselves, I think. If only every citizen realised he (or she) is a member of their country's diplomatic service—unpaid ambassadors in fact—friendships would be formed which neither tactless governments nor indiscreet newspapers could break. It was not long before the men from America were joined by war-seasoned veterans from Sicily and the Italian 'beaches'— fellow countrymen—and those boys, battle-scarred and enthusiastic, were simple, charming friendly people, grateful for the poor hospitality a rationed small-town could give. Childlike almost in their 'let's be friends' attitude, eager in their impatience to 'get going' and finish the war. It is true that in certain quarters bitterness and jealousy was felt as young un-schooled Americans were put in command over ourselves. As they were paying the piper they had the right, it must be faced, to call the tune from time to time. Looking back now I can't help likening the American expeditionary forces in Britain to tempestuous puppies barking and snapping at the tail of an old dog who is wearied but refuses to give up mastership or admit defeat. There were difficulties, misunderstandings and —hurdles—on both sides; as a woman I sometimes was able to see and understand the mutual indignations and impatience of both sides. I was frequently accused of being pro-American, but surely it is better to understand one's ally than to fight him?

In the autumn of '43 I joined the Home Guard, which of course made me a target of fun, the more so as I, with two other women friends, were in 'Intelligence'. Our headquarters was in a once-charming uninhabited house several miles from Fowey, where we met as a rule twice a week, at night, and I enjoyed the whole business enormously. Much of our instruction had a maths-like quality which totally defeated me, and there was a great deal which was absolutely useless knowledge to women. There were about a dozen of us in all, the rest men. A great deal of fun was got out of it (or so I found); one shared infantile jokes. . . . I shall always remember the calm way in which one of the men said to me: "I see you have driven much on the continent", as I sped along the wrong side of the road (a bad habit of mine) one night; and the earnest voice of another's remark: "Quite a lot of ladies drink rum these days. *In a nice way*, of course, I mean."

There was always the shadow of invasion and enemy para-troop-landings hanging over us, and in that event we all knew what was expected of us, and what our duties would be and where we should go. And I for one was extremely surprised (*and* relieved) to find that I was not called out to some outpost for an indefinite period when D-Day was declared.

At Christmas 1943 Daphne moved into Menabilly. My brother-in-law had been overseas for a long time, and she had been living in a small house in Fowey, during which time she realised her dream sufficiently to rent Menabilly, 'doing it up' as far as she was able. With a household of influenza'd children she moved in at Christmas time and we saw it on December 25th for the first time cleaned, redecorated, furnished, inhabited. It was after Christmas that Jeanne was taken so ill, with a rare internal complaint necessitating bed for some time and many weeks of rest, and for the next few weeks—or months possibly—I worked Pont alone.

By May it was obvious that 'der tag' was not far off. American craft of all sorts and sizes filled the harbour, and more and more men appeared, and a hush-hush atmosphere filled the air. In May Daphne was asked to give a secret party for the American war correspondents who were down here hidden. '*Not a soul was to know*', even Daphne's own staff had to be sent out on a picnic and negro naval staff replace them, bringing food and drink and crockery, etc, in trucks from Fowey H.Q.! I could not help being reminded of the old Drage advertisement of 'plain vans'. Mummie and I were sworn to secrecy, for we were 'ordered' to be present as co-hostesses. There were sixty—I think—war correspondents in this party which was supposed (though we only surmised it naturally!) to be eve-of-D-Day. It is a matter of history now that the wind was averse or the tides, and that D-Day was at a moment's notice cancelled. Be that as it may, the Menabilly party was a great day, interesting, enjoyable, amusing and up to a point instructive. When the Great Day finally came, June 6th, Jeanne and I were putting in tomato plants by the hundred. Only those who have planted outdoor tomatoes on a large scale will appreciate the fact that as far as we were concerned June 6th was Tomato Day, and it was not until we looked out of the windows that evening and saw *an empty harbour* that we realised the significance. There was something stupendous, something wildly exciting, something profoundly horrible in the realisation. Boys and men we knew so well, whom we'd seen twenty-four hours ago, had sailed . . . some never to return. And then came that first Radio announcement, telling us the stupendous news that the D-Day landings had been made victoriously and with singularly little mishap.

I was spending the week-end on the Bodmin moors when news of the Arnhem airborne battle was announced on the wireless. Knowing as I did that my brother-in-law must be heavily involved the announcement was breath-taking; the days went by and the news of the battle and set-backs became worrying and desperate, and there was the horrible moment when a reporter rang Daphne up at six a.m. to know whether it was true Tommy had been taken prisoner. Knowing nothing but that he was in the thick of it all, her feelings can perhaps be imagined; certainly her letter to *The Times* about the brutality of such tactlessness was to the point.

By the end of the year our branch of the Home Guard was disbanded; it was felt, I suppose, that our need was no longer necessary! It had been a thoroughly enjoyable experience, especially the 'ragging' I had to endure when I refused to divulge *what* I did for Intelligence! Jeanne had for a considerable time been a member of the N.F.S. and as far as I remember that continued until even after V-Day. She was on duty certain nights throughout every week, as of course she was working Pont in the day-time. 'Muffet' was in the family by now; the tiny ball of fluff had been brought back from London just a few weeks before the American influx. We had tried being dog-less for a while after the death of Mummie's Belinda, but it was a miserable house without them, and in '42 a tiny Blossom was procured, followed a year later by Muffet, who Blossom thought she had miraculously given birth to. It was adorable to watch the ecstatic joy the tiny little year-old parti-colour took in the grey ball of fluff, who I fear to say only too soon mastered her and battered her although she was very fond of her at heart. A tiny stray cat—Timoshenko—was also added to the household by Jeanne who found him lost and pitiful on a wall one night. Muffet was Jeanne's shadow from the first, possibly due to the illness which caused Jeanne to remain for so long in bed, on which 'Tuffy' mounted guard and was in constant attendance. Mummie and I used later to dread Jeanne's N.F.S. nights more on poor Muffet's account than Jeanne's, for she would remain like the wife of Ulysses *gazing*—and hopeless—till her return. It is extraordinary to realise that this little creature who could not bear Jeanne out of her sight is now—apparently—content to winter à deux with me with great affection.

It was at the beginning of 1945 that *my* tummy once again began to play havoc, and after X-rays and one thing and another it was considered that the (now fashionable) gall-bladder was misbehaving, and I was stopped work. I cannot pretend that this caused me nights of patriotic sleeplessness. I was tired and felt unwell and was heartily sick of the searing pain that was ever keeping me awake at nights. Moreover it gave me the opportunity and chance I had longed for: time to write. So I settled down to *Lawrence Vane*, which some people thought the best of my books but which because of the 'colour' question has never found a film company brave enough to tackle what I frankly believe to be a first-class film story. *Treveryan* was bought up for films, but so far nothing has come of it or to it. It is my misfortune that whenever I write a novel I picture it as a film as I'm writing. And this is queer, because I am not a particularly zealous 'fan'. I suppose I see movement and action, and the theatrical blood in me wants drama to have spoken outlets. But I certainly filmed in my mind's eye *The Spinning Wheel*, *Treveryan* and *Lawrence Vane*.

In the meantime the war was nearing excitedly and miracu-lously its end. The horrified surprise which numbed us when Roosevelt died suddenly was overshadowed by the amazing death of Hitler, and then like Alice—'faster, faster'—before one had realised it V-Day was upon us.

I wonder why it is that the fourteen-year-old Angela recol-lects November 11th 1918 with far greater strength and reverence than the forty-odd Angela remembers May 7th 1945. Is it that one's memories of youth stand out in greater per-spective than our own adult years? It is certainly true that I remember incidents of childhood with infinitely greater clarity than many of greater importance of more recent years. Pos-sibly incidents and happenings occurred with little frequency and so appeared isolated, but I don't believe that is the sole reason.

When I was asked in the war days what I longed for most I invariably replied 'the end of black-out' and 'petrol and cars'. The glory of light once again was indeed heaven-sent (or so it seemed), and in June when basic-petrol was allowed we thought our troubles were over and 'peace in our time' had really come at last and to stay, poor benighted fools that we were.

Alas, the summer of 1945 which should have brought every-one joy brought to me personally great sadness. Olive, who had been unwell for some time grew rapidly and suddenly much worse, and died in the Oban Cottage Hospital at the beginning of July, after but a few days of severe illness and pain. I had little thought the autumn before, when I had gone as usual to Scot-land, that I should never see her again. One of the things I regret so much for so many people's sakes is that Olive Guthrie never wrote her Memoirs. For she had led the most surprising and wonderful life, had known people in every walk of life—kings, statesmen, poets, bandits, singers, writers—had travelled

the globe from one end to the other in strange and uncon-
ventional ways, had herself worked in the City doing a man's
job as Chairman of a great bank when her husband was dying,
and afterwards when she took his place; she had a fund of
stories and anecdotes unparalleled, which only an Irishwoman
such as she was could have told with just that right amount of
wit, or pathos, or credulity. I know that Lennox Robinson
wanted her to write her life-story, as did many of her Irish
friends, and there were times when she used to say to me that
when the war was over we would do it together. Her courage,
both moral and physical, was unsurpassed; I know of no one
who suffered more appalling injuries than she had done in a
motor smash; no one but Olive would have lived with the
amount of bones broken and multiple lacerations she suffered
and internal injuries which caused untold pain at times for the
rest of her life. Life had been both beautiful and bitter to her,
kind and cruel, yet I think she was brave enough to accept
whatever fate had ready. When we were alone she told me so
much of glamorous Edwardian days, and of youthful Irish
childhood, of her ecstatically happy marriage to Murray
Guthrie—the wonderful life they shared in London and Scotland and abroad for so brief a time alas, for she was widowed
before she was forty, and left with four young children, Torosay and Murray Guthrie's business to run. She was the most
remarkable woman I ever knew; her letters were like her, they
brimmed over with her own personality and fun. She had the
ability and integrity of a man, the fascination of a woman, the
enthusiasm of a child and the imagination of a fairy. When her
spirit departed from this world on July 3rd 1945 the light
dimmed and the sun lost its glory for many who loved her.

Brigit and Bobs, her two daughters, had kept me au
courant by telephone and telegram those sudden fatal last few
days, and when she died they asked me to go and bid her
farewell.

The week was a nightmare. The Election was thrust suddenly on a country unready and still bewildered by years of war, on a people many of whom ignorantly imagining Churchill would continue to lead them whichever party they voted into power. In the early hours of July 5th after registering my vote for the Prime Minister's party I left Cornwall once again for Scotland, and arrived next day on Torosay's beach, to hear in the distance a Lament, being played on the bagpipes; then—out of the teeming rain—came mourners, so numerous that one could not count them through one's own veil of tears, and slowly the cortège came to a halt and Olive was laid to rest beside Murray, her husband, under the massive granite cross which stands alone in splendid isolation on Torosay's most eastern shore looking forever to Loch Linnhe, Ben Nevis and the rising sun.

I was with Olive's younger grandson when the news of Labour's victory swept the country with mixed feelings of bewilderment, joy and despair some weeks later. I remember we were having lunch at the Café Royal. I for one was mildly glad at the result. I had voted for Churchill's Conservatives because I could no more have denied him or his banner than I could deny the Christian faith. But I felt that Socialism 'had something', that far too many people of my own class were diehard and critical in their attitude to the Labour Party's ideals and I felt that here was a chance for that party to prove their greatness, their ability, their patriotism and worth. (I also felt that if a state of chaos was to ensue after six years of warfare, as was generally supposed must happen, better another party and another man shoulder responsibility and blame than Churchill!) Like many others I had not believed Winston Churchill's own gibes against Socialism in Britain, had felt his antagonism and bitterness to it to be old-fashioned and misleading. There were many in England in 1945 who did not realise that the margin between Socialism and National Socialism (i.e. the Nazi doctrine) was but an invisible thread, and that we were in for years of dictatorship by a bureaucracy masquerading under the name of democracy.

In August the Japanese war came to an end with strange suddenness, and in quiet little seaside and country towns like Fowey bells rang, and flags were hoisted and churches held services of Thanksgiving, and we thanked God that six disastrous years were now behind us. Men slowly returned from fronts, and arms were outstretched and hearts overflowed to husbands, fathers, sons and brothers set free from tortured years of prison camps.

X

And Post War

THERE was still plenty to do in various theatres even with the war over and I now found myself in the Women's Land Army. Not as 'digger and delver' but as a welfare worker. I fear the reason for this sudden decision on my part was not patriotism but the fact that I badly needed new tyres for the Morris 8!!! By becoming a welfare worker I got 'E' coupons for petrol and 'E' coupon holders alone were entitled to new tyres. . . . In actual fact the work was extraordinarily interesting and I grew really attached to the girls I visited regularly every month over a fairly extensive district, and was more than sorry when the W.L.A. dispensed with 'Reps'. I must have worked for about three years I think, and it was interesting coming into contact with girls of many different types, listening to grievances, enjoying (occasionally) little personal confidences, hearing too the employers' side of the picture. And above all realising the conditions under which girls on farms and on the land do live.

Many people I suppose went back to London when the war was over. I am sure it was expected of us! I am sure there were plenty of people who imagined one had chosen safety in Cornwall as opposed to dangers in London, and that the moment war and raids were over we should hurry back. By now however one's roots—Jeanne's and mine at any rate—were more firmly fixed than ever in the soil of the countryside. And although neither of us felt we ever wished to hold a trowel or a spade in our hands again, neither did we wish to return to what little civilisation London was left with. Jeanne said she would never live in London again; and there was something very final in that decision. I was still refused permission to put Achnacroish (my Mull cottage) in order and as I by this time had far more interests—music and theatres apart—in Cornwall than in London I did nothing to persuade Mummie into returning to Hampstead. Providence Corner had, moreover, been let for some time, and it seemed a far better solution to remain country bumpkins.

London, poor battered war-scarred London, was indeed a grim city to visit in those early post-war months and years. During and after the blitz, and in the era of flying-bombs and V.2's it gave the appearance of wounded gallantry, but as 1946 slowly passed each succeeding visit only reasserted the dismal fact of its growing shabbiness and 'gone-to-seed'-iness. Bomb craters and bombed sites were one thing—they were the legitimate sign of all she had been through. It was the stripped plaster and dilapidated walls of unbombed but disused houses, rows upon rows of them, that filled one with depression and made one feel that the 'centre of the universe' would never be the same again. And, alas, in some ways I think London has changed for ever. It is not the face of London that has changed, it is its manner. And its people. I am aware, every time I go to London—which for all I live in Cornwall is pretty frequently— that Londoners are different: that in fact half the people who live there *are not Londoners*. That very many are not British people at all. I went into a world-famed store, I remember, one day (in 1946 or '47) and I hardly heard a word of English spoken. Some people may find this cosmopolitan and interesting, I do not. Maybe that after many years I have become insular. To me it is a matter of sad regret that much of England, and a great deal of London, has lost the grace and graciousness of the past, not only with the passing and destruction of its buildings but with the strange and inexplicable departure of its inhabitants.

It was in the early part of 1946 that I went to Covent Garden for the first time since 1939. The occasion was a performance of *The Sleeping Beauty*—I believe it was the opening night, and that the Queen was present. I and the friend with whom I went naturally wore our best evening dresses; we had stalls, and I had been properly brought up as far as Covent Garden was concerned. I think we were the only people 'dressed'; beside us was a man in plus-fours, the rest of the audience wore day clothes, many had hats and a considerable number of women hid their shopping-bags under their seats. Shades of Melba, shades of de Reszke, of Patti . . . of Nijinski, of Pavlova; of 1939 days for that matter. One realises of course the argument for the mackintosh and jumper . . . the no-car, go-to-the-play-by-tube, the seven o'clock early hour, the lazy comfort of *not* returning to change, and a mere quick drink and wash of the hands. But are not some theatres, some evenings, some entertainments worth an eight o'clock opening, where patrons can be clothed decently and in honour as it were of the function they are attending? Haven't opera, ballet—and Covent Garden in particular—a tradition which we would do well to keep if only as the one phoenix rising from the '39–'45 ashes? People who can afford the price they pay for 'dressed' seats at Covent Garden can afford to dress, and by the looks of London streets neither motor cars nor taxis are unpatronised. Perhaps I am old-fashioned, I am probably most unpopular in my ideas, but I *long* for a compulsory order that to sit in the stalls, boxes and stalls-circle, etc, at Covent Garden, one must be in evening dress; and for the operas and ballets to start later in order to allow people to be able to do this. I should be the first to grumble and suffer, I am the first to like sitting snugly in a wool frock and with a warm scarf round my neck, but I disapprove of the laxity with which post-war men and women take their pleasures. The marriage garment in fact . . . and those who know their Bible will remember what happened to that wretched individual who did not wear it, yet was forced to appear.

The Sleeping Beauty, with Margot Fonteyn, Helpmann and Beryl Grey, was the first of many nights of rapture that I was to recapture at Covent Garden in the years which have followed. Indeed I had not expected such beauty or such superb talent from an English company, Diaghilev and de Basil snob that I was. Such beauty made me cry, and of all the many Sadler's Wells productions which I have seen in the last four years—and I have seen most—I still think that first *Sleeping Beauty* remains as the greatest pleasure in my memory. Perhaps it was the surprise element about it that caused such ineffable pleasure to one's jaded mental palate, used in the last years to mere spectacles in Glorious Technicolor.

Not only great dancing, but great acting was to be seen in London now that wars were over and done with: Olivier and Gielgud with their superb productions . . . the Old Vic has surely never bettered that *Œdipus*, that *Lear*. Performances which made one proud to be British and connected with the British theatre. Indeed, with my love of music and of the theatre I admit it is not always easy to choose between a city's culture and the two hundred and forty miles which separates it from Cornwall. Either/or . . . it was the old question of the cake. In my case I decided to cut the occasional slice and eat that.

One therefore, with little jaunts to London—expensive little jaunts with theatres nightly—lives one's life in the country; writing, sitting on committees and interesting oneself in matters calculated to give one's sophisticated London friends giggles (but no matter), growing daily happier in the choice of the roots one has decided upon.

1946 was Airborne's Derby, which, because of Tommy's past connection in that line, was an obvious bet, and one which subsequently paid handsomely for a holiday!

It was in 1946 that all the Hickses returned from Africa. It did not seem possible that so much had happened, that so many miles, so many seas, had divided us. Bet's son, a tiny baby when I had last seen him, was now a person to be reckoned with—and I felt more nervous about the meeting with seven-year-old Rob than I ever had with his father. All went well however, and he is one of the surprising New Young to whom one finds oneself talking on straight and adult lines about everyday matters. Not many months went by before Willie Spillane appeared from Cape Town, and Bet changed her name. Willie is one of those people who becomes a friend at once; from the moment we met—during their honeymoon in Cornwall—we became firm and lasting friends.

I think I expected to find both Seymour and Ella very changed, but I need not have worried. Courage is the middle name of all members of that family, courage and fortitude, and I rather think that those two qualities, which Seymour and Ella had so abundantly in their years of anxiety and late middle age, kept them miraculously youthful to the joy of their friends who loved them devotedly. When Seymour died I felt I had lost a father for the second time; 'Uncle Ted' was someone very special in my life, a friend whose memory I shall always bless. And Ella . . . one hesitates to write with a full heart of people who are living, for fear of sounding sometimes over-fulsome or exaggerating in praise. To know Ella is to know Good. To me she is a mixture of a statue of Our Lady and Bluebell in Fairyland. I do not think I have ever met anyone who radiates saintliness and also glorious fun to the degree she does. Nor have I ever known anyone keep her unspoilt girl-hood with such charm and lack of affectation. I collided with her in the passage of Bet's house not long ago, and I could have sworn the little person in a quilted dressing-gown, with two plaits neatly tied in ribbons, was one of my own nieces. It wasn't, it was Bluebell—in perpetuity.

Jeanne, by the time 1946 was half through, was again wedded to the paint-brush, and in November went off for the first of her many winters abroad—which she has continued to achieve ever since to the surprise and envy of many people, myself amongst them—whilst we of the Cornish Riviera battled with snow feet deep, burst pipes, impassable roads and old-fashioned winters so pretty in Christmas cards and so awful in reality.

It was during the bad cold spell in the early spring of 1947 as far as I can remember that Robert Boothby came down to address the Unionists of S.E. Cornwall, and Douglas Marshall our member brought him to Ferryside. I had met him years ago, but had never heard him speak on the platform till he came to Liskeard. By now I had become extremely interested in politics, and S.E. Cornwall's in particular, and had (like better men than myself) turned from hue to hue, finally convinced that the Bad Old Tory Party was the only one to put the country back on to her feet. Possibly like the mobs in Shakespearean plays (and mobs in general for that matter) I am swayed by forcible rhetoric, certainly the visits in our own constituency of Robert Boothby and Harold Macmillan, and later Lady Tweedsmuir (at that time Lady Grant), forcibly instilled enthusiasm into me which has taken all forms from tub-thumping to writing my last novel, *Reveille*. There have even been moments when I have seriously wondered whether I should leave home, and chuck what little success I have achieved and may achieve further as a writer, and try to stand for Parliament myself. All I have however is conviction and I do not believe that is sufficient. Mine is not a head that carries facts, I cannot argue, I speak ungrammatically and stammer and lisp when in a tight corner, and suffer the nerves of the damned when addressing meetings. For several years now I have for some reason or other had public speaking 'thrust upon me'; this I tried to take in my stride for one reason and one reason only: my father never refused to speak on behalf of anything when he was asked (unless of course it was for some cause he disapproved); he had stringent ideas that he was a public servant and must do his duty as such whenever called upon. I am not, I suppose, a public servant, but I have always felt that to refuse to speak (when asked) would be to shirk my duty, and that Daddy would disapprove strongly of sliding out of things that one could do merely because such a task gave one 'first-night' nerves. All went well until at one political meeting of certain magnitude at which I was called on to speak, *every word left me* . . . all I saw was a yellow wall in front of me and rows of faces below; and the best speech which I had ever thought up and memorised went with the wind and I was forced to extemporise—slip-shoddedly at that—and make of myself, let's face it, a sorry spectacle. That has probably seen the last of me as a platform speaker!

The war over, it behoved me to start writing once more. *Lawrence Vane*, which my cousins Peter and Nico Davies had published after Michael Joseph had refused it, now belonged to the past, yet my mind was a blank and barren of ideas, and I was convinced that I would remain incapable and useless until I went abroad again. Not only was I certain that I needed an entirely new environment but I felt that my brain had become rusty and thwarted with the lack of the right stimulants to the body. I knew that I needed meat to eat, wine to drink and if possible citrous fruits to eat and drink. I am firmly of the idea that certain people are in need of certain foods which are now unobtainable or so heavily rationed that it comes to the same thing. And as for wines, the ordinary man and woman just cannot afford to drink them in the everyday fashion that their fellow men and women do on the continent. I am certain that the wine of the country stimulates the brain, as does red meat, and that half the reason we in England have become slow, dull-witted and mediocre is due to the fact most of us are forced to live out of tins, and drink more beer (admittedly my favourite drink)—and occasionally revive our jaded frames with spirits at an exorbitant cost—instead of feeding upon the roast beef of old England or partaking daily from the grape as they have never ceased to do in France, in Italy, in Switzerland, in Spain and in all Mediterranean countries.

I was right. Three weeks in Italy, spent at the lovely Bella Riva hotel at Fasano, on Lago di Garda, revived my brain and working power as if a hypodermic needle had injected me. Ideas for stories crowded into my head, and I could hardly wait for the return to England and the winter through which I intended to write.

It had been eight years since my last visit to Italy; the changes that struck me forcibly were the extreme degrees of poverty and wealth: extremes which in the days of Mussolini one was unaware of, whether they had existed or not. I shall never forget my horror as, dining at Biffi's my first night in Milan, I saw the beggars collect half-smoked cigarettes from under tables, wait for the scraps of food from unfinished plates, linger for anything that might be given them. Nor shall I readily forget the anxiety of the little man who took me through devious ways and channels to some black market or other by which the English traveller could obtain a better exchange of currency, in the hopes that he would make a paltry (or possibly not so paltry) bit for himself. One discovered that the wretched worker was indeed a poor man, that meat and butter and even milk were commodities only dreamed of, and that although the peasant in the countryside lived as well or better than his fellow-man in rationed England, those in the towns were in a hopeless state as far as food was concerned, with prices which seemed extortionate. My ideas of steaks daily faded, but in the country it was different and the food and wines and general comfort provided by the Giorgettis, the stimulating conversation I had from Micky Jacob, who had moved from Sirmione to the Fasano side of the lake, and above all the glory of Italian sun and views, all too soon helped me to forget the misery in the cities, and compare favourably the Italian post-war conditions in the campagna to those of country dwellers in Great Britain.

I returned to England after the worst journey I have ever known which was fully described in 'This was the Russian's Train' in my book of short stories which, under the title of *Birkinshaw* I spent the following several months writing. Probably the appalling journey would not have been necessary had I been content to wait, but I was impatient to return to England for several reasons, not the least being to attend *Salome* which the Vienna Opera were to do at Covent Garden, and which proved worth all the horror of the preceding forty-eight hours' hell, and which incidentally far surpassed the recent (and I submit rather regrettable) production in 1949.

Salome indeed was one of the high spots of 1947, as was *Edward, My Son*—to me the best-acted play since the war. Superb 'theatre' and faultlessly played when I saw it, by Robert Morley and Peggy Ashcroft. I do not remember being so thrilled by a modern play for many years, thrilled that is to say by the sheer perfection of production and acting. Another play, alas not a success as was *Edward*, which caused the same enthusiasm in me was *Adventure Story*, in which Paul Scofield as Alexander the Great showed himself a very worthy rival, young as he is, to Olivier and Gielgud, and Gwen Ffrangcon-Davies gave the most exquisite performance as the queen-mother of Persia. I went to the play alone, sometimes a good thing to do. My father and I were always totally unable to stay our tears when emotion got the better of us, and doubtless have been popular on dressing-room visits when it has been all too hideously obvious that the power of the actors—and possibly the playwright—have been too much for us! I do know that when I finally reached Gwen's dressing-room after the performance was over of *Adventure Story* I dissolved once again in

streaming tears and it took not only Paul Scofield and Gwen
to comfort me, but Mario and the Caprice as well. Fay Compton's performance in that beautiful play *Family Portrait* is
another treasure I keep to remember post-war productions of
the London Theatre.

One more 1947 glory was the French tapestries at the Victoria and Albert Museum. This was for me, a great lover of
tapestry, the most beautiful exhibition I have ever seen, and
although the Munich collection of pictures shown later at the
National Gallery gave me the greatest pleasure I have ever had
from an exhibition of pictures, that of the French tapestries
took my breath away in the same manner as had the Sadler's
Wells production of *The Sleeping Beauty* the year before. One
appeared to lose oneself in some fairyland.

Mummie and I went up to London early in '48 for Gladys
Cooper's long-awaited return to England and to go to her
opening night in London once again. This was an occasion that
recalled the glamour of pre-war days, and the wonderful
acclamation Gladys received on her first entrance must have
made her realise that she was as beloved by her London
audiences as she had ever been. 1948 was a year of returns.
Kirsten Flagstad's to Covent Garden when Mary Newcomb
and I went together to watch her Isolde; it had seemed impossible that her pre-war renderings could be bettered, but that
was the case, one was spellbound by the magic of that voice and
the really great quality of her whole performance.

1948 brought Gwen and Marda back from Africa; Gwen, it
is true, had been home more than once within the past few
years, but it had been early in 1940 that I had said good-bye to
Marda before they sailed away; and now, one evening in
September at Lostwithiel, I met a train from Stratford-on-
Avon and out of it stepped Marda, and we forgot the eight
years which had come and gone, and soon realised that no
years can destroy true friendship; and before her visit to us was

over she had arranged for a winter in Basutoland and the Cape for Jeanne, who had returned from her second Teneriffe winter voiceless and far from fit.

1948 also saw my return to Stinsford, a Stinsford entirely unaltered by years of war, or so it seemed. A Stinsford where roses and lilies, delphiniums and giant lupins still grew in beauty, where the eye was fed as well as the stomach (and where that too seemed in no way unkindly rationed). No horrible pre-fabs had arisen to distort the view, that broad expanse of meadow-land which stretched away and beyond the gardens to the distant horizon; the lark still sang in the summer sky, and pretty and unexpected plates appeared with the different courses.

What other bright memories are there? London memories mostly. The superb acting of Eric Portman in *The Browning Version*, to which play I went with Gwen and Marda. The film of *Monsieur Vincent*, the greatest and most poignantly acted film I can ever remember; a holiday in Italy, another in Scotland.

And there are other memories too lovely and too personal for this book.

Micky lent me the villa at Fasano to which a friend and I went for the month of May, a May spent happily and peacefully amid the olive groves of Garda's hills where the nightingale sang as we looked across a valley to the magic of Bezzuglio; where one walked accompanied by a brown adoring Pekinese, Baldo, and an enchanting naughty wayward chicken-killing terrier, Mario. A May spent showing cypress trees and olive trees, the lemon groves of Bezzuglio and Limone, the enchantment of San Vigilio, Maderno, Malcesine and Gardone Sopra to one who had never before seen Italy, and discovering San Michele —high above Gardone and Salo—after hours spent on the hillside when the sun was setting and in the distance the mountains turned slowly purple as evening approached.

As I had once recognised the necessity for warmth, sun, food, wine and Italy, so again was I suddenly aware of the vital need of Scotland, and the scent of peat-laden air, and Douglas firs, and pines, of bracken turning red with late autumn tints, and the sound of a stag's roar on the mountainside. Mull was a finished chapter and Achnacroish a precious but stillborn dream. Loch Rannoch, in spite of the beauty of Schiehallion and the glory of silver-birch glades turned golden, suffered in comparison with Argyllshire, for there were no firs or pines or peat-laden air, and never a sign of deer in the forests; but it was Scotland, and I suppose gave me the added and necessary fillip without which I felt I could not write, and almost immediately I had returned the seed of *Reveille* took root.

The lack of success (and I will not call it failure) with which *Birkinshaw* was greeted was a bitter disappointment, as from all sides people thought fit to tell me it was by far my best achievement. I had been duly warned, admittedly, that short stories are not popular, either with the general public, publishers or critics, and certainly the latter in a body ignored the volume. Yet from friends, literary and otherwise, whose opinion I value, I received letters of praise and congratulation which had not come my way before. It was a disappointment because I realised, as Daphne had done some years before, that my métier *was* the short story, and I know that cameo sketches and light painting is my 'thing', as people say nowadays.

As I look back, now that 'forty year' has come and gone, I realise that I have achieved little in many ways. In many ways life has been too kind and too soft. In some ways I think that the fact that I have come of an illustrious family most of whose members have worked hard for their recognition—while I have been idle and content to dawdle—has been something of a handicap. Yet to me has been given in fuller measure than to some of the others a gift for which I can never be too grateful: that of enthusiastic appreciation. I do not think I ever realised this until one day my mother and I were lunching at the Ivy with Ivor Novello and Bobby Andrews, and Ivor said suddenly: "I love Angela! she's so excited about things she enjoys." I wonder how many people also love Ivor for that same reason. With the exception of my own father I can think of no one who has derived such pleasure and enthusiasm from other people's performances as Ivor, whose appreciation is joyous indeed, and who gives praise without stint, with a heart brimful of largesse. I have known during my lifetime more people in the theatrical profession than any other, and they are not lacking in 'panners', whether of personalities or stage performances. But in all the years I have known Ivor (thirty of them) I have never once heard him say an unkind word, and his acts of kindness must be legion.

For myself I'm glad that even now my heart misses a beat when I enter the foyer of Covent Garden, that tears well in my eyes at beauty such as Salisbury Cathedral, Winchester College, one's first glimpse of the Highlands after an absence, at perfection in any form, whether it be Moira Shearer's Cinderella, Toumanova's art in almost any ballet, a bank of deep blue delphiniums, a line of Yeats. How dull life would be if one's own emotions lay fallow and one took but an academic interest and suffered neither joy nor sorrow. Took the view, in fact, that so many *young* people nowadays appear to take, that life is altogether rather a bore, unless led with a speed that leaves no time for either the enjoyment, or even the academic interest. "What are your hobbies?" I am asked. Does it sound the reply of a prig, a poseur, if I answer: "My friends, the people I love, and little everyday ploys that could have no interest in these pages."

"You who once led a full (if useless) life, who met daily people of interest, who travelled often, whose time was taken up flitting butterfly-wise an hour here, an hour there—surely you must find your present life, buried in Cornwall, deadly?"

How often has that been said to me and how difficult I find it is to convince people that all I want now is peace in country living, time in which to write; that church parish councils and little Unionist committees and the lives of the people near whom I live are fraught with interest as far as I'm concerned, and that although part of me misses the culture that it's possible to find in city life I would miss country lanes, the smell of the sea, all my present 'roots' infinitely more.

I think that middle-age is definitely a bridge, a cross-roads. In these days of heavy taxation it is nearly impossible to keep two homes going; one must choose a city life with all its gaiety, all its culture, the grime of the chimney-pots, the noise from the streets, *or* the quiet perhaps humdrum life of the country-dweller, who must depend on the radio and library and an occasional visit to the cinema for mundane pleasures, but who, if he's like me, is content to exchange the theatre for birds singing, restaurant life for a tramp over cliffs, smart clothes for macs and wellingtons, a host of friends for one or two.

I should be a liar if I pretended that London now holds no joys for me. It does, in plenty. But they are joys I cannot afford except on brief occasions, and in any case I would never miss the worldly pleasures and gaieties of the city as I would—and do—the quiet and simple life spent in the country. A time may yet come when I shall finally achieve what I want most: that small low cottage in the Western Highlands of Scotland where in May I can hear an eider call to his mate, and in the late autumn the vibrant thrilling grunt which precedes the stag's roar, the filling silence of a Highland night with the sound of its power and primeval beauty.

Menabilly, January—
Isle of Eriska, May 1950